Academic Languaging and Historical Thinking

Cultivating Students' Language Skills for Argument Writing

Undarmaa Maamuujav and Jacob Steiss

University of Michigan Press
Ann Arbor

Published in the United States of America by the
University of Michigan Press

ISBN 978-0-472-04008-7 (paperback)
ISBN 978-0-472-22244-5 (e-book)

First published January 2026

Authorized Representative: Easy Access System Europe, Mustamäe tee 50, 10621 Tallinn, Estonia, gpsr.requests@easproject.com

Academic Languaging and Historical Thinking

Contents

List of Figures

List of Tables

Acknowledgments

This book has grown quite a bit from our initial four-page document describing language support for argument writing in history and the accompanying Academic Language Toolkit developed for the WRITE Center's professional development intervention for middle and high school history teachers. The WRITE (Writing Research to Improve Teaching and Evaluation) Center at the University of California, Irvine, funded by the Institute of Education Sciences (IES; Grant R305C190007), extended evidence-based practices from three nationally recognized interventions—the Pathway to Academic Success Project; College, Career, and Community Writers Program (C3WP); and Self-Regulated Strategy Development (SRSD)—into history classrooms with the goal to provide teachers with the professional learning needed to improve their students' writing.

We would like to express our sincere gratitude to the teachers and students whose work is featured in this book. We are inspired by the resolve and resilience of the many teachers who support learners with diverse needs, backgrounds, and experiences. The strategies we include in this book have been tested by teachers and students who participated in the WRITE Center intervention. Their work is important in advancing our understanding of language and writing development and contributes to our collective goal of supporting culturally and linguistically diverse learners for academic literacy.

Our deepest appreciation goes to our doctoral advisor Carol Booth Olson, who was the principal investigator and director of the WRITE Center. Her support, guidance, and trust have been instrumental not only in this project with the WRITE Center but also in our professional journeys of growing as scholars and researchers. Her commitment to causes beyond her own and her drive to improve teaching and extend educational opportunities to underserved youth have always inspired us.

This book builds on the important work of many scholars who have influenced our learning. We acknowledge the intellectual contributions of major scholars such as Sam Wineburg, Chauncey Monte-Sano, Jeffrey D. Nokes, Nicole Gilbertson, Mary Schleppegrell, Bob Bain, Luciana C. de Oliveira, Michael Halliday, and Caroline Coffin. Their innovative ideas in inquiry-based history instruction and language development have been instrumental in the conceptualization and creation of this manuscript.

We are especially grateful to the University of Michigan Press staff, including Katie D. LaPlant, Haley Winkle, Juliette Snyder, and Danielle Coty-Fattal, as well as Bailey Odom, for providing clear guidance throughout the writing process. Without their support, this book would not have come to fruition. We are also grateful to the reviewers for providing us with thorough and thoughtful feedback that helped us improve and strengthen the content of the book.

Finally, we extend our heartfelt gratitude to our families for their understanding and unwavering support. Writing this book while managing our demanding full-time roles as research scientists was a challenging endeavor that often took time away from precious family moments. Some of these chapters were crafted amidst soccer practices in the evenings and during halftime and water breaks of weekend games. The support of our loved ones—Todd, Maika, Anu, Otgonbayar, Maggie, and Mia—has been a source of strength. Their understanding and encouragement reinforce the importance of our work and its impact on education.

Preface

To succeed in college and career, students are expected to master specialized language and communication skills used in academic and professional settings. However, they often receive insufficient instruction and guidance in developing these skills. Many teachers recognize the importance of developing language skills for academic communication but may lack the pedagogical language knowledge (Galguera, 2011) necessary to support learners with diverse linguistic backgrounds and needs. In light of this issue, this book provides instructional guidance to practicing and pre-service teachers, teacher educators, instructional mentors, homeschooling parents, college professors, and all other educational stakeholders who support secondary and postsecondary students' argument writing development.

In this book, we demystify the *academic languaging* practices that are used in historical argumentation. We are intentional in our use of the term "academic languag*ing*" with the "*ing*" suffix emphasizing the dynamic nature of language use that not only reflects linguistic flexibility but reinforces the importance of context in shaping how we communicate. Our choice of this term highlights the nuances of communication, illustrating how language adapts and transforms across different contexts and how we adjust our language to suit varying audiences and purposes as we shift from informal conversations to more structured academic discourse.

To help students use language more effectively in historical argumentation, we unpack the language structures and patterns underlying historical reasoning—an important disciplinary literacy skill set that students need in order to make evidence-based arguments of the past. We make explicit how language functions in argument construction and provide instructional guidance that supports students in expanding their linguistic repertoires and language knowledge. In doing so, we aim to promote pedagogical language knowledge, which is essential for guiding students to make linguistic choices skillfully and strategically. Such language support and guidance can help students not only bolster the clarity and strength of their arguments but also develop their reasoning and historical thinking skills.

Our primary focus is on developing language skills for source-based argument writing in history and beyond. Curricular and instructional mandates for literacy development in U.S. secondary schools have placed a considerable emphasis on students' argument writing. For example, the College, Career, and Civic Life (C3) Framework for Social Studies State Standards stresses the need for secondary students to develop proficiency in argument writing in the content areas as it is central to postsecondary educational attainment, career success, and civic engagement (National Council for the Social Studies, 2013). Similarly, the Common Core State Standards (CCSS) for English Language Arts & Literacy in History/Social Studies, Science, and Technical Subjects describe argument literacy as "essential to both private deliberation and responsible citizenship in a democratic republic" (National Governors Association Center for Best Practices & Council of Chief State School Officers, 2010, p. 3). The significance of argument writing in content areas is also emphasized by Steve Graham and Dolores Perin (2007), who assert that writing effectively in academic contexts is "not just an option for young people—it is a necessity," as it is "a predictor of academic success and a basic requirement for participation in civic life and in the global economy" (p. 3).

Despite the emphasis on argument writing and disciplinary literacy in national and state standards, there is little guidance on how to meaningfully support the disciplinary language and literacy development of diverse secondary and postsecondary students, particularly multilingual learners of English (MLEs) who are learning to write in their second or an additional language. Even the Common Core State Standards explicitly state that defining the range of instructional supports that are available for students developing their proficiency in English is "beyond the scope of the Standards" (California CCSS, 2013, p. 5). How to support language development may be beyond the scope of the standards, but it is certainly not beyond the scope of classroom teachers who are responsible for finding ways to meet the diverse linguistic needs of adolescent students in argument writing and disciplinary literacy. We feel compelled to assist teachers in this mission.

We focus on language pedagogy for inquiry-based literacy, with the goal to help teachers and students recognize the functions and structures of language underlying historical inquiry and disciplinary literacy. Building on Sam Wineburg's (2001) work on thinking like a historian and Peter Seixas and Tom Morton's (2013) Big Six Historical Thinking Concepts, we highlight how language is used to represent historical thinking and offer instructional tools and scaffolds that enable students to engage in such academic languaging practices. In addition to practicing the thinking and reasoning skills necessary for historical inquiry, students must develop language skills to express their thinking and reasoning. This book offers practical strategies and guidance for teachers to effectively support their students in developing language skills for argument writing.

Introduction

With a premium placed on argument writing and disciplinary literacy—subject-specific ways of reading, thinking, and writing that perform the distinct tasks of a discipline—adolescent students are expected to develop several advanced skills. Students must analyze and interpret complex texts, synthesize multiple sources, and formulate compelling arguments supported by reliable evidence and sound reasoning. These higher-order tasks require students to be proficient in and knowledgeable about the specialized languaging practices of academic written discourse. Just as adolescents learn distinct discourse patterns for socializing with friends, they also need to master the discourse patterns used in disciplinary writing and use language strategically as they move between discourse communities.

Students who are developing their disciplinary literacy skills need to be provided with language support because the *academic languaging* practices underlying disciplinary thinking are obscure to many of these students. This means content area teachers share the responsibility for students' academic literacy development. George C. Bunch and colleagues (2014) underscore the shared responsibility among teachers by stating that a vision of career and college readiness requires students to learn the conventions of disciplinary literacy, and "literacy instruction involves collaboration among teachers across disciplines" (p. 3). Similarly, Laura Schall-Leckrone (2022) contends that all teachers need pedagogical language knowledge to support their students in increasingly multilingual classrooms with linguistically diverse students.

While this is the case, content area teachers are not equipped to teach language and provide language support to their linguistically diverse students. For example, Nicole Gilbertson (2012) noted that most history teachers are unfamiliar with the linguistic research and language structures underlying history content. While history teachers have content expertise, they are not accustomed to teaching language and writing (Schall-Leckrone & Barron, 2018). With a lack of guidance, resources, and time to develop instructional materials, secondary teachers in content-area classrooms, such as history, find it challenging to address the varied linguistic needs of their students. Therefore, it is crucial to support teachers in their efforts to help students develop academic literacy in content-area classrooms.

Recently, efforts have emerged to equip teachers to build students' disciplinary literacy skills in history, such as the explicit adoption of literacy standards by states and the allocation of funding for professional development to support the implementation of disciplinary literacy instruction in history (see California History-Social Science Project; Read.Inquire.Write; Stanford History Education Group, renamed as Digital Inquiry Group; the WRITE Center). Jeffrey D. Nokes (2017) has described an ongoing shift in the U.S. history classroom toward greater inquiry-oriented literacy instruction. In light of these developments, this book doesn't merely draw on the bodies of research around historical inquiry and disciplinary literacy but rather puts them in conversation with each other to help teachers enhance students' historical thinking, argument writing, and academic languaging.

While building historical thinking and argumentation skills is beneficial in itself, the recent emphasis on literacy instruction in history is partially due to the capacity of social studies instruction to build critical thinking and communication skills that students can apply in social and civic domains. Disciplinary literacy skills central to history (e.g., sourcing, evaluating documents, and resolving conflicting claims through evidence-based reasoning) can transfer beyond the history classroom as students answer important civic questions and engage in democratic deliberation (Nokes & De La Paz, 2023). Just as language underlies sound historical discourse, the strategic use of language is also essential for productive civic deliberation and argumentation. Thus, this book can help those concerned with building language skills for argumentation more broadly.

By addressing a gap in language pedagogy related to argument literacy and historical inquiry, we hope to enhance language and writing instruction in content-area classrooms. Our emphasis on language and the use of a functional language approach based on Systemic Functional Linguistics (SFL) offers teachers the understanding and tools to transform concepts into pedagogical moves to deepen students' knowledge and skills in historical argumentation. We focus on four key areas: making claims, using evidence, expressing reasoning, and addressing counterclaims. The use of effective language to communicate historical, social, and civic arguments is a key competency future citizens need. This is why we are compelled to respond to a pressing issue facing many teachers in both secondary and postsecondary contexts: a lack of pedagogical knowledge about language use. Such knowledge is essential for addressing diverse linguistic needs of students and for helping them become confident academic writers and competent language users.

What to Expect

The book consists of six chapters. The first two chapters provide a rationale for linking academic languaging with historical thinking, make a case for language support in history classrooms, and provide evidence for language-focused instruction to develop students' disciplinary literacy. Each of the remaining chapters (three through six) focuses on

1. *a key historical thinking concept* to provide an overview;
2. *disciplinary language features* that underlie the specific historical thinking skills; and
3. *instructional strategies* for teachers to build pedagogical language knowledge to better support students in improving their academic languaging practices and disciplinary thinking concurrently.

Each chapter opens with guiding questions that frame the discussion and organize the content. We provide a brief synopsis of each chapter below.

Chapter 1 describes the inextricable link between language and thinking and elucidates how proficiency in *both* facilitates success in source-based argument writing genres. We describe the need for students to build language skills to effectively communicate in an academic context, as well as higher-order disciplinary reasoning skills for college, career, and civic preparedness. We also argue that although the development of thinking and language are intertwined, more attention has recently been given to reasoning, thinking, and making sense of historical documents than to language.

Chapter 2 describes the language demands of constructing and developing arguments in history and the challenges facing students and teachers in meeting these demands. We explain why focusing on language and providing contextualized language support are integral in multilingual classrooms. Based on a review of the literature and research on the SFL approach at the intersection of language and history, we make a case for a language-focused approach in history classrooms and discuss how teachers can provide meaningful language support to meet the linguistic needs of their diverse learners.

Chapter 3 focuses on **making claims** as a key disciplinary practice. The various reasons for making claims and the norms for argumentation in history necessitate strategic linguistic choices. For example, historians hedge their claims given the tentative nature of history and thus use *modal verbs* like *would, can, could, may,* and *might*, as well as *introductory verbs* like *appear, seem,* and *suggest* to qualify their claims. Such academic languaging practices recognize that claims are limited by available evidence, perspectives, and historical contexts. After unpacking the languaging practices used in making claims, we provide guidance to help students build language skills for formulating claims with varying degrees of sophistication.

Chapter 4 discusses **sourcing and integrating evidence**, calling attention to key rhetorical moves, such as attributing, questioning, evaluating, and integrating sources, and the accompanying disciplinary language choices for integrating evidence from multiple sources to support arguments. For example, writers may use *infinitive phrases* to show the purpose of sources (e.g., *to record, in order to persuade*), and they may use *modifiers* (e.g., *the New York Times* article *published in 1918)* to provide important contextual details about a source. We then provide guidance for teachers to explicitly teach the language skills students need to source, contextualize, evaluate, and integrate evidence.

Chapter 5 focuses on the **reasoning** involved in historical arguments—contextualization, causal thinking, counterfactual reasoning, corroboration, and interpretation. We outline how reasoning is expressed in specific language moves. For example, students may need to leverage multiple pieces of evidence to advance a claim. Using *linking words* (e.g., *both . . . and, similarly, whereas*) can facilitate corroboration and allow students to make more persuasive arguments. Students also need to learn how writers express causality through different linguistic choices such as *causal verbs* (e.g., *contribute to, engender, produce, precipitate*), *causal nouns* (e.g., *consequence, effect, reason, byproduct*), and *causal connectors* (e.g., *since, as, consequently*). Expressing evidence-based reasoning to support or challenge claims is also a core civic competency that teachers must cultivate in students.

Chapter 6 focuses on **presenting and addressing counterarguments** in historical inquiry. As multiple perspectives and claims about historical events should be considered to best understand a complex past, writers make specific linguistic choices to express this tentative disposition. To effectively present and address counterarguments, students need language to introduce and respond to an alternative view by acknowledging, conceding, and refuting counterclaims. We provide instructional activities to help students expand their linguistic repertories so that they can make informed and effective language choices. Further, as social-justice-oriented educators may choose to directly challenge oppressive or hegemonic interpretations of the past, the nuanced language skills we outline in this chapter would facilitate students' construction of effective and clear counterclaims as they *rewrite* or *critique* problematic interpretations of the past.

Language skills and historical reasoning should be addressed jointly as they mutually support each other's development and are maintained by the same disciplinary understanding of history. Addressing both of these areas simultaneously will help students develop disciplinary thinking, construct compelling arguments, and communicate effectively by making strategic and intentional language choices.

CHAPTER 1

Language, Thinking, and Historical Argumentation

Guiding Questions

- How are language and thinking linked?
- What role does language play in historical argumentation?
- Why is it important to engage students in argument writing in history?
- Why cultivate students' language skills for argument writing in history?

During a unit on Medieval Europe as part of the World History curriculum, a seventh-grade teacher poses a question: *What caused the decline of feudalism?* Students explore this question through historical inquiry—analyzing multiple primary and secondary sources, establishing historical evidence, and forming interpretations. They then write an argument essay that synthesizes evidence from multiple sources to respond to this historical question. Completing this writing task requires each student to

- make a claim about the cause or causes that contributed to the decline of feudalism,
- support their claim with evidence from various sources,
- provide reasoning why the evidence supports their claim,
- address alternative explanations for the decline of feudalism, and
- organize all of these rhetorical components into a coherent text.

Importantly, they will have to strategically use language to externalize their thinking to an audience, expressing complex ideas in a clear and cogent manner. This is no easy feat!

Students who have yet to develop historical reasoning and academic language skills will find this task daunting. They may resort to summarizing the sources they read instead of formulating a compelling argument supported by evidence. They may use familiar language, common in narration or everyday conversation, as seen in the following example:

> Black Death killed 1/3 of the European people and had an effect on the social structure of Europe. The deaths and peasants trying to escape the plague made it hard to find people to work on the land. This killed the feudal system.

The language used to construct the text above exhibits features of a summary rather than reasoning and argumentation. The sentences list events in an additive style, leaving the causal links between ideas implicit.

On the other hand, students who are equipped with historical reasoning skills and disciplinary language resources will likely craft more effective arguments. Let's look at an example by another student who made the following interpretive claim about what led to the decline of feudalism:

> Although the Magna Carta and Hundred Years War both contributed to the decline of feudalism, the Black Death played a key role in the deterioration of the social system due to the impact it had on the supply of labor.

The language used to construct this claim reflects historical reasoning that not only acknowledges the role of multiple forces that contribute to a historical outcome but also expresses a stance more clearly, using language that explicitly conveys causal relationships—*contributed to, played a key role, deterioration, due to.* We use these two examples to illustrate how constructing effective historical arguments requires both historical reasoning skills and language resources. Students must develop the skills to make strategic language choices to effectively communicate their thoughts and reasoning.

The Link Between Language and Thinking

The connection between language and thinking has been investigated and discussed extensively by linguists, philosophers, cognitive psychologists, neuroscientists, and others. The German philosopher and linguist Wilhelm von Humboldt (1999) argued:

> *Intellectual activity*, entirely mental, entirely internal, and to some extent passing without a trace, becomes, through sound, externalized in speech and perceptible to the senses. *Thought and language are therefore one and inseparable from each other.* (p. 54; italics added)

Language enables the expression of ideas, externalizing underlying thinking, reasoning, and mental representations. Tilbe Göksun (2020) contends that language "not only facilitates thought communication but also shapes and diversifies thinking" (para. 1). When language is used to describe abstract ideas that go beyond the concrete things we see and experience, it helps us think and form new concepts (Göksun, 2020). Language and thinking influence and interact with each other in a facilitative way—language plays a critical role in the development of analytical thinking, and the development of analytical thinking, in turn, expands language skills. Such a contention has been supported in writing research (Kim & Graham, 2022), and our work shows language and reasoning skills are strongly related (Steiss et al., 2024). This bidirectional relation between language and thinking is important to acknowledge when developing students' historical argumentation.

How language connects to thinking is also underscored in Systemic Functional Linguistics (SFL; Halliday, 1978, 1994) that takes a functional-semantic approach to understanding how language is used in specific contexts. As an analytic approach that describes and interprets language use and patterns in context, SFL focuses on how meaning is made, knowledge is communicated, and thinking is externalized in and through language. Regarding the relationship between language and thought, Michael Halliday and Christian Matthiessen (2014) emphasize that language needs to be connected to the underlying concepts and thinking as "we seek to understand the nature and the dynamic of a semiotic system as a whole" (p. 20). Because the key function of language is to represent thinking and communicate thoughts, it cannot be separated from thinking. In the context of disciplinary discourse, like historical argumentation, thinking becomes more complex as it revolves around abstract concepts like causation, changes, and consequence. Thus, the language that construes the concepts and expresses the thinking also becomes more complex (Schleppegrell et al., 2004).

In the context of argument writing in history, students not only need to develop discipline-specific *thinking* skills, but they also need to learn to use *language* aligned with disciplinary thinking. For example, Carol Berkenkotter et al. (1991) assert that writing in the discipline requires an ability to use "discipline-specific rhetorical and linguistic conventions to serve their purposes as writers" (p. 191). Therefore, to participate fully in disciplinary discourse, students need to understand the distinct rhetorical and linguistic choices made in disciplinary writing (i.e., how meaning is constructed, organized, and presented using language in a written form). By fostering this understanding, students cultivate critical language awareness (Shapiro, 2022) that enables them to make informed and intentional language choices, realize the rhetorical effect of their choices, and learn to adapt their language and communication styles effectively in various contexts.

The Role of Language in Historical Argumentation

As the discipline of history studies people, events, and their interactions across time and space, historical argumentation is the process through which historians analyze evidence, synthesize information, and construct reasoned interpretations of the past. To engage effectively in this practice, they must develop a specialized language. In fact, students' language use is a crucial factor underlying effective rhetorical moves and overall writing quality (Maamuujav, 2022). In our research, we find evidence that the linguistic features of writing are strongly correlated with the disciplinary components (Steiss et al., 2024). Word- and sentence-level linguistic features of students' source-based argument writing are related to the rhetorical features such as source use, text cohesion, and the ways students integrate evidence and reasoning in their writing (Maamuujav, 2022). We also find that students who improve their linguistic skills improve their reasoning skills, and vice versa (Olson et al., 2023). Similarly, Charles A. MacArthur et al. (2018) found that linguistic features of students' argument essays predicted writing quality, and the changes in response to instruction resulted in improvement in language use.

To better see the role of language in expressing historical thinking, let's take a look at the following excerpt from student writing that seeks to advance an argument about what led to the success of the Delano Grape Strike and Boycott. As you read the passage, notice the student's language choices, where they display complex reasoning, and whether the argument is clear and compelling.

Student Sample on Delano Grape Strike and Boycott

> There were some we'll know names in this protest, one being Cesar Chavez others might say he was the main reason for the success as

> he was the leader of the protest and is the one who organized all the marches. He also wrote a letter to the public stating please do not buy any grapes from California that the bosses treat their workers unfairly. He also stated in that letter sent out to the public for them to join him and the farmers in their march and he was very influential. That is all good. The article where I found these facts was very reliable and trustworthy; its just that he is not the main reason for the success. Ceaser Chavez had a real impact for the success but still the main reason for the success is the public; because they could have ignored his letters and speeches but they didn't. They followed the boycott by not buying grapes, getting the bosses to lose money and which eventually led to an official agreement. The public didn't only boycott they also went and involved themselves in the marches giving the farmers protection and the feel of togetherness.

First, we note that this student does a lot of things well. They display complex disciplinary reasoning as they

- *acknowledge* that there are *many potential forces* (e.g., *letters sent to the public, leadership during marches*) that should be weighed when engaging in causal analysis; and
- use *counterfactual reasoning* to frame the letters as causal agents that required future commitment to reach the end goal of the boycott (e.g., *because they could have ignored his letters and speeches but they didn't*).

However, the use of colloquial language—phrases, expressions, and syntactic construction that are common in informal conversation—makes the argument less persuasive, if not opaque. As language is the vehicle for transporting complex disciplinary thinking to a discourse community, here it does not do so effectively. Neglecting to use precise and specialized language that aligns with disciplinary norms obscures students' complex thinking. While *mastery* of language enhances thinking and expression, *misaligned* language use prevents students from articulating their reasoning.

Recognizing this student's potential for growth as a communicator, we see clear paths for helping them make their thinking and reasoning more explicit and effective. A revised version of the following excerpt exhibits different language choices—achievable through instruction and scaffolded practice—that more effectively convey the same ideas and historical reasoning originally presented.

Original Writing

> . . . but still the main reason for the success is the public; because they could have ignored his letters and speeches but they didn't. They followed the boycott by not buying grapes, getting the bosses to lose money and which eventually led to an official agreement.

Revised Version

> The public's participation in the boycott ***shaped*** the eventual success of the boycott. The public could have ignored Chavez's letters and speeches, but they didn't. ***If the public did not devote themselves to the cause . . .***

The revised version shows the use of a *causal verb* (*shaped*) to foreground the role of the public and center the causal link between public participation and the success of the boycott. The addition of a *conditional clause* (*if the public did not devote themselves to the cause* . . .) indicates consideration of the likelihood of other plausible outcomes.

The inextricable link between *language* and *thinking* necessitates an instructional approach that addresses these two complex skills alongside each other. Such an approach needs to make visible how language works. This can be done through functional language analysis (we will discuss this in greater detail in chapter 2) that involves deconstructing and unpacking texts to make visible the underlying language patterns and structures (Schleppegrell & de Oliveira, 2006). This approach helps students understand how language is used to communicate disciplinary thinking. Such understanding is essential for them to make strategic and intentional language choices aligned with the norms and expectations of the disciplinary community.

Textual deconstruction is an important method for showing how language functions, as it reveals the underlying linguistic choices that are made in constructing meaning. It makes apparent the relationship between disciplinary thinking and the languaging practices involved in historical argumentation. In this regard, Mary Schleppegrell (2004) remarked:

> To achieve advanced literacy and disciplinary knowledge, students need to be able to understand how language construes meanings in content-area texts and how the important meanings and concepts of

school subjects are realized in language. In other words, disciplinary knowledge is not taught in isolation from language (p. 68).

We use the SFL-based functional language analysis to deconstruct texts and demystify languaging practices in connection to historical argumentation and reasoning. Our goal is to help teachers and students to recognize language features, markers, and patterns in context and build knowledge of language use and disciplinary concepts.

Developing language skills in conjunction with historical thinking can enable students to communicate their thoughts powerfully and effectively. While we emphasize the importance of cultivating language and reasoning skills *jointly* to promote disciplinary literacy, we want to briefly illustrate the distinct and growing calls for students to build these skills in the following section.

The Importance of Argument Writing in History

Engaging students in argument writing in history plays a pivotal role in developing their inquiry, argumentation, and reasoning skills, which are essential in both history and civic life. As mentioned in the preface, U.S. researchers, policymakers, and teachers are increasingly prioritizing students' inquiry skills and argument writing (De La Paz et al., 2017). While we interpret this trend positively, it also reflects a lack of literacy instruction previously (Monte-Sano & Allen, 2019) and a lack of training in writing instruction for history teachers (Tate & Collins, 2022). Without training in writing and language instruction, history teachers face challenges in effectively guiding students to develop language and writing skills essential for constructing historical arguments.

Still, many educators today are rising to meet the challenge of literacy-based instruction in content areas through authentic disciplinary inquiry (Cowgill II & Waring, 2017). This means thinking about the tasks, language, and purposes of literacy in a specific discipline: *What is history for? What does communicating in history look like given its purposes? What are the skills, norms, and practices we use to answer historical questions?* The shift from memorizing facts and dates to constructing interpretations of the past through inquiry and defending claims with evidentiary thinking has been aided by innovative teaching methods that develop reading and inquiry skills (Monte-Sano & De La Paz, 2012; Wineburg, 1991). Writing is foundational to these skills as it provides students with an opportunity to express and externalize their thinking, make connections between different concepts, organize and synthesize information, and learn to communicate effectively.

Argument writing in history also has immense civic and social importance as future citizens need to be prepared to construct evidence-based claims and reason in the "intertextual reality" of the twenty-first century (Bråten et al., 2011, p. 49). Defending claims with sources of evidence that have varying degrees of reliability is just one key competency for civic life that teachers can build in daily classroom instruction. Keith Barton and Linda Levstik (2004), for example, contend that developing argumentation through reasoned judgment about the past is critical to prepare students for democratic citizenship. They argue:

> Reflection on the causes of historical events and processes, their relative significance, the potential outcomes of alternative courses of action, the impact of the past on the present—all these require the deep and sensitive reasoning characteristic of humanistic study. (p. 36)

Argument writing, then, is an important way to foster reasoning skills. In fact, arguing a position based on reasoning and evidence is a key attribute of civic writing and a critical component of advocating civic engagement and action as indicated in the National Writing Project's Civically Engaged Writing Analysis Continuum (CEWAC).

Despite its importance, less time has been devoted to developing the language skills needed for argument writing in history. The shift toward disciplinary reading and writing requires addressing new linguistic challenges for students, as the demands of language differ across genres and the rhetorical tasks within specific disciplines. While curricula and lessons exist to develop historical inquiry skills like sourcing, which involves questioning and evaluating sources, these lessons spend less time emphasizing the specific languaging practices underlying the thinking and inquiry process.

Cultivating Language Skills for Argument Writing in History

Developing language skills for argument writing in history augments students' existing linguistic resources, allowing them to construct meaning and communicate complex thinking. Argument writing is an academic writing genre that is characterized by its interpretive stance, informational purpose, and impersonal style. It exhibits specialized patterns of language use and grammatical complexity that students learning to write in an academic context must acquire

(Schleppegrell, 2001). In essence, students need to develop knowledge, skills, and awareness of the disciplinary language features to become effective academic writers.

Writing involves both the "language system" and the "cognitive system for memory and thinking" (Kellogg, 2008, p. 2). However, students who haven't developed the necessary language skills are often cognitively overloaded. For these students, developing proficiency in argument writing is constrained by various factors affecting language development, including their exposure to disciplinary literacy practices and formal instruction, previous development of linguistic knowledge, and the extent to which they pay attention to words, phrases, and sentence structures (Olson et al., 2015). Through exposure and explicit focus on language in connection to historical thinking, teachers can help student writers expand their linguistic repertoires and develop awareness that linguistic choices are shaped by many factors, including disciplinary thinking practices, rhetorical goals, and the context of communication.

While language development is vital for all students' college, career, and civic preparedness, it is particularly important for multilingual learners whose home language differs from the language used in disciplinary communication. For many of these students, school serves as a space where they build the language skills necessary for disciplinary reading, writing, and thinking. Yet, research shows that multilingual learners of English in college who have completed their secondary education in U.S. schools often have lower writing performance and exhibit limited knowledge of formal language because they are likely to develop their proficiency in language by immersing themselves in casual, nonacademic situations (di Gennaro, 2013; Reid, 2006). Pedagogy geared toward meeting the disciplinary language and literacy needs of these students in history classrooms is a critical effort to level the playing field for this student population.

We can better support linguistically diverse students in developing language knowledge and skills alongside historical thinking. We can help them become effective communicators, confident writers, and critical thinkers. We can achieve these goals by using an integrated pedagogical approach that makes language, thinking, and content visible and tangible through writing (Figure 1). Such an approach is at the core of disciplinary literacy development, which emphasizes evidentiary thinking to foster accurate interpretations of the past. An instructional approach that connects language development, historical thinking, and content knowledge is critical for enhancing students' academic writing and historical argumentation skills.

Emphasizing the connections between language, thinking, and content in developing disciplinary understanding, we provide rationale and evidence for

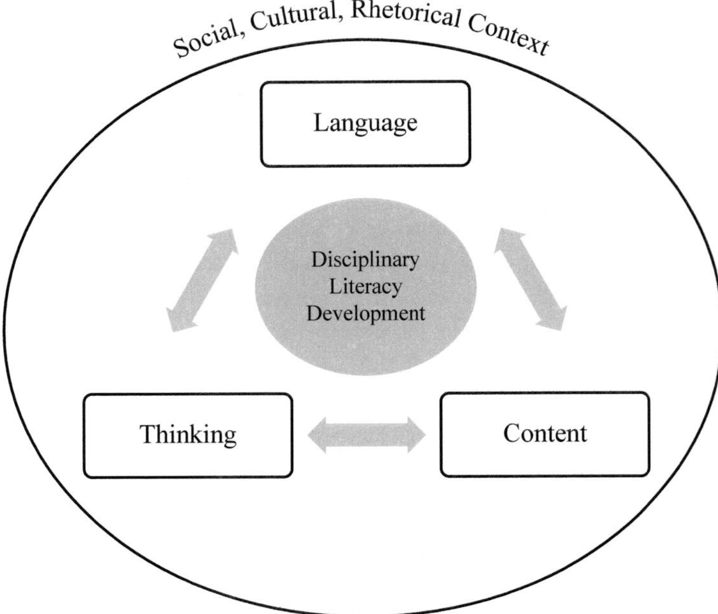

Figure 1. Disciplinary Literacy Development

language-focused instruction and further explore the language demands and support for historical argumentation in the following chapter. This exploration draws on research and literature at the intersection of history content, language, and thinking.

CHAPTER 2

Language Demands of and Support for Argumentation

Guiding Questions

- What are the language demands of historical argumentation?
- What are the challenges facing students and teachers in argument writing?
- How do we reframe the challenges as opportunities in the history classroom?
- Why provide language support to multilingual learners of English?
- What is academic languaging and why support it?

When history teachers, such as the seventh-grade teacher mentioned in the previous chapter, ask students to write an argument essay in response to questions like *What caused the decline of feudalism?* or *How did the women's suffrage movement succeed in passing the Nineteenth Amendment?*, they provide an opportunity for students to do the work of history. Students engage in complex reasoning and argumentation, moving beyond the tasks of recalling and retelling. This engagement in historical reasoning and argumentation depends heavily on language resources. Mary Schleppegrell and Mariana Achugar (2003) state that it is "through language and in language" that argumentation and disciplinary reasoning are constructed and communicated (p. 21). Despite the fact that language is the conduit through which higher-order disciplinary thinking is carried out, the disciplinary language and literacy practices for historical argumentation are often obscure to students.

While students draw on their existing linguistic resources to construct arguments in history, they need to further develop language resources to participate in disciplinary discourse. Participation in such discourse requires students to move beyond what Carl Bereiter and Marlene Scardamalia (1987) refer to as "knowledge telling," a skill that relies primarily on retelling and summarizing. Instead, students need to reach an advanced level of "knowledge transformation" (Bereiter & Scardamalia, 1987). Transforming knowledge requires complex rhetorical problem solving as students analyze, synthesize, corroborate, consider multiple interpretations, evaluate sources, and extract evidence from multiple sources to construct arguments.

Similar to Bereiter and Scardamalia, Caroline Coffin (2006) asserts that constructing an argument in history requires students to go beyond what she refers to as recording genres that include historical accounts and recounts, as well as autobiographical and biographical recounts. Students have much more exposure to recording genres than arguing genres as the former are prioritized in earlier grades and in history curriculum (Coffin, 2004, 2006). Thus, students develop linguistic repertoires to narrate and record their own lived experiences and historical events early on. Students lacking the language resources for constructing historical arguments tend to summarize or recount information as these language resources are more readily accessible. To transition to knowledge transformation, students need language resources for argumentation.

To illustrate this point, we use two sample student responses from an eleventh-grade U.S. history class. Both of these responses address the essential question: *How did the women's suffrage movement succeed in passing the Nineteenth Amendment?* To complete this task successfully, each student has to

- make a claim that responds to the question,
- read multiple sources to extract evidence to support their claim,
- evaluate the reliability of the sources,
- provide reasoning on why and how the evidence presented supports their claim,
- present a potential counterargument or an alternative view, and
- convince readers of their argument's strength through evidence and reasoning.

They also need to situate the event in its historical context and comment on the significance of the event in the present day. These tasks require students to go beyond simply retelling what the sources say—they require academic languaging and historical thinking.

As you read Sample Response 1, pay attention to the specific language choices made, consider how these choices contribute to the overall effectiveness of the argument, and observe the structure of the text.

<u>Sample Response 1</u>

> In the 1890, the women's suffrage movement was one of the decade's struggles which helped women win the right to vote for women in the United States. During the women's suffrage movement in the United States, the people that were called "suffragists" were anyone (male or female) who supported extending the right to vote (suffrage) to women. The women's suffrage movement was a decade-long fight which took nearly over 100 years for the womens to win that right. The women's suffrage movement was started in the early 19th century during the trouble against slavery. The women's suffrage movement succeeded in passing the 19th amendment because after a battle, the womens has the right to vote. Anthony and the first introducer in 1878, said that "The right of citizens of the United States to vote shall not be denied or abridged by the United States or by any State on account of sex." This statement by Anthony and the first introducer in 1878 helped the women's suffrage movement to succeed more than anything else. The 19th amendment is also known as Anthony Amendment, named for Susan B. Anthony since she was the person who made the women's suffrage movement to succeed. In 1848, a group of abolitionist gathered in Seneca Falls and discussed the problem of women's rights. They were invited there by the reformers Elizabeth Cady Stanton and Lucretia Mott. The group argued that American women had the right to vote. In the Declaration of Sentiment, they stated "that all men and *women* are created equal, that they are endowed by their creator with certain inalienable rights, that among these are life, liberty, and the pursuit of happiness." Their statement also helped the women's suffrage movement to succeed. In addition, the women's suffrage movement succeeded with the help of Susan B. Anthony, Elizabeth Cady Staton and Lucretia Mott. They helped the women's suffrage movement pass the 19th amendment and be a right for itself. What we can learn from the success of the women's suffrage movement by knowing that sex and gender or race does not matter in this world and everyone have the right to vote in the United States.

In Sample Response 1, although a claim is presented—*This statement by Anthony and the first introducer in 1878 helped the women's suffrage movement to succeed more than anything else*—there is no explanation of *why* or *how* the statement helped the women's suffrage movement succeed. When we closely look at the structure of the text, we see that it follows an "orientation and account" structure that is typical of the recounting genre (Coffin, 2006; Derewianka & Jones, 2023). Instead of analyzing why events led to the passage of the Nineteenth Amendment, the student mainly engages in **orientation** (providing background information responding to who, what, when, where things happened) and **account** (recording events as they unfold in chronological order). In other words, the writer engages in knowledge telling, recounting what they read without synthesizing source material to make an interpretative argument about the past.

When examining the syntax of the passage, we notice that the student starts multiple sentences with the same subject-verb pattern: *The women's suffrage movement was*. The student then focuses on the key actor (*Anthony, the first introducer, she*) and actors (*a group of abolitionist, they, the reformers, Elizabeth Cady Stanton, Lucretia Mott, the group*). These language features that focus on concrete elements are more reflective of a recounting genre than an arguing genre that often deals with abstract ideas. As Coffin (2006) points out, in historical *recounts* an emphasis is often placed on people, groups, and other concrete elements, while *arguing* genres emphasize change, continuity, and other abstract notions. This student could benefit from instructional support to develop language resources for expressing abstraction and causation.

The next response from a different eleventh-grade student shows language that moves beyond retelling to argumentation. As you read Sample Response 2, take note of how it differs from the previous response in terms of language use, text structure, and argument development.

<u>Sample Response 2</u>

> The women's suffrage movement was a decades-long struggle that eventually led to the passage of the 19th amendment granting American women the right to vote. Many contributed to the movement, including state-level suffrage organizers, national protests by the National Women's Party (NWP), and early suffragists who laid the foundation for the larger women's rights movement. Although early suffragists generated interest in the cause of women's suffrage, the actions and tactics of the National Women's Party were most directly responsible for the passage of the 19th amendment because they put crucial pressure on national political figures.
>
> The protests and demonstrations of the National Women's Party were the most critical contributor for passing of the 19th amendment. We first see evidence of their progress in the 1915 NY Times article. The

article describes a suffrage amendment being voted on in Congress, but being defeated by a "vote of 174 to 204." While at first this seems negative, it does show progress in changing national lawmakers' opinions on the issue of suffrage in 1915. In the article, Dr. Howard Anna Shaw claims, "Suffrage is no longer a local question because the National House of Representatives has discussed suffrage . . ." This shows that the movement is finally making progress towards a national amendment, progress that had not yet been seen since the Seneca Fall Convention 60 years ago.

Because there was still work to do, the NWP staged a number of public demonstrations over the next five years so that the President and others in Congress began to change their stances on suffrage. We see protests by the NWP in the NPS article (Source 6), the 1918 NYTimes article (Source 5), and the Women's suffrage overview (Source 1). These protests, including picketing and hunger strikes, applied pressure needed for the movement to progress. Alice Paul, leader of these demonstrations and the NWP, notes the progress of the movement: "President Wilson made a magnificent speech calling for the amendment as a war measure Without action on a national stage in the form of pickets, protests, and the accompanying press, the President and then Congress may not have ever passed the amendment. The NPS article (Source 6) also confirms the impact of the NWP's picketing on the President and Congress' changing perspective on women's suffrage.

Others may argue that there would have been no political action without the advocacy of early suffragists like Susan B. Anthony. Anthony references the Constitution and citizenship rights in her speech given in 1872: "it was we, the people; not we the white male citizens; nor yet, we the male citizens; but we, the whole people who formed this union." However, none of the documents indicate her speech was effective in moving public opinion or producing legislation leading to the 19th amendment. There is actually much evidence her words were ineffective. The timeline of the Women's Suffrage movement notes that congressional amendments failed multiple times in the 19th and 20th centuries; these failures occurred years after her speeches and writings and years after her death indicating that her speeches were not pivotal to the passage of the 19th amendment.

As leader of the NWP, Alice Paul ends her interview noting, "I always feel . . . the movement is a sort of mosaic. Each of us puts in one little stone, and then you get a great mosaic at the end." Although the contributions of early leaders in the Women's Suffrage Movement were important, it was Paul's leadership and the catalyzing efforts that were the cornerstone in the mosaic, without which the 19th amendment may not have been passed. What we can learn from this is that while speeches may bring attention to a movement, it takes a more national action targeted to influence people in power to make lasting change.

Sample Response 2 presents a clear and nuanced claim, provides reasoning for why evidence from various sources supports the claim, and acknowledges and refutes a counterargument. This evidently moves beyond the typical recounting genre structure of orientation and account sequence. The writer also makes critical choices about language to advance a sophisticated historical argument. For example, they use

- *qualifying language* to express reservation and acknowledge an alternative cause (e.g., *Although early suffragists generated interest in the cause of women's suffrage . . .*);
- *complex noun phrases* to express abstract ideas (e.g., *the actions and tactics of the National Women's Party; the protests and demonstrations of the National Women's Party; the cornerstone in the mosaic*);
- *causal verbs* to express reasoning and causality (e.g., *led to, contributed to, generated*);
- *causal expressions and collocations* to show cause-and-effect relationships between events and concepts (e.g., *laid the foundation for, most directly responsible for, the most critical contributor for*); and
- clause-linking strategies using *connectors* (e.g., *although, because, while*) to make explicit the relationships between ideas.

These language resources are essential for an argument about causes and consequences. We see that there is a clear difference between the two responses. In the following section, we elaborate on this difference and discuss the language demands of historical argumentation.

Language Demands of Historical Argumentation

The two sample responses illustrate that historical argumentation is a genre with unique language demands. It builds on language used in historical accounts or narratives but draws on explanatory resources that involve not only considering different interpretations but arguing for and against a particular interpretation of the past (Coffin, 2006). Unlike recording genres that deal with concrete events and people, historical arguments focus on abstract trends, causes, and consequences (Coffin, 2004). Thus, argument writing in history often has an abstract style and a structure that is logical (e.g., arguing why their interpretation is best supported by evidence) rather than chronological (e.g., recounting events in sequential order without interpreting their significance). This distinct way of organizing and constructing a text requires linguistic resources that are distinct from everyday language, as well as the language commonly used to narrate, summarize, sequence, and record historical events.

The linguistic features of historical arguments also differ from those of other historical genres, such as the recording genres, because the genres reflect different cultural and rhetorical purposes for writing (Coffin, 2006). Sometimes historians communicate to simply inform others what has happened, but often they communicate interpretations or arguments about significance, causality, or effects. This matters for language-based instruction because research has provided empirical evidence that different writing genres exhibit distinct linguistic features and, thus, demand disparate language skills (Crossley, 2020). The languaging practices for historical argumentation are shaped by the discipline-specific ways of reasoning, including sourcing, corroboration, and contextualization to substantiate claims (Goldman et al., 2016; Monte-Sano, 2012). Such disciplinary reasoning requires "language that construes those concepts [and therefore] becomes more complex and distanced from ordinary use of language" (Schleppegrell et al., 2004, p. 68). In essence, the language demands of argumentation in history are distinctly challenging and increasingly abstract.

By uncovering how language works in different domains and what linguistic choices are made to externalize thinking and reasoning in that discipline, SFL-oriented research and pedagogy have played a central role in identifying and mapping the linguistic demands of various genres of historical writing. Such mapping can help us identify and then teach the language moves students need. The SFL-based pedagogy uses functional language analysis to unpack the underlying linguistic patterns of written texts that represent different genres (Accurso & Gebhard, 2021). Essentially, SFL literature at the intersection of history content and language has provided insight into how language choices are shaped by discourse domains (e.g., historical discourse, academic written discourse), text types (e.g., arguments, recounts), and rhetorical moves (e.g., attributing sources, addressing a counterargument).

In this book, we expand on the important work done on the language of history from an SFL perspective but focus on the genre of historical arguments given the importance of argumentation in civic engagement and the increased emphasis placed on it in national and state standards (CCSS, 2010, 2013; NCSS, 2010, 2013). In each chapter, we use the SFL approach to unpack the language patterns underlying historical reasoning and argumentation to foster history teachers' pedagogical language knowledge (Bunch, 2013; Galguera, 2011). With such knowledge, history teachers are better equipped to help their students, especially multilingual learners of English, to meet the language demands of argumentation and to develop disciplinary literacy and reasoning skills. We also provide evidence-based strategies to expand students' linguistic resources so history teachers can build students' writing skills and foster metalinguistic knowledge and language awareness.

Challenges Facing Students and Teachers in Argument Writing in History

Although literacy standards have prioritized argument writing, developing written argumentation remains challenging for students, especially multilingual learners of English (Ferretti & Graham, 2019). For example, Marianne Perie et al. (2005) reported that only 15 percent of the twelfth-grade students who scored proficient in writing could compose essays containing a clear arguable claim and consistent supporting evidence. Other studies have found that students are challenged by developing warrants that explain why and how their evidence supports their claim and acknowledging and refuting potential criticisms of their positions (Kuhn, 1991, 2005).

The results of the National Assessment of Educational Progress (NAEP) also present a bleak picture of students' writing performance; only about one quarter of graduating high school students show solid performance in academic writing and only 1 percent of English learners in the eighth and twelfth grades perform at or above the proficient level in writing (U.S. Department of Education, National Center for Education Statistics, 2012). The NAEP reports released by National Center for Education Statistics in 2012 and 2019 suggest that the majority of the students, especially English learners, find it challenging to meet the expectations set forth by rigorous national and state standards. The continued underperformance of student writing on national assessments calls for effective instructional support for students to develop argument literacy skills.

A significant factor that contributes to students' low performance in argument writing in history is that instruction featuring argumentation is infrequent, leaving students with a lack of exposure to language used to construct and develop arguments (Coffin, 2006). In this regard, Coffin (2006) makes an important observation that textbooks used in history classrooms do not exemplify historical argumentation discourse. In fact, "contemporary textbook writers are reluctant to argue explicitly for or against a particular version of the past" and "tend to separate primary from secondary sources rather than weaving them into their argument as evidence" (Coffin, 2006, p. 87). Bob Bain (2006) has also noted that dominant modes of textbook instruction in the United States undermine the interpretative, inquiry stances students need to develop reasoning and writing with multiple sources.

Further, while the primary and secondary sources students read and analyze in the history classroom, such as diaries, letters, interviews, photographs, newspaper articles, and government documents, may be conducive to forming arguments of interpretation, they do not typically model argument writing. Coffin (2006) points out that "students have few models of effective argumentative historical discourse exemplifying, for example, strategies such as 'putting forward a thesis,' 'using sources to support the thesis,' 'making a concession' or 'integrating alternative views' " (p. 87). Given the importance of model texts for writing development (Graham et al., 2016), students' lack of exposure to the discourse of historical argumentation presents an obstacle for history teachers.

As mentioned previously, students who haven't developed language resources for argument writing and disciplinary literacy resort to *knowledge telling*—retelling the details from the sources in chronological and additive orders even though they are prompted to write an argument essay (Maamuujav, 2022; Olson et al., 2023; Steiss et al., 2022). However, we find that instruction that emphasizes key rhetorical moves and academic language used for argumentation helps such students grow in the quality of ideas, evidence use, and language use (Olson et al., 2023). These findings point to the importance of instructional support that models effective historical argumentation, highlighting language choices and rhetorical moves such as qualifying claims, integrating sources, and addressing counterarguments.

To help students expand their linguistic resources for effective argumentation, teachers also need support and guidance. Given students' low performance on argument writing, the complexity of developing argumentation skills, and the shifting instructional focus toward argument literacy in history, there is a greater responsibility placed on history teachers to find effective ways to provide language support for their increasingly diverse students. However, history teachers are not accustomed to providing language instruction and are challenged to meet the linguistic needs of their students (Schall-Leckrone & Barron, 2018).

The challenges for history teachers are further compounded by numerous constraints, including "the need to cover a prescribed curriculum" (Barton & Levstik, 2004, p. 252), lack of time and inadequate instructional materials

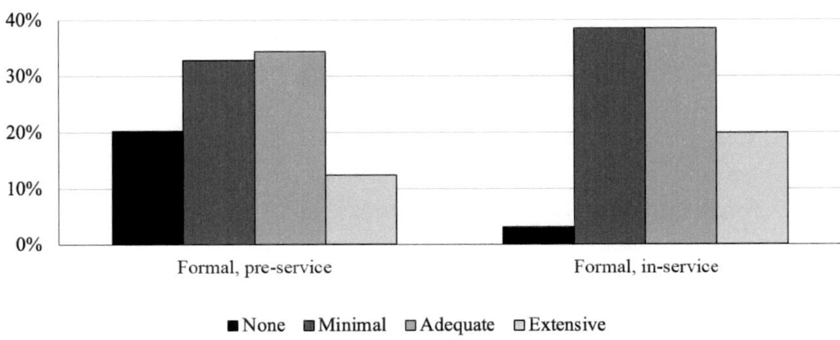

Figure 2. History Teachers' Report on Writing Instruction Training

(Cho & Reich, 2008), and insufficient training for writing instruction (Ray et al., 2016). Barton and Levstik (2004), for example, found that many history classrooms show little evidence of instruction that engages students in analyzing sources and developing interpretations. While many history teachers have content expertise, they have not had the opportunities to develop comparable expertise in teaching writing and language (Schall-Leckrone, 2022).

We have similar findings in our work with history teachers. In Figure 2, we share results from a survey administered to seventy-eight history teachers. Overall, more than half of the teachers reported receiving no training or a minimal amount of training in writing instruction before entering the field. About 40 percent received no training or a minimal amount of training when in the field. Thus, providing support to history teachers to integrate language focus into their instruction, which is our goal in writing this book, is an important step toward addressing these challenges.

Reframing Challenges in the History Classroom as Opportunities

While it is crucial to address and acknowledge the *challenges* students and teachers face on the path to developing proficiency in argument writing and language, it is equally important to explore *opportunities* presented by these challenges. First, a shift toward inquiry in curricular frameworks presents exciting possibilities for students to develop disciplinary literacy and language skills. This shift may be especially beneficial for multilingual learners of English who need opportunities to develop disciplinary literacy skills. Accordingly, Laura Schall-Leckrone and Debra Barron (2018) point out, "history classrooms have great potential to equip emergent bilingual learners (BLs) with content, language, and thinking skills associated with academic achievement and civic engagement, such as explaining significant phenomena or advancing an argument" (p. 205).

Through instruction, scaffolding, and a literacy-rich curriculum, history teachers can help students develop critical inquiry skills alongside the language resources and metalinguistic knowledge needed for historical argumentation. But for this to happen, history teachers need to develop *pedagogical language knowledge*: knowing key language skills needed for success in a discipline and how to teach students to develop this language (Galguera, 2011). Pedagogical language knowledge is critical in assisting multilingual learners of English to develop disciplinary language skills needed for argumentation and college and career readiness (Bunch, 2013). Similarly, Tomas Galguera (2011) argues that pedagogical language knowledge is a crucial component in preparing teachers to integrate language focus into their instruction in order to help students "use language to describe complexity, higher-order thinking, abstractions," and to integrate "evidence for support that is nuanced, qualified, and objective" (p. 90). Building teachers' pedagogical language knowledge enables them to respond to language demands placed on students and better support their students to not only learn language but to also learn *about* and *through* language (Derewianka & Jones, 2023). With such knowledge, history teachers can empower students to engage in disciplinary literacy practices by making visible languaging practices used to construct historical arguments. Building this knowledge is the primary goal of this book.

The emerging body of SFL-oriented research at the intersection of language and history suggests that equipping history teachers to teach disciplinary language and literacy based on functional language analysis has a powerful impact on both teacher and student learning (Accurso & Gebhard, 2021). Drawing on the review of 136 studies on SFL praxis in U.S. teacher education spanning from 2000 to 2019, Kathryn Accurso and Meg Gebhard (2021) found that SFL-based pre-service and in-service teacher professional development has been effective for supporting teachers to build language knowledge and critical language awareness, develop pedagogical knowledge, and gain confidence to engage in disciplinary literacy and language instruction. Thus, integrating functional language analysis into the professional learning of history teachers can help them develop a critical understanding of language in their discipline.

Importantly, Mary Schleppegrell and Luciana de Oliveira (2006), based on their work with hundreds of history teachers across California, reported that history teachers are motivated to engage in SFL-based pedagogy that involves deconstructing texts to uncover language patterns and choices. Teachers find this approach as helping students "see" the language patterns and evaluate language choices. Schleppegrell and de Oliveira (2006) conclude that providing opportunities to understand the role of language in constructing historical knowledge helps students comprehend texts and write effectively. Coffin's (2006) study in the context of Australian secondary schools also reported that integrating language-focused instruction into history teachers' professional development had a positive effect on "teacher attitudes and behaviors regarding the role of language in learning history" and improved student writing (p. 413). We add and argue that the skills students develop in deconstructing texts to see the underlying language structures for *historical argumentation* is transferable to other content areas and civic reasoning.

The Importance of Language Support for Multilingual Learners of English

Focusing on language in the history classroom is especially important for multilingual learners of English (MLEs) who are developing their English language proficiency. In history classrooms in the United States, MLEs must learn new content in a new language. Further, the academic languaging practices they are expected to use are often not transparent. The challenge of engaging in highly demanding historical argumentation and reasoning is enormous for this student population.

A lack of preparation in disciplinary literacy and academic writing is pervasive among MLEs who represent language-minority students, underrepresented racial and ethnic populations, and low-income immigrant students from underserved communities (Kanno & Cromley, 2015). While enrollment of these students in public schools with English as the language of instruction has been increasing, literacy and opportunity gaps remain, and the challenges posed by the demands of disciplinary literacy make those gaps more glaring (Goldenberg, 2013). For many MLEs, school may be the only place where they have opportunities to develop disciplinary language and literacy skills. Yet, they are often placed in sheltered courses with watered-down academic content. Rigorous instruction that prioritizes complex interpretative and rhetorical problem-solving skills is often reserved for honors students or those deemed "English proficient" (Kanno, 2022). Such instructional and institutional barriers can cause many MLEs to become "long-term" English learners (Kanno & Cromley, 2015). Lack of access to rich literacy practices and language support to meet the demands of disciplinary literacy is an equity issue.

Providing language support while engaging MLEs in rigorous literacy instruction and disciplinary practices is a way to promote equal access and level the playing field for this student population. In this regard, Schleppegrell (2004) contends, "In the absence of an explicit focus on language, students from certain social class backgrounds continue to be privileged and others to be disadvantaged in learning, assessment, and promotion, perpetuating the obvious inequalities that exist today" (p. 3). To support diverse MLEs in developing their disciplinary language and literacy skills, it is essential to provide them with multiple opportunities to engage with complex and challenging content. In this vein, Schleppegrell et al. (2008) note, "When a challenging curriculum is supported by strategies for talking about language in meaningful ways, students who may otherwise be unlikely to succeed can demonstrate strong growth in history achievement" (p. 186).

Academic Languaging

Developing disciplinary language and literacy skills entails learning to use language for academic purposes—academic languaging. It is important, however, to acknowledge the controversies surrounding academic language. Some scholars have problematized the prioritization of academic language as this can stigmatize, devalue, and suppress the linguistic practices of language-minoritized populations in the United States (Flores & Rosa, 2015; Garcia & Solorza, 2020). The raciolinguistic ideologies, the term coined by Nelson Flores and Jonathan Rosa (2015) to refer to the interrelationships between racialized bodies and linguistic practices, extend the critique of academic language. These scholars argue that the language of minoritized groups is devalued as a consequence of the prioritization of academic language in formal schooling contexts.

In response to these critiques of academic language, the term *academic languaging* has been suggested as a way to move away from prescriptive and exclusionary framing to a more holistic view of language use (Sembiante & Tian, 2021). The addition of the "*ing*" suffix, though it might seem a minor tweak, alludes to the fluid and multiple languaging practices used in linguistically pluralist societies. The term "languaging," in general, has been used to foreground the dynamic, reconstructive nature of language rather than seeing it as a static product (Swain, 2006; Shapiro, 2022). We adopt the term academic languaging not only to recognize the dynamic use of language but also to situate the academic languaging practices within the disciplinary ways of communicating.

While it is crucial to be mindful of the critical stances toward language, the deeper systemic and structural barriers confronting MLEs cannot be ignored. For example, one of the most pressing issues facing MLEs is lack of support they need to meet the demands of rigorous standards. In a society where academic language proficiency continues to be a gatekeeper for access to college and professional careers, multilingual students who haven't developed language skills necessary to participate in disciplinary discourses continue to be marginalized, excluded, and restricted in their access to academic communities, as well as college and career opportunities.

Language educators and educational linguists, including those who problematize academic language, recognize the value of helping students to become language users who are able to make linguistic choices strategically, whether that be their home language or a language needed for college and career advancement. In a culturally pluralistic society in which multilingual speakers "shuttle between communities and enjoy multiple memberships" (Canagarajah, 2002, p. 35), strategic language users are conversant with distinct language conventions and make linguistic choices considering the linguistic practices of various communities they shuttle between. They are aware of their audience and the rhetorical situation and choose language tactically to negotiate meaning in different communicative contexts.

Participation in academic communities and disciplinary discourses entails being proficient in the linguistic practices of these communities. Thus, instead of rejecting academic language, we need a way to support students in their effort to become well-versed in academic languaging while upholding the rich linguistic practices of their homes and communities. In this regard, Shawna Shapiro (2022) advocates for a "both/and" approach as a way of building language knowledge and resources, as well as cultivating critical language awareness in multilingual classrooms. This important pedagogical goal aligns with the principles of linguistic diversity, social justice, and equitable educational opportunities.

Collectively, educators can support students, particularly MLEs, in expanding their linguistic repertoires and developing critical language awareness. For example, Culturally Sustaining Systemic Functional Linguistics (CSSFL) centers the dynamic cultural and linguistic practices of multilingual students while supporting them in "building up their rhetorical, civic and academic repertoires within their new cultural context" (Harman & Burke, 2020, p. 18). As implied from its name, CSSFL draws on culturally sustaining pedagogy and systemic functional linguistics to foster linguistic pluralism and raise critical language awareness while simultaneously supporting students to expand their language resources to meet the demands of disciplinary literacy.

As teachers engage students in complex reasoning and argumentation in history, it is important to respond to the language demands of the genre and provide language support. History classrooms can be a stimulating learning environment in which linguistically diverse students are included in, rather than excluded from, opportunities to participate in academic languaging practices while, at the same time, developing their historical reasoning skills. Teachers have the opportunity to foster knowledge of language, text, and discourse to help their students *argue* cogently, *language* competently, and *write* confidently.

CHAPTER 3

Making a Claim for Historical Argumentation

Guiding Questions

- What is a claim in historical argumentation and what claims do historians make?
- How is language used to formulate historical claims?
- How can teachers help students articulate clear and compelling claims about historical topics?

In an eighth-grade U.S. history class, students engage in historical inquiry around the Louisiana Purchase and the subsequent expedition led by Lewis and Clark to explore the newly acquired territory. As part of their inquiry, students are asked to consider different factors and reasons for the success of the expedition in reaching the Pacific Ocean and to write an argument responding to the question: *Why did the Lewis and Clark expedition succeed?* Students will arrive at their claim for why the expedition succeeded only after careful reading and synthesizing of information from multiple sources. In argument writing, however, the claim comes first as the central point of the argument.

Paying attention to the claims different eighth graders write in response to this question, we see a wide range of skills students have in historical reasoning, argument writing, and language use. For example, one student made the following claim: "*This expedition was successful because of Lewis and Clark's experience.*" This claim is simple, uses accessible language, and directly responds to the historical question. In fact, this type of claim—simple but lacking specificity or supporting reasons—is typical in the writing of secondary students in history classrooms (Steiss et al., 2024). However, given language support and instructional scaffolding for argument writing, the student can improve their writing and construct a more effective claim.

Another student showed a more strategic use of language and historical reasoning in their claim: "*Though the team's personal and navigational skills were important, the help they received from Native American peoples along the way is one of the most important reasons the expedition succeeded.*" By acknowledging an alternative factor that contributed to the success of the expedition and qualifying their claim using hedging language, this student shows more effective language use and reasoning aligned with disciplinary norms in history. Though this type of claim is less common in student writing, secondary students across all grade levels can reach this level of sophistication when provided with explicit instruction that focuses on both language use and historical thinking (Moon et al., 2024).

This chapter will help push students forward in their articulation of clear and compelling claims aligned with disciplinary norms. Because making a claim is a key disciplinary practice in history and a core rhetorical component of argumentation, students need to learn to construct defensible and debatable claims supported by evidence and reasoning. To do so, they need both a conceptual understanding of what claims are for historical argumentation and a strong grasp of how to use language effectively to present convincing claims. The goal of this chapter is to foster understanding of the concept of a claim, to make visible the language patterns and markers associated with historical claims, and to provide pedagogical guidance for cultivating the language skills students need to articulate effective claims. The chapter is organized in the following sequence:

I. **Conceptual Overview:** Understanding Claims in Historical Argumentation
   - What is a claim in historical argumentation?
   - What do historians make claims about?

II. **Language Focus:** Languaging Practices for Formulating Historical Claims
   - How is language used to express a stance in historical claims?
   - What language choices can be made to explain reasoning in historical claims?
   - How is language used to qualify historical claims?

III. **Instructional Support:** Cultivating Language Skills for Effective Claims
   - How can teachers cultivate language skills for an effective claim?
   - How can teachers build metalinguistic knowledge and awareness?
   - What should teachers consider for effective instruction?

I. Understanding Claims in Historical Argumentation

What is a claim in historical argumentation?

To understand what a claim is, we first situate it in the context of a larger argument. A claim is the point, the arrowhead, of an argument that communicates a stance, view, interpretation, evaluation, or belief. The claim, along with the supporting evidence and reasoning and treatment of alternative claims, represents the argument (Toulmin, 1958). In other words, making an argument means providing a claim and succinctly providing evidence for why the claim is sound or makes sense. In many disciplines, making claims appropriate to the task and grounded in available evidence is a key practice for successful communication (Shanahan & Shanahan, 2012). Specific disciplines have their own conventions of how to put forth claims and how to provide evidence and reasoning to support these claims. Thus, we first consider why and how historians make claims.

What Is a Claim?

A claim communicates a **stance**, informed by evidence-based **reasoning**, about a historical topic. Claims are **bounded** by the scope of inquiry, available evidence, and other plausible interpretations.

To understand the claims historians make, we start with the purpose of history as a discipline and its norms for generating knowledge. Phrased most succinctly, *historians make evidence-based interpretations about the past* (De La Paz et al., 2017; Monte-Sano, 2010; Nokes, 2013). They make these claims using historical reasoning and inherently limited sources of evidence while acknowledging the tentativeness of their interpretations. Thus, claims in a historical argument (1) communicate a stance about a historical topic, (2) informed by evidence-based reasoning and (3) bounded by the scope of inquiry, available evidence, or other plausible interpretations. We briefly describe these three features of a historical claim before discussing what types of claims historians make.

When historians make arguments, they communicate a **stance** about a historical question, sharing knowledge about a time, place, event, or people that contributes to our collective understanding of the past. Because claims in history are about the real world, taking a stance is inherently a social act (Renier, 2016). There is a certain level of objectivity governing the claim-making practices of historians (VanSledright, & Maggioni, 2016) that is different from some disciplines, such as literature, which permit writers to make subjective stances (e.g., "*Romeo and Juliet* is not a love story; it is a story about how teenagers' hormones will lead them to early deaths if unchecked"). To illustrate, there is an objective and true account of what led to the Boston Massacre, even if we still debate the conflict today. To build this account, historians use available artifacts—stories and documents created about the past and in the past—to interpret the past and build meaning that is relevant to the present (Howell & Prevenier, 2001).

Embedding supporting **reasons** into a claim is a key practice in history. Ultimately, claims in history try to describe and explain what actually happened in the past—what is true. For example, a historian may make a claim that the effects of the U.S. Reconstruction policies on African American communities were mostly negative. This stance matters not only for our conception of the past but also for what policymakers and citizens think we should do in the present to redress past racial injustices. Still, it is toward a true and comprehensive account that historians orient their inquiry efforts and eventual arguments. Thus, historians have an epistemological commitment to making true and comprehensive accounts of the past through evidence-based inquiry and reasoning.

Because historical claims are built on artifactual evidence, a true account of the past may not be easily accessible if there are holes in the "historical record." The claims we make, therefore, are limited or **bounded** by available evidence and perspectives. Historians then make *tentative* claims that can be disproved (Monte-Sano & De La Paz, 2012). Because claims can be disproved as we find new historical evidence (e.g., a declassified report about the Cuban missile crisis), historians make some claims with the understanding that they are limited in scope and eligible to be revised with new evidence or reasoning. Historians, according to Martha Howell and Walter Prevenier (2001), are "skeptical about the kinds of truths [they] can discover, about the kinds of truth buried in sources" (p. 16). Therefore, effective and compelling claims, as we will show later, *qualify* or *limit* their positions.

What do historians make claims about?

Historians make claims not only about what happened, but also about why and how it happened, what is significant, and what the consequences of events and actions were. As historians specialize in noticing and examining changes focusing on the questions of how and why, they use "analytics of causality, action, and consequence" to uncover "who did the changing, and how [we can] be sure they were the agents" (Guldi & Armitage, 2014, p. 14).

To list all types of claims one could make in history would be a herculean, if not quixotic, endeavor. Fortunately, Peter Seixas and Tom Morton's (2013) Big Six Historical Thinking Concepts offer a useful taxonomy for the types of claims historians might make. Historical thinking is a process of chronological reasoning, which means wrestling with issues of significance, evidence, continuity and change, cause and consequence, historical perspectives, and ethical dimensions of the past (Seixas & Morton, 2013). Claims respond to historical questions in each of these concepts, such as taking a stance on why and how an event was significant in the Cold War, what caused the Cold War, what its consequences were, and what important lessons we should learn from the Cold War. Focusing on each historical thinking concept, we explore what claims historians might make and offer explanations, along with sample questions and examples of potential claims students might make.

Establishing Historical Significance: Historians make claims about what is significant in the past. As stated by Howell and Prevenier (2001), "They choose the events and people that they think constitute the past, and they decide what about them is important to know" (p. 1). Events are not inherently meaningful or significant; instead, we *impose significance* on events for particular reasons. For example, *Read.Inquire.Write* produced by the University of Michigan features the following inquiry question:

A SAMPLE QUESTION: What is one significant cause of the Trail of Tears that you think people should know about today?

A POTENTIAL CLAIM: In my opinion, the role of institutionalized racism is one cause of the Trail of Tears that should be emphasized today.

A question of historical significance is best answered with a stance supported by evidence and reasoning, using language that bounds, contextualizes, or justifies the opinion.

Using Sources for Evidence: Historians make arguments about how we can reliably come to know about the past and what evidence is most relevant or reliable for a given inquiry. As the accuracy of claims is dependent on reliable evidence, historians take precautions that "the evidence upon which their narrative was based must be subjected to methodical probing" (Renier, 2016, p. 21). Thus, it is important for students to learn analytical methods for evaluating evidence. For example, students can take stances on the usefulness and reliability of primary sources when answering a question about what took place in Boston on March 5, 1770 ("The Boston Massacre").

SAMPLE QUESTIONS: What sources are you using for evidence? Are these sources reliable?

A POTENTIAL CLAIM: The Captain's account of what happened cannot be fully trusted because he was a British officer on trial for a crime and, therefore, might have provided an account that unfairly favored him.

In using sources for evidence, we make a claim about a source's reliability and its relevance to the argument at hand.

Identifying Continuity and Change: Historians make claims about when eras begin, when they end, and what major themes/periods should be used for interpreting the past. Jo Guldi and David Armitage (2014) explain, "Historians learn how to argue about changes by means of narrative, how to join explanation with understanding, how to combine the study of the particular, the specific, and the unique with the desire to find patterns, structures, and regularities" (p. 14). This involves making claims that classify, describe, and explain historical events and periods.

A SAMPLE QUESTION: What marked the decline of the Roman Empire?

A POTENTIAL CLAIM: The decline of the Roman Empire was centuries long, but the pivotal moment of decline came with the rise of the Ottoman empire.

Making claims about continuity and change often involves causal reasoning—putting events in order and considering how multiple forces interact with each other.

Analyzing Causes and Consequences: Historians make claims about why events happen and how they influence future events. Historians recognize that understanding past experiences and events is essential for future consequences (Renier, 2016). Thinking causally involves thinking about *multiple* forces and their *relative* contributions. For example, one might make an argument about why and how the Montgomery Bus Boycott succeeded.

SAMPLE QUESTIONS: What contributed to the success of the Montgomery Bus Boycott? Why is one person/event more influential than another? Did the context and conditions make one cause more or less influential?

A POTENTIAL CLAIM: The distribution of flyers by the Women's Political Council was particularly important because it leveraged strong communal ties to disseminate a call to participate widely.

While one might be tempted to make a strong claim that force A caused force B, using hedging language becomes important because it recognizes how many forces are layered and embedded in historical contexts.

Taking Historical Perspectives: Space and time are two important elements of historical perspectives, and historians are concerned with "how to extend their work across ever greater expanses of [space and time]" (Guldi & Armitage, 2014, p. 15). Attending to the lived realities of historical actors and understanding them as people with unique and varied experiences can help us better understand the past and present. Perspective-taking requires an understanding of the difference between the past and present, and arguments of interpretation can be made about historical periods and actors. The following sample question is from *Read.Inquire.Write*:

A SAMPLE QUESTION: Was Reconstruction a tragedy or triumph for African Americans?

A POTENTIAL CLAIM: Given the impact of Jim Crow policies on local communities in the 19th and 20th centuries, Reconstruction was mostly a tragedy.

Responding to such questions fully requires a complex understanding of a collective experience and necessarily requires nuance in a claim.

Ethical Dimensions: Historians also consider what lessons can be learned while avoiding "presentism," imposing contemporary morality on past actors. One might ask: *To what extent was the United States justified in going to war with Mexico?* Such a claim may be qualified with a consideration of important political doctrines of the time that both the United States and Mexico arguably abided by, but the actions of the United States might also be considered alongside its frequent and uninvited excursions into sovereign nations of Central and South America. Given another question, *When can the government suspend civil rights?*, one might also consider pressures and concerns of the historical context. Alternatively, one could focus on Japanese internment and remind present readers of past injustices, using the historical record to advocate for a more just future. For historians, "critical engagement with the records of the past can produce useful knowledge about the past," but it is also important for them "to unseat easy assumptions about the certainty of our knowledge about the past" (Howell & Prevenier, 2001, p. 3).

A SAMPLE QUESTION: To what extent was the United States justified in going to war with Mexico?

A POTENTIAL CLAIM: The United States was not justified in going to war with Mexico because the United States was first to violate the treaty and was first to commit an act of aggression in Texas.

Although the types of claims historians make differ depending on the concepts and rhetorical goals, there is a common thread to these claims that is reiterated here: Claims communicate a stance about a historical topic, informed by evidence-based reasoning and bounded by the scope of inquiry, available evidence, or other plausible interpretations. In short, making claims about the past is a socially significant act, telling us what is true, what really happened in the past, and what (or even whose stories) matter most. Taking a stance should be done responsibly by offering supporting reasons and justification based on evidence as well as qualifying and hedging one's stance. Key languaging practices allow this communication to happen clearly.

II. Languaging Practices for Formulating Historical Claims

The claims students make in history will be diverse in their function and content, but they share common linguistic features. The languaging practices associated with making a claim in history can be demystified by closely examining the rhetorical components of the claim and how these components are realized/expressed in language. If a claim communicates a stance about a historical topic, informed by evidence-based reasoning and bounded by the scope of inquiry, available evidence, and other competing claims, then the key components of a claim involve ***stance***, ***reasoning***, and ***qualification***.

A student with a strong understanding of each component of a claim and the underlying linguistic choices associated with these will be able to communicate their stances on historical topics effectively. To illustrate how a student might build these components of the claim incrementally, we examine the claim made by an eleventh-grade student in their argument writing on the women's suffrage movement that we shared in chapter 2:

> *Although early suffragists generated interest in the cause of women's suffrage,* **the actions and tactics of the National Women's Party were most directly responsible for the passage of the 19th Amendment** <u>because they put crucial pressure on national political figures.</u>

> *What Is a Clause?*
>
> A clause is a sentence within a sentence. It contains a subject and a verb. A clause is either independent (can stand alone as a complete sentence) or dependent (cannot stand alone as a complete sentence).

As we deconstruct the claim into its key rhetorical components (stance, reasoning, qualification), we see that the **independent clause** (bolded) communicates a **stance** or the writer's central position, responding directly to the essential question: How did the women's suffrage movement succeed in passing the Nineteenth Amendment? The independent clause is followed by a dependent clause that offers reasoning (underlined), using the causal connector because. To *qualify* the claim (italics), another dependent clause with the concessive connector *although* is added to the main clause. This claim contains three clauses, each serving an important rhetorical function.

Breaking down the claim, explicitly identifying key components and describing their language features and rhetorical purposes, can help build an understanding of how language functions in context.

In the following sections, we further discuss the language features associated with these three components of a claim—expressing a **stance**, explaining reasoning, and *qualifying* a claim. Our goal is to provide guidance so teachers can attend to each in their instruction. At the end of the chapter, we provide a series of instructional activities as a guide to build language knowledge and awareness for making claims at varying levels.

How is language used to express a stance in historical claims?

Stance, which refers to "the speaker's or writer's feeling, attitude, perspective, or position as enacted in discourse" (Strauss & Feiz, 2014, p. 103), is the most

Table 3.1. Deconstructing a Claim

Rhetorical Components of a Claim	**Qualification:** Acknowledging an alternative view	**Stance:** Writer's central position, perspective, or viewpoint	**Reasoning:** Based on reliable evidence
Student example	Although early suffragists generated interest in the cause of women's suffrage,	the actions and tactics of the National Women's Party most directly contributed to the passage of the 19th Amendment	because they put crucial pressure on national political figures.
Language features	A dependent clause added to the independent clause with a concessive connector *although*	The independent clause that states the central position. It can stand on its own when the dependent clauses are removed.	A dependent clause added to the independent clause with a causal connector *because*
Rhetorical purposes	To acknowledge an alternative view and the prospect of multiple causes as contributing factors	To express the writer's central position, stating a claim about the key contributor for the passage of the 19th Amendment	To provide a reasoning or rationale for taking the stance

central component of a claim. Because of its centrality, a writer's position is typically expressed in an independent or main clause in a complex sentence or as an independent sentence of its own (e.g., *the actions and tactics of the National Women's Party most directly contributed to the passage of the 19th Amendment*).

To further illustrate the clause structure that expresses a writer's stance, we examine a claim made by a student in grade 10 World History class about the thirteenth-century Mongols. Note that the claim has a structure similar to the one presented earlier, though the historical topic is different:

> *Even though the Mongol conquests were marked by extreme violence and brutality,* **Mongols exhibited key practices of a developed and civilized society during their rule in the 13th century that people often overlook**. The Mongol rule facilitated the diffusion of trade, allowing it to flourish, and promoted religious tolerance and the spread of various cultures and ideas.

The claim is expressed in a multi-clause, multi-sentence construction. In the first multi-clause sentence, **the bolded independent clause** clearly and markedly expresses the **central position** of the student writer. This clause can stand on its own and can be taken out of the multi-clause sentence to show how it clearly answers the inquiry question. A qualification that acknowledges the other side is added to the main clause through clausal embedding using the concessive connector *even though* at the beginning of the sentence. Reasoning is provided in a new sentence.

From a functional language perspective, each clause has "the character of message or quantum of information in the flow of discourse" (Halliday & Matthiessen, 2014, p. 88). Each clause has a rhetorical purpose, carrying discrete yet related ideas. While the independent clause carries the central idea, the dependent clauses complement the main clause by providing additional information to contribute to the whole message. Ensuring that a stance or the central position is clearly expressed in a claim is arguably the most integral part of constructing an effective argument.

A systemic functional approach to language identifies two thematic parts of a clause—**theme** and **rheme**—that together constitute a message (Halliday & Matthiessen, 2014). While the **theme** "serves as the point of departure of the message," guiding readers to form their interpretation of it, the **rheme** is what comes after and where the clause moves after the point of departure (Halliday & Matthiessen, 2014, p. 89). Using this theme/rheme notion from a functional grammar approach, we can deconstruct a main clause into two parts: a topic of

Table 3.2. Deconstructing the Independent/Main Clause

Topic of Discussion (What or Who: Theme)	+	**Comment on the Topic** (What about it: Rheme)
Mongols		exhibited key practices of a developed and civilized society during their rule in the 13th century that people often overlook.
The actions and tactics of the National Women's Party		were most directly responsible for the passage of the 19th Amendment.

discussion (theme) and comment on the topic (rheme). Table 3.2 deconstructs the independent clauses of the previous claims to illustrate the two-part thematic structure.

The **topic** of discussion (theme) is accompanied by a **comment** or what the writer states about the topic (rheme). The rheme can take many forms. For example, the rheme in the main claim about Mongols is about historical perspective, commenting on the historical and temporal context and the lived realities of historical actors. On the other hand, the rheme about the actions and tactics of the National Women's Party deals with causes and consequences.

For a claim to be compelling, the topic/theme needs to be clear and specific. While some topics can be clearly expressed in a simpler noun phrase structure (e.g., *Mongols* as a single noun), other topics are expressed in complex noun phrases. For example, the topic *the actions and tactics of the National Women's Party* is expressed in a complex noun phrase structure. The coordinated nouns, *actions and tactics*, are followed by the prepositional phrase *of the National Women's Party*. A clearly specified topic of discussion in a clause serves as the point of departure, naming the topic with clarity.

For instructional purposes, teachers can explicitly describe these two parts of a main clause and have students identify and evaluate the topic and comment using models before asking them to evaluate their own claims. They can first identify the what or the who before identifying the comment. Students can then evaluate whether the writer used specific and precise language for the topic and the comment to express their stance clearly and effectively. The following steps can guide their inquiry:

- Identify the topic of discussion: *What or who is the topic of inquiry?*
- Identify the comment made about the topic: *What is said about the topic? Is it justifiable and defensible?*
- Evaluate the language used to construct the claim: *Is the language used precise and specific? Does it express the central point clearly?*

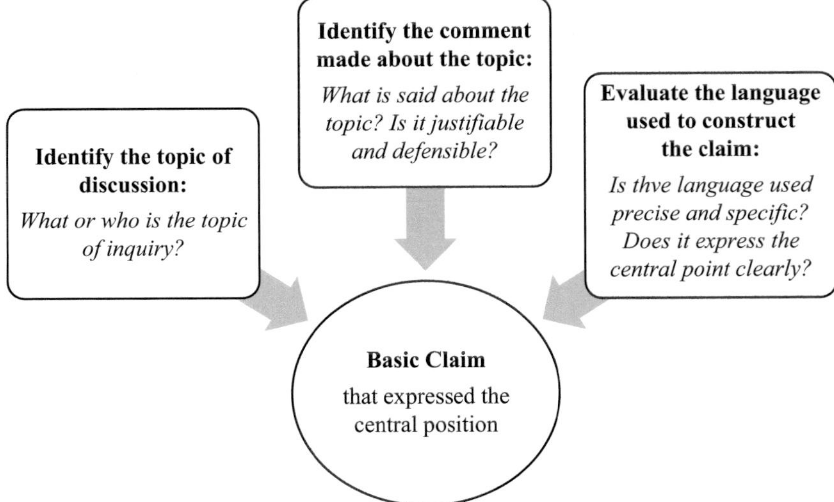

Figure 3. Steps to Evaluate a Claim

In a process-based approach to writing, having students self-assess and evaluate their claims can build their metalinguistic knowledge.

What language choices can be made to explain reasoning in historical claims?

While a reasonable first step in writing instruction is ensuring each student has a central position expressed clearly, a reasonable next step is to have students strengthen this claim by including supporting reasons. A statement of rationale added to the claim, explaining why and how a claim is made, intends to convince the audience by providing some backing and outlining the argument that will follow. As such, reasons serve to answer the following questions:

- Why and how did you come to this conclusion?
- What compelling reasons and evidence can you offer to convince your readers?

After students articulate a clear position in the form of an independent clause, asking these questions can lead students to express supporting reasons that strengthen the claim. This point is illustrated below by comparing a claim without a rationale and the same claim with reasoning.

A Claim without Rationale

> Susan B. Anthony's statement in 1878, "The right of citizens of the United States to vote shall not be abridged by the United States or by any State on account of sex" helped the Women's Suffrage Movement to succeed more than anything else.

A Claim with Rationale

> Susan B. Anthony's statement in 1878, "The right of citizens of the United States to vote shall not be abridged by the United States or by any State on account of sex" helped the Women's Suffrage Movement to succeed more than anything else because it brought national attention to the issue of gender discrimination and argued for civil rights.

Without an explanation or reasoning, the claim appears as a mere assertion without backing. The added reasoning, however, makes the claim more effective by offering justification.

Table 3.3. Common Languaging Practices for Constructing a Claim

Claims (with reasoning underlined)	**Linguistic Choices**	**Language Markers**
The Black Death plague was the most significant cause for the decline of feudalism *as* it took out a large number of the peasants which feudalism needed.	Reasoning in a dependent clause that is added to the claim with a causal connector *as*.	as, since, because, for the reason that
Though Lewis and Clark's navigational skills were important, the help from Native American people along the way should be considered as a reason for the success of the Lewis and Clark expedition. *Evidence shows* multiple tribes helped the expedition for months at a time and their guide Sacagawea played a key role in their journey.	Reasoning expressed in a separate sentence. *Note that the first sentence of the claim is a complex, multi-clause sentence with an acknowledgment of other contributing factors.	As shown by, This is due to, This is because, Evidence shows, This is supported by, This is true on the grounds of
The California Grape Strike and Boycott was ultimately successful *due to* the march led by Roberto Bustos and the immense support of grape workers and citizens.	Reasoning in the form of complex noun phrases with a connecting phrase: *due to*.	due to, thanks to, because of, as a result of, on the account of, as a consequence of

There are various ways of adding reasoning to a claim. As shown in the example above, rationale can be expressed in a dependent clause added to the main clause with a causal connector *because.* This clause-linking technique is a rather common languaging practice used in both writing and speech. When asking even a very young child *why* they caused some household mischief, one is not surprised to hear a causal connector used in response (e.g., *because my brother told me to*). For secondary writing instruction, developing the metacognitive knowledge that a rationale is needed to back the claim will help students move toward formulating more nuanced claims.

While the use of a connector such as *because* will suffice in many cases, there are other ways to add reasoning to a claim. Table 3.3 shows three common ways reasons are added to a claim. Students can practice using these language moves by revising model texts or their own writing, expressing reasoning in various ways. It is important to note that the language features presented here are not an exhaustive list but rather examples of common linguistic patterns. Various other languaging practices used to express reasoning and causality in historical arguments will be explored further in chapter 5.

How is language used to qualify historical claims?

Historians are oriented toward objectivity, but they also acknowledge that what we think about history today could be proven wrong tomorrow given new evidence and interpretations. These beliefs directly inform the academic languaging practices used to make claims in history, specifically the inclusion of language that equivocates, hedges, and expresses reservations.

Historians *qualify their claims* in relation to other claims and within the limits of their own knowledge and available evidence. For example, they may acknowledge the limits of their claims if only one side is presented, if the claim is only about a specific period, or if other potential explanations exist (McCullagh, 2004). Because the validity of a claim is determined by available evidence and reasoning, adding qualifications that address the *limitation* of a given claim actually improves its rhetorical power. This is something student writers may not be aware of.

We examine the linguistic practices used to qualify a claim and express caution when making a claim based on various rhetorical purposes:

- expressing the degree of certainty/conviction: *Ghandi's Salt March was mostly a success . . .*
- expressing the scope of limitation: *The ideals of the enlightenment are somewhat reflected in the Bill of Rights of the U.S. Constitution . . .*
- situating the claim among other plausible interpretations: *Even though the Colonists did provoke the British soldiers, the soldiers are ultimately*

responsible for the violence that precipitated . . .

- avoiding overgeneralization: *The Delano grape boycott and strike succeeded because of the march led by Cesar Chavez to Sacramento in which many farm workers participated . . .*
- distancing oneself: *In the view of many historians, . . .*

These rhetorical purposes guide writers in their use of hedging language that equivocates and expresses reservations. In what follows, we discuss common linguistic hedging devices used to qualify a claim. We also share how students can be explicitly taught these linguistic choices and practice using them when engaging in a historical inquiry and constructing an argument.

Use of Modifiers. One way to qualify a claim is through modifying nouns and noun phrases that name key actors, events, and actions about whom or which the claim is made. The use of modifying words and phrases (e.g., *some, many, most, a large number of*) can help writers avoid problematic overgeneralizations. For example, the underlined noun phrase *farm workers* in Example A can be modified to reflect a more accurate account of what happened as it is most likely that not all farm workers joined the march. The use of the modifier in Example B more accurately reflects the truth of the claim and avoids overgeneralization.

A. *The Delano grape boycott and strike succeeded because farm workers joined the march to Sacramento which was led by Cesar Chavez.*
B. *The Delano grape boycott and strike succeeded because a large number of farm workers joined the march to Sacramento which was led by Cesar Chavez.*

Key nouns and noun phrases can also be specified by the use of modifying adjectives, nouns, and prepositional phrases that add specificity. Comparing the two sentences below, we see that the use of the noun phrase "*The Mongols*" in Example A generally refers to the entire ethnic group, and it is not fair to generalize the statement to all who identify as Mongols. However, the general noun phrase can be modified by using a more precise noun "*invaders*" and the prepositional phrase "*of the 13th century*" to specify that the statement does not apply to all Mongols or Mongols in general but to a specific group within a specific time frame.

A. *The Mongols engaged in the mass, unnecessary slaughter of many people and promoted drunkenness and polygamy within their society.*
B. *The Mongol invaders of the 13th century engaged in the mass, unnecessary slaughter of many people and promoted drunkenness and polygamy within their society.*

Adding specification to generic nouns and noun phrases is often necessary to acknowledge that the claim does not apply to all cases, conditions, and contexts. Students often have the linguistic knowledge to use modifiers, but they may need to develop a rhetorical understanding of hedging language and its role in historical argumentation. Therefore, a simple instructional strategy focused on specifying nouns through the use of modifiers can help students add nuance in their claims and avoid overgeneralization.

Use of Modal Verbs. Another linguistic practice expressing the tentative nature of a claim is the use of modal verbs such as *may, might, can,* and *could.* Modal verbs are versatile because they convey varying degrees of certainty. Again, students might be able to use these in day-to-day speech, expressing varying degrees of commitment to studying for next week's test: some *will* study every day, some *might* study. But it is important to explicitly teach students that these verbs also have a place in historical argumentation. Modal verbs add nuance to a claim by presenting it as a tentative interpretation rather than an objective truth or a declarative statement. Consider the following claim made by a seventh-grade student that is expressed as a definitive statement: *The Black Death plague **is** the most significant cause for the decline of feudalism.* The certainty of this statement, indicated by the singular present form of the verb "be," belies the multivariate nature of causality in history.

A more appropriate claim would use a modal auxiliary verb to express less certainty. Varying degrees of certainty can be expressed through the use of modal verbs as exhibited in the following examples. Determining which degree of certainty should be expressed is informed by the scope of the historical inquiry and available evidence, but explicitly teaching the language to express varying degrees of certainty will help writers communicate effectively using cautious and careful language.

Degree of Certainty	**Modal Verbs**	**Examples**
Highest	will	*The Black Death plague <u>will</u> be the most significant cause of the decline of feudalism.*
	would	*The Black Death plague <u>would</u> be the most significant cause of the decline of feudalism.*
	can	*The Black Death plague <u>can</u> be the most significant cause of the decline of feudalism.*
	could	*The Black Death plague <u>could</u> be the most significant cause of the decline of feudalism.*
	may	*The Black Death plague <u>may</u> be the most significant cause of the decline of feudalism.*
Lowest	might	*The Black Death plague <u>might</u> be the most significant cause of the decline of feudalism.*

Use of Hedging Verbs. Another hedging practice involves using verbs such as *seem, appear, tend, suggest.* These verbs help writers avoid stating their claims in absolute terms by removing themselves from fully committing to their claims. In Example A below, the claim sounds like a definitive statement. However, the hedging verb *appears* is added in Example B to attenuate the conviction of the claim, presenting it as a plausible interpretation rather than a definitive statement.

A. *The Black Death plague is the most significant cause of the decline of feudalism.*
B. *The Black Death plague appears to be the most significant cause of the decline of feudalism.*

This type of tempering is a common practice among scholars and historians who make claims with the understanding that their claims are limited in scope and eligible for revision with new evidence or reasoning.

Use of Adverbs. Writers can also moderate the strength of their claims by using adverbs. Two types of adverbs that are commonly used to soften the conviction of claims in academic writing are adverbs of frequency (e.g., *occasionally, generally, usually, often, sometimes, commonly, typically*) and adverbs of stance, which are sometimes called modal adverbs (e.g., *probably, presumably, perhaps, relatively, likely*). These qualifying adverbs often answer such questions as how, how often, how much, how certain, or to what degree. Thus, they are used to express reservation and the scope of limitation. Consider the two claims below:

A. *The Black Death plague was the most significant cause of the decline of feudalism.*
B. *The Black Death plague was probably the most significant cause of the decline of feudalism.*

The example sentence A leaves no doubt and presents the claim with absolute certainty, but the addition of the adverb "*probably*" expresses some doubt and avoids overstatement. The use of such adverbs communicates that the claim is made based on what the writer knows so far. It acknowledges that the claim can be revised as additional evidence emerges or becomes available.

Use of *It*-Clauses. Adding *it*-clauses (e.g., *it is plausible that . . ., it is reasonable to conclude that . . .*) is a common sentence-level manipulation to modify the strength of a claim. An *it*-clause is often followed either by a *that*-clause or the infinitive (e.g., *to conclude*) when used for qualification. In examples B and

C below, we highlight these two features using the claim made by an eighth-grade student about the Lewis and Clark expedition:

A. *The help from Native American peoples along the way is the most important reason the Lewis and Clark expedition succeeded.*
B. *It is likely that without Native American aid, the expedition would have failed. Therefore, the help from Native American peoples along the way is the most important reason the Lewis and Clark expedition succeeded.*
C. *Given the countless times they were aided, it is reasonable to conclude that the help from Native American peoples along the way is the most important reason the Lewis and Clark expedition succeeded.*

The claim expressed in Example A above sounds much more definitive and absolute. However, the use of *it*-clauses in Examples B and C softens the claim, presenting it as a plausible interpretation rather than a factual statement.

Adding Clauses and Phrases. Another sentence-level hedging strategy writers commonly use to qualify their argument is adding a dependent clause and prepositional phrase that introduces an alternative view or counterclaim. From a functional perspective, this language structure "enhances the meaning of another by qualifying it in one of a number of possible ways: by reference to time, place, manner, cause, or condition" (Halliday & Matthiessen, 2014, p. 476). For example, one can make a concession by adding either a dependent clause or prepositional phrase (underlined):

DEPENDENT CLAUSE: *Even though the 100 Years' War contributed to the decline of feudalism, the Black Death plague played a more important role.*
PREPOSITIONAL PHRASE: *Despite the efforts taking over a year to be recognized by the British government, the Salt March was a successful event that brought Indians together against colonial rule.*

The rhetorical purpose of such clauses and phrases is to situate the claim among other competing claims or prior interpretations. As such, qualifying clauses and phrases often use concessive connectors such as *although, even though,* and *while* and prepositions and prepositional phrases such as *despite, in spite of,* and *regardless of.* To show the rhetorical effect of adding a clause of concession to a claim (underlined in Example B), we use the claim about the success of the Lewis and Clark expedition.

A. *The help from Native American peoples along the way is the most important reason the Lewis and Clark expedition succeeded.*

B. *Even though Lewis and Clark's personal and navigational skills were important, the help from Native American peoples along the way is the most important reason the Lewis and Clark expedition succeeded.*

In Example A without the dependent clause, the claim sounds presumptuous and leaves no doubt. However, the addition of a clause with concessive connector *even though* in Example B enhances the claim by acknowledging the importance of Lewis and Clark's personal and navigational skills, which can be seen by some as another important contributing factor to the success of the expedition. This also previews a potential counterclaim the writer will address later in their essay.

Making a historical claim is complex; writers and historians recognize that they do not know everything about people, places, and events in their historical contexts and that they form interpretations based on limited evidence. Linguistic hedging is a communication strategy that writers use to express the limits of their knowledge, the degree of their certainty, and the limitations and the situatedness of their claims. Using precise and cautious language helps writers avoid overgeneralization and bias. However, for students learning to write in an academic context, linguistic hedging practices can be obscure. It is important for teachers to help students learn to use the right amount of hedging and make effective language choices while considering their rhetorical purposes.

In sum, by deconstructing a claim to understand the linguistic components in connection to their rhetorical functions, teachers can help students construct clear and compelling claims. Teachers can support students who might be challenged by the linguistic demands of academic writing by making explicit the languaging practices that allow writers and historians to present nuanced claims. In the following section, we provide some guidance on how teachers can cultivate students' language skills for making claims.

III. Cultivating Language Skills for Effective Claims

How can teachers cultivate language skills for an effective claim?

In this section, we provide several instructional strategies and activities to support students in formulating clear, compelling, and nuanced claims. You should modify and contextualize these resources based on your students' needs and course content. The key pedagogical focus is to provide explicit instruction on the components of an effective claim, using mentor texts to showcase the essential parts. Explicit teaching is an evidence-based strategy shown to improve secondary students' writing (Graham et al., 2016). We provide several teaching moves you can integrate into your instruction to scaffold students' language development for evaluating and articulating effective claims.

Teaching Move 1: Explicitly teach key parts of a claim using mentor texts

Using the Model→Practice→Evaluate instructional cycle (Graham et al., 2016), you can help students understand and internalize the features of claims. Teacher modeling can help students observe and notice the thinking and actions of an experienced writer. Students then practice emulating the features of model texts before they evaluate their claims. Table 3.4 shows different components of a claim—qualification, stance, and reasoning—using a sample claim made about the Lewis and Clark expedition.

The following steps can be used to scaffold instruction and engage students to read, annotate, and deconstruct various claims:

- Have students read and annotate a sample claim for what is done effectively.
- Highlight the first part of the claim, noting that the claim starts with a *qualifying* statement. You can share why hedging is important in history and for this particular question.
- Pinpoint the language markers such as *even though*, explaining their function to qualify the argument.
- Ask students to identify the main/independent clause that communicates the writer's central position or stance.
- Explain the rhetorical function of the sentence that offers reasoning.

Table 3.4. Claim Components

Components of a Claim	**Model Text**
Qualification: Concession of an alternative view	Though Lewis and Clark's navigational skills were important,
Stance: Writer's central position or perspective	the help from Native American people along the way should be considered as a reason for the success of the Lewis and Clark expedition.
Reasoning: Informed by available evidence	Evidence shows multiple tribes helped the expedition for months at a time and their guide Sacagawea played a key role in their journey.

This deconstruction approach using mentor texts can help make the language features and rhetorical functions transparent for students. To deepen students' understanding, you can use the following activities.

Activity 1: Model, Practice, Evaluate

You can first model annotating a sample claim before students practice annotating a different claim and assessing their own claims.

Students annotate a different claim independently or in pairs and evaluate their own claims. This activity can be done after students have drafted their tentative claims.

Activity 2: Sentence Expansion

You can integrate the sentence expansion activity to guide students through each part of constructing a claim by using a mentor text to support their thinking. This scaffolded technique can help students construct a complex claim and promotes the skillful use of language.

Once students understand the function of each part of a claim, you can target building proficiency in specific components of the claim. This builds linguistic knowledge more intentionally. Though all parts are related, specific parts of the claim are connected to different reasoning processes and

Table 3.5. Model an Annotation

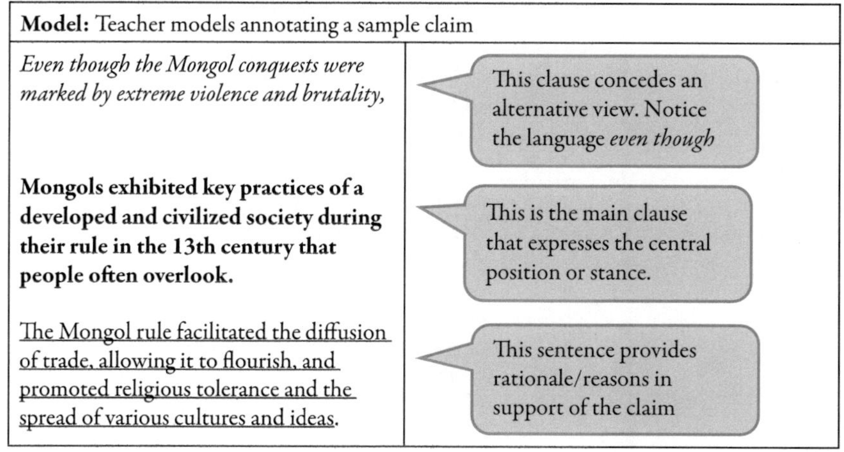

Model: Teacher models annotating a sample claim	
Even though the Mongol conquests were marked by extreme violence and brutality,	This clause concedes an alternative view. Notice the language *even though*
Mongols exhibited key practices of a developed and civilized society during their rule in the 13th century that people often overlook.	This is the main clause that expresses the central position or stance.
The Mongol rule facilitated the diffusion of trade, allowing it to flourish, and promoted religious tolerance and the spread of various cultures and ideas.	This sentence provides rationale/reasons in support of the claim

components of the larger argument. For example, adding supporting reasons references evidence from sources while hedging language can allude to other plausible interpretations.

Table 3.6. Practice and Evaluate

Practice: Students annotate a different claim independently or in pairs	
Although early suffragists generated interest in the cause of women's suffrage, the actions and tactics of the National Women's Party were most directly responsible for the passage of the 19th Amendment because they put crucial pressure on national political figures.	Annotation Notes:
Evaluate: Students evaluate and annotate their own claims	
My claim (copy your claim here and evaluate): *My claim is effective/ineffective because . . .*	

Table 3.7. Sentence Expansion Activity

Instructions/Steps	Example
State your topic of discussion	**Susan B. Anthony's statement**
Specify your topic by using modifiers and adding details	Susan B. Anthony's statement in **1878, "The right of citizens of the United States to vote shall not be abridged by the United States or by any State on account of sex"**
Formulate your commentary or opinion on the topic	Susan B. Anthony's statement in 1878, "The right of citizens of the United States to vote shall not be abridged by the United States or by any State on account of sex" **made a major contribution to the women's suffrage movement**
Explain your reasoning based on evidence from reliable sources	Susan B. Anthony's statement in 1878, "The right of citizens of the United States to vote shall not be abridged by the United States or by any State on account of sex" made a major contribution to the women's suffrage movement **because it brought national attention to the issue of gender discrimination and argued for civil rights.**
Qualify your claim by adding an alternative view/other plausible cause or by using hedging language	**Although early suffragists generated interest in the cause of women's suffrage,** Susan B. Anthony's statement in 1878, "The right of citizens of the United States to vote shall not be abridged by the United States or by any State on account of sex" made a major contribution to the Women's Suffrage Movement because it brought national attention to the issue of gender discrimination and argued for civil rights.

Teaching Move 2: Deconstruct the main clause that expresses the central point

You can help students build a clear and concise **main/independent clause** using specific and precise language that clearly states the topic and comment. You may choose to start with this teaching move first. To do this, you can first deconstruct the main/independent clause that expresses the writer's central position in a sample claim. You can use Table 3.2 from the previous section to show the two parts: topic (what or who) and comment (what about it). You can also simply underline the topic and italicize *the comment* as shown below:

- Mongols *exhibited key practices of a developed and civilized society during their rule in the 13th century that people often overlook.*
- The actions and tactics of the National Women's Party *were most directly responsible for the passage of the 19th Amendment.*

Here you can point out how some topics are simple nouns while others are expressed in complex noun phrases. But the key focus here is to encourage students to use precise and specific nouns and to avoid vague expressions. Students can then practice constructing basic claims using a Do/What chart (Olson et al., 2023).

Activity 3: Do/What Chart

A Do/What chart is an evidence-based strategy that helps students make a plan for composing by breaking down the tasks and by developing a roadmap (Olson et al., 2023).

Table 3.8. Do/What Chart

Do	**What**
Practice	writing a simple but clear claim
Identify	the who or what (the main subject/topic in inquiry question)
List	possible nouns and noun phrases that function as actors, events, causes, or consequences in the essential question. For example: • Sojourner Truth • The National Women's Party
Specify	the noun and noun phrases to clarify and to provide additional information. For example: • Sojourner Truth, an African-American abolitionist and civil rights advocate, • The National Women's Party that was established in 1916 to fight for women's suffrage
State	your opinion/comment about the topic (what about it)

Teaching Move 3: Highlight and practice adding reasoning/rationale into a claim

Once students have a basic claim, asking them or having their peers ask them "*why?*" can be the first step to adding justification. To illustrate, two students meet and share claims with each other. One at a time, they listen and ask their partners: *Why do you think so? What is the rationale for this? What made you come to this conclusion?* Together they justify the claim, given they have both read the sources, and practice expressing their reasoning succinctly.

You can further support students by explicitly focusing on common languaging practices used to express reasons of support. This can be done by showing how reasoning is integrated in sample claims and by providing language resources, such as sentence stems, that show how students can communicate in varied and purposeful ways. "Because" will likely occur frequently, but awareness of other language choices can help students communicate with precision when needed. When using mentor texts, you can ask students to analyze the choices writers make to express their reasoning. These choices are not merely stylistic but help communicate meaning more clearly. Having students analyze these choices can help them build metalinguistic knowledge. You can use Table 3.3 from the previous section to show how reasoning is added in various ways. You can also simply list several examples and underline the reasoning as shown below:

- The Black Death plague was the most significant cause for the decline of feudalism **as** it took out a large number of the peasants which feudalism needed.
- Though Lewis and Clark's navigational skills were important, the help from Native American people along the way should be considered as a reason for the success of the Lewis and Clark expedition. **Evidence shows** multiple tribes helped the expedition for months at a time and their guide Sacagawea played a key role in their journey.
- The California Grape Strike and Boycott was ultimately successful **due to** the march led by Roberto Bustos and the immense support of grape workers and citizens.

After reviewing examples that show various ways reasoning can be provided, you can ask students to practice adding reasoning to a sample claim or to their own claims.

Activity 4: Practice Adding Reasoning

Helping students practice with reasoning can build fluency for independent writing later on.

Table 3.9. Language Resources for Reasoning

Provide Reasoning	**Language Choices & Resources**
1) The actions and tactics of the National Women's Party most directly contributed to the passage of the 19th Amendment (provide reasoning) 2) Add your basic claim and provide reasoning	___ Add a dependent clause to the claim using a causal connector. ○ as . . . ○ because . . . ○ since . . . ___ Add a new sentence that provides rationale. ○ Evidence shows . . . ○ This is because . . . ○ This is due to . . . ○ As shown by . . . ○ This is supported by . . . ○ This is true on the grounds of . . . ___ Add a prepositional phrase that provides reasoning in your main clause. ○ due to . . . ○ because of . . . ○ on the account of . . . ○ thanks to . . . ○ in view of . . .

Teaching Move 4: Facilitate dialogue and practice qualifying a claim

To practice qualifying or hedging, students can benefit from interactions with peers. Given the collective goal of advancing the best possible interpretation of the past, sharing claims with others in order to refine them, acknowledge their shortcomings, or compare them to competing expectations reflects the disciplinary practice of historians. It also helps students learn! Such an activity can begin after each student formulates a claim. Then, each student shares their claim with a partner who listens and considers if the claim is properly scoped, qualified, or distinguished from counterclaims.

To facilitate the dialogue around different ways of qualifying a claim, you can first model by modifying a claim. For example, you can point out that because there are many potential causes of World War I, adding the phrase "*most significant*" is a small, but more precise way to express their view about this historical event. It is helpful to offer a way to qualify or temper the claim with a handy list of adverbs—*occasionally, generally, usually, often, sometimes, commonly, typically, probably, presumably, perhaps, relatively, likely*—with some suggestions for how they can qualify their claim.

- The Black Death plague was the most significant cause of the decline of feudalism
- The Black Death plague was *likely* the most significant cause of the decline of feudalism.

Because the word *likely* indicates there are other potential answers to this question, students consider a relatively advanced but attainable move, a two-part claim. You can show this by adding a counterargument to a claim:

- *Although the 100 Years' War played a significant role in the decline of feudalism,* the Black Death plague was *likely* the most significant cause for the decline of feudalism.

After you model, you can ask students to try the same. You can provide them with a list of language resources that they can use to qualify their claims. It is helpful to provide scaffolding phrases and sentence stems such as *although, even though, while, given that,* and *provided that.* You can use the following steps to scaffold students' practice:

- Ask students to write their initial claims and share with one another.
- Ask students to provide their reasoning after they share.
- Ask peers to suggest potential counterclaims. Peers evaluate each other's claims to see if they are properly scoped or qualified.
- Ask students to write revised claims with qualifiers.

You can project the following chart that summarizes various hedging devices used to qualify a claim. Though students are probably familiar (notice our hedging language!) with these language resources, they may need additional support in using these tools strategically to add nuance to their claims.

Activity 5: Practice Hedging Claims

Having students practice qualifying claims using a variety of language resources can help them see that they can make various language choices.

Table 3.10. Summary of Language Resources for Hedging

Choices	Language Markers	Rhetorical Purposes
Use a modifier or modifiers	*most, many, much, some, several, a majority of, a large number of,* *specific adjectives, nouns,* and *prepositional phrases for contextualization*	to avoid overgeneralization; to express the scope of limitation
Use a modal verb	*may, might, can, could, would*	to express the degree of certainty or conviction
Use a hedging verb	*seem (to), appear (to), tend (to), suggest, indicate,*	to distance oneself
Use a qualifying adverb	<u>Frequency</u>: *usually, typically, often, commonly* <u>Stance:</u> *likely, probably, perhaps, arguably* <u>Adverb phrases:</u> *in some case, in certain situations*	to express the scope of limitation; to express the degree of certainty or conviction
Use an *it*-clause	*It is likely/plausible that . . .* *It is reasonable to conclude . . .* *It is assumed that . . .* *It is widely accepted that . . .*	to express the scope of limitation; to express the degree of certainty
Add a dependent clause	<u>Connectors</u>: *although, even though, while granted that, given that, provided that*	to situate the claim among other competing claims or prior interpretations
Add a prepositional phrase	*despite, without, in spite of, regardless of*	to situate the claim among other competing claims or prior interpretations

Table 3.11. Practice Hedging Claims

Instructions/Steps	Practice (with this claim or your claim)
Version 1: Unhedged	The help from Native American peoples along the way is the most important reason the Lewis and Clark expedition succeeded.
Version 2: Qualify the claim using *it*-clause	
Version 3: Hedge using a modifier or adverb	
Version 4: Add an alternative view	

How can teachers build metalinguistic knowledge and awareness?

The instructional strategies and activities in the previous section will help students expand their linguistic resources and develop an understanding of linguistic choices to meet rhetorical and disciplinary goals. While exposure to mentor texts and deconstruction of these texts help students see effective ways of communicating by making the language structures and patterns visible, asking students to reflect and evaluate texts and language choices can push them to develop metalinguistic knowledge and awareness. You can engage students in evaluating various types of claims for rhetorical effectiveness and linguistic choices. Such activities show how choices about language matter for writing.

Activity 6: Evaluating Claims

This activity engages students in evaluating and ranking various claims. Students explain their reasoning for their ranking by answering the question: *What makes them more or less effective?*

Table 3.12. Evaluating Claims Activity

Sample Claims	**Ranking**
The grape boycott and strike succeeded because Cesar Chavez appeared on television to make his cause known and because of a march to Sacramento which many farm workers participated in.	_ Beginning _ Developing _ Advanced
The National Women's Party was most directly responsible for the passage of the 19th Amendment.	_ Beginning _ Developing _ Advanced
There were many factors that led to the decline of feudalism in Europe, such as the Black Death plague, the Magna Carta, and the Hundred Years' War. The Black Death plague was the most significant cause for the decline of feudalism because it took out a large number of the peasants which feudalism needed.	_ Beginning _ Developing _ Advanced
The Black Death plague was the most significant cause for the decline of feudalism as it took out a large number of the peasants which feudalism needed.	_ Beginning _ Developing _ Advanced
Though Lewis and Clark's personal and navigational skills were important, the help from Native American peoples along the way is the most important reason the Lewis and Clark expedition succeeded. Evidence shows multiple tribes helped the expedition for months at a time and their guide Sacagawea played a key role in their journey.	_ Beginning _ Developing _ Advanced
Bonus: Edit two of the claims to make them more effective.	
Revised Claim:	
Revised Claim:	

You can use anonymized claims from your students or write sample claims around topics of historical inquiry. Though choices are key, students benefit from models and guided practice. Then, students can make their own decisions about language choices as they construct their own claims. Before having students craft their own claims or include hedging language, you can provide models and sentence frames. Models and sentence frames are particularly beneficial to multilingual learners of English who need language support.

Activity 7: Practice Using Sentence Frames for Claims

You can ask students to review the following sentence frames and practice using these frames as they make a claim about the causes of events. You can prompt them to notice the various ways causality is expressed. Then, students evaluate the sentences to see which one works best for their own claim and explain why it works best and how they can modify to make it better. This activity helps students see different choices and encourages them to make intentional choices for their claims.

1. ____________ was one of the most significant reasons that ____________ succeeded because ____ ____.
2. Even though ____________ partially led to the success of ____________, ______________________________ was the most significant cause because ____.
3. ____________ would likely be one of the most important causes of ______________________________. This is based on the evidence that ____.
4. ____________ made a major contribution to ____________. Without ____, ____ would not have happened.
5. ____________ most directly led to/gave rise to ____________. Therefore, ______________________________ was the most significant reason for ____ ______________________________.

6. Although some argue ____________, the decline/fall/change in ____________ is best marked by ______________________. This is supported by ____.
7. The ____________ [event/actor/time/period] is best characterized as ____________. This is due to ___________________________ and ____.
8. Despite the contributions of ___________________________, it is also significant/important to note that ______________________.

Sentence frames can serve as a scaffolding technique that is helpful in accelerating learners' development of complex sentence structures needed in crafting nuanced claims. You can refer to these sentence frames to engage students in constructing or revising their claims. The idea is for them to experiment with various language choices to construct their claims, and then reflect on those choices to build metalinguistic knowledge.

During this instructional phase, students can also benefit from access to additional language resources. For example, when students are practicing writing and revising their claims after discussion with peers, you can project a chart with language resources for students to use as shown in Table 3.13. Alternatively, you can model revision using the chart and then assign students to revise their claims as an exit ticket or bellwork activity.

Table 3.13. Language Resources for Constructing a Claim

Features	Language Resources
Adjectives of Value	important, significant, crucial, consequential, momentous, far-reaching, major, critical, vital, pivotal, decisive, substantial, key
Causal Verbs	contribute to, lead to, cause, give rise to, be the cause of, result in, produce, generate, engender, precipitate, prompt, provoke, promote, foster, trigger, create, bring about
Causal Nouns	contribution to, cause of, the reason for, participation in, involvement in, the basis for, the grounds for, the success of, pressure on
Causal Connectors	**Phrase Linkers:** because of, due to, on account of, as a consequence of, as a result of, thanks to, on the grounds of **Clause Connectors:** because, since, as, so that, so, for **Sentence Connectors:** thus, therefore, as a consequence, as a result, accordingly, for that reason, consequently
Concessive Connectors	**Phrase Linkers:** despite, in spite of, regardless of **Clause Connectors**: although, even though, while, though, yet, but **Sentence Connectors:** however, still, nevertheless, regardless

Reflect!

- What language choices did you make to construct the claim?
- How effective are your language choices given the rhetorical goals?
- How would you modify your language to improve the claim?
- How else can you express a similar meaning?

We suggest that you engage students in reflection through quick writes or dialogic interaction after each activity to promote metalinguistic knowledge and awareness. To facilitate reflection and interaction, you can provide your students with guiding questions to write, discuss, and reflect on languaging practices used to construct claims.

The pedagogical strategies and activities we suggest closely align with the following WIDA standards for English Language Development (ELD) for Social Studies (WIDA, 2020):

ELD-SS.6-8.Explain.Expressive and ELD-SS.9-12.Explain.Expressive

Construct social studies explanations that

- Establish perspective for communicating outcomes, consequences, or documentation
- Develop reasoning, sequences with linear and nonlinear relationships, evidence, and details, acknowledging strengths and weaknesses
- Generalize multiple causes and effects of developments or events
- Introduce and contextualize multiple phenomena or events

ELD-SS.6-8.Argue.Expressive and ELD-SS.9-12.Argue.Expressive

Construct social studies arguments that

- Introduce and contextualize topic
- Establish perspective
- Show relationships between claims and counterclaims, differences in perspectives, and evidence and reasoning

What should teachers consider for effective instruction?

Students in diverse classrooms have varying levels of proficiency in historical understanding, argumentation, and language skills. In our own work, the average student in grades 6 through 12 scored a 3.5 out of 7 in presenting a clear and compelling claim. This means that the historical claim an average student made was simple and somewhat clear, but could be improved, especially in the areas of reasoning and qualification.

Student artifacts and writing also show that about half of the students need support in building a basic claim and half need support improving their claims. While all students can benefit from explicit instruction that contextualizes language in content, identifying student needs and their level of mastery based on standards and skills in claim-making can help design future instruction and shape instructional practice to meet the demands of argument writing. In other words, instructional decision-making needs to be guided by where students are in articulating their claims about historical topics and what grade-level learning objectives they need to attain in argument writing. The instructional strategies and activities we have provided can be intentionally selected, modified, and integrated into instruction to meet the diverse needs of students.

With this in mind, we return to an eleventh-grade student's claim that adequately addresses the prompt, but we add layers to the claim construction as shown in Table 3.14. The descriptions that focus on both rhetorical and linguistic features within each area/layer can guide you in evaluating students' thinking and writing. You may consider using examples that are contextualized within the content you are teaching and the topic of historical inquiry your students are engaging in.

A Simple Argumentative Claim. A simple argumentative claim addresses the historical inquiry question and communicates a stance, clearly stating the topic of discussion (*The actions and tactics of the National Women's Party . . .*) and commenting on the topic (*were most directly responsible for the passage of the 19th Amendment*). The student writer shows both some understanding of the historical content and the linguistic knowledge to communicate a stance. Affirming these abilities can help developing writers internalize the basic criteria for making an argumentative claim.

Because historians are ultimately concerned with bringing us closer to the truth about the past, the claim should also be justifiable and defensible based on the available facts and evidence. You may need to guide students in formulating a justifiable and defensible claim to move them away from stating the obvious or summarizing a fact. This may include directing students back to historical content. The following questions can serve as an instructional guide:

Table 3.14. Layers of Claim Construction

Layers	Examples	Descriptions
A simple argumentative claim	The actions and tactics of the National Women's Party were most directly responsible for the passage of the 19th Amendment.	**Rhetorical Features:** • Communicates a stance • Is justifiable and defensible **Linguistic Feature:** • One-clause sentence that expresses a stance/perspective clearly
A reasoned argumentative claim with rationale	The actions and tactics of the National Women's Party were most directly responsible for the passage of the 19th Amendment because they put crucial pressure on national political figures.	**Rhetorical Features:** • Communicates a stance • Is justifiable and defensible • Provides reasoning **Linguistic Features:** • Independent clause expresses a stance • A multi-clause complex sentence • A dependent clause expresses reasoning
A reasoned, qualified, and contextualized claim with rationale	Although early suffragists generated interest in the cause of women's suffrage, the actions and tactics of the National Women's Party were most directly responsible for the passage of the 19th Amendment because they put crucial pressure on national political figures.	**Rhetorical Features:** • Communicates a stance • Is justifiable and defensible • Provides reasoning • Qualifies the claim by acknowledging an alternative view. **Linguistic Features:** • Independent clause expresses a stance • A multi-clause complex sentence • Dependent clauses that express reasoning and alternative view

- Is the claim arguable?
  - Could anyone disagree with the claim?
  - Are there other possible explanations that better explain the historical inquiry?
- Is the claim justifiable based on evidence?
  - What evidence do you have for this claim?
  - Can you defend the claim based on available and reliable evidence?
- How is the claim expressed?
  - Is the topic of inquiry/discussion clear and precise?
  - Does the comment on the topic express a stance and viewpoint?

Asking these questions can help students with the basic construction of a simple arguable claim. It is important to note that close reading and rereading multiple sources and making meaning from sources are needed to build the content knowledge.

A Reasoned Argumentative Claim with Rationale. A well-reasoned claim addresses the historical inquiry question and provides a rationale or reasons. For students who have not included reasoning, the next step in a student's developmental progression in claim-making is to include rationale—a supporting reason or reasons for their claim. Reasoning is an essential part of justifying a claim; it can serve as a signpost for further discussion as the writer expands their ideas and provides evidence as they develop their arguments.

A simple question of *why* can help students move toward the direction of adding the rationale and making their reasoning visible. Linguistically they also need the skills of embedding clauses and prepositional phrases to construct complex sentences. You can guide students in adding reasoning by asking the following questions:

- Is the claim justified with reasoning?
  - What is your reasoning behind your claim?
  - What evidence do you have for this claim?
- How is the reasoning added to the claim?
  - What language marker(s) can help your readers see your reasoning more clearly?

You may need to guide students to provide sound reasoning based on available and reliable evidence as evidence-based reasoning is an essential part of historical inquiry. This means that students will have read, evaluated, and analyzed multiple sources to extract key evidence to support their claims. At the same time, students may benefit from sentence stems provided in the previous section.

A Reasoned Claim That is Qualified and Contextualized. At this level, the claim addresses the historical inquiry question, provides rationale and reasoning, and has an additional layer of qualifying and contextualizing the claim. Qualifying a claim within the context of the historical question and other relevant interpretations is challenging conceptually and linguistically. The following questions can serve as instructional guides to move students in this direction:

- Is the claim qualified and contextualized?
  - Is the claim contextualized within a relevant historical period and events?

  - Is the claim situated among other competing claim(s) or prior interpretations?
  - Does the writer avoid overgeneralization and/or address the scope of limitation?
- How is the claim qualified and contextualized?
  - How is the degree of certainty expressed in the claim?
  - What language marker(s) indicate qualification and contextualization?

Finding effective ways of contextualizing and qualifying a claim requires not only an understanding of a relevant historical context within which the claim is situated but also knowledge about languaging practices used to communicate the tentativeness of the claim.

In this chapter, we have provided an array of instructional tools, resources, and strategies you can use and modify to provide your students with meaningful language support for making an effective claim for historical argumentation. By providing language support, you can cultivate your students' language skills and expand their linguistic repertoires so that they can formulate clear and compelling claims.

CHAPTER 4

Sourcing and Integrating Evidence

Guiding Questions

- Why and how do historians use multiple sources for historical argumentation?
- How is language used to integrate sources in argument writing?
- How can teachers help students build language skills for sourcing and integrating evidence?

In an eleventh-grade class focused on twentieth-century U.S. history, students analyze major social problems, tracing their causes and consequences (California Department of Education, 2000). In one class, students are asked to respond to a historical question: *What contributed to the success of the Montgomery Bus Boycott*? To answer this question, students read various sources, both primary and secondary, with different perspectives and authority. They must also use a sophisticated skill, sourcing—thinking about the source's origin and context, questioning who created it for what purpose, evaluating whether it is credible, and describing how it contributes to our interpretation and understanding of the past (Wineburg, 2001).

To use and integrate sources effectively in argument writing, students must discern important information in and about the sources and select relevant evidence to support their arguments. When writing, they use language strategically to weave in source information and materials to build their arguments. The strategic use of language requires knowledge of disciplinary conventions for sourcing, as well as proficiency in languaging practices used for attributing, contextualizing, evaluating, and integrating sources. These skills can be challenging for students, especially those who are not familiar with the conventions of source use in argument writing. To see how the integration of sources might be challenging for students, we examine two paragraphs for source use.

The paragraphs we present here are written by two different students in an eleventh-grade class. As you read Sample Paragraph 1, pay attention to the use of sources for evidence, as well as the language choices made for source integration.

Sample Paragraph 1

> The most significant reason the Montgomery bus boycott succeeded was the carpool system set up by Dr. Martin Luther King Jr. and Rufus Lewis, and here is evidence from source 3 that supports my claim: "the success of the carpool is at the heart of the movement, Lewis said at the meeting. It must not be stopped." This evidence supports my argument that the carpool system most helped the boycott succeed because it clearly states, "the success of the carpool is at the heart of the movement." Other evidence from source 3 supports my argument: "It thus became necessary for the Black leaders to find an alternative—the carpool. They set up 23 locations where people could gather to wait for free transportation." This evidence supports my claim because it states that the only alternative (other than walking) to help the people participating in the boycott get to their jobs was the carpool system. Of course, other people might say that the handouts were the most important reason or the people who helped the handouts get printed, and they're absolutely right! There is no right or wrong answer here but the carpool system is simply the most important reason because in source 3 it clearly says, "the success of the carpool is at the heart of the movement," this suggests that if the carpool had failed the boycott might have failed along with it.

In this example, the student uses a single source for evidence to support their argument. However, the evidence is not clearly attributed to the source, preventing readers from identifying where the evidence comes from. Quotations from a single unidentified source, along with a repetitive pattern of quotes followed by explicit statements (*This evidence supports my claim . . .*), do little to strengthen the argument.

The next student example, on the other hand, exhibits more sophisticated use of source material to support the claim. As you read Sample Paragraph 2, observe how it differs from the previous paragraph in source use and language choices.

Sample Paragraph 2

> One might think that an important reason the Montgomery Bus Boycott succeeded was because of the strategic planning of the boycott. This is a valid point as there is evidence from "A Timeline of the Montgomery Bus Boycott" published by Beacon Press, explaining each of the crucial steps in this movement. This timeline gives insight into the progression of the boycott until it reached the point where the Supreme Court deemed segregation of city buses illegal and thus leading to the desegregation of Montgomery buses. However, even the best plans cannot succeed without the determination, perseverance, and passion of the participants/citizens. This is evident in multiple sources, including Jo Ann Robinson's memoir and Bayard Rustin's diary, both of which are primary sources that provide first-hand accounts of the events leading to the boycott. For example, in his diary written on February 24, 1956, Rustin states how he was introduced to "two men, one of whom has walked 7 miles and the other 14 miles, every day since December 5." He then explains how, even though 28 of the carpool drivers had been arrested, the remaining ones scattered through the city, pledging that they'd risk being arrested until their hard work was paid off. The carpool system of the boycott provided the Black citizens with a ride to the places they needed to go and was significant during this movement. To put in all this work, every person was okay with suffering the punishments inflicted by the city officials, like being arrested or harassed. Similarly, the memoir written by Jo Ann Robinson, the president of the Women's Political Council, recounts her and her students' involvement in the boycott by making thousands of copies of handouts with boycott messages and mapping out to deliver these handouts to black homes. If these people didn't care or had no passion to end segregation, the boycott wouldn't have succeeded. Each of them made huge sacrifices so that their suffering can aid the others. Therefore, despite other rational arguments, still, the Black citizens' dedication helped the boycott succeed.

This example demonstrates the use of multiple sources for evidence with clear attribution, naming the authors (*Bayard Rustin, Jo Ann Robinson*), the title (*"A Timeline of the Montgomery Bus Boycott"*), and the type of sources (*timeline, diary, memoir*). The student contextualizes the source by providing when the source was written (*on February 24, 1956*) and establishes credibility by providing additional information about the source (*both of which are primary sources that provide first-hand accounts; Jo Ann Robinson, the president of the Women's Political Council*). Finally, paraphrases, quotations, brief summaries, evaluative statements, and reasoning are strategically woven together.

Through explicit instruction and language support, teachers can help students build both language and sourcing skills as seen in the second student example. This chapter provides guidance to support students in learning to attribute evidence to sources, articulate sourcing moves, and effectively integrate evidence in their argument writing. Our goal is to foster an understanding of why we use sources when engaging in historical argumentation and to make visible the languaging practices used for attribution, integration, and evaluation of sources. The chapter is organized into three main sections:

I. **Conceptual Overview:** Using Multiple Sources for Historical Argumentation
   - Why do we source documents in history and beyond?
   - How do historians integrate evidence from multiple sources to build arguments?

II. **Language Focus:** Languaging Practices for Integrating Sources in Argument Writing
   - How is language used to attribute evidence to sources?
   - What language choices can be made to evaluate sources?
   - How is language used to integrate sources in support of a claim?

III. **Instructional Support:** Cultivating Language Skills for Source Integration
   - How can teachers cultivate language skills for source integration?
   - How can teachers build metalinguistic knowledge and awareness?
   - What should teachers consider for effective instruction?

I. Using Multiple Sources for Historical Argumentation

Why do we source documents in history and beyond?

Recognizing that evidence comes from distinct sources is a key first step in historical reasoning. The next step is to understand sources as *historically situated* and *constructed* in particular times and places. To illustrate, consider a student who wants to learn more about the impact of fossil fuels on the environment. They find a website claiming there is little evidence that climate change is caused by human activity. They also find that the website is supported by donations from a number of large energy corporations that have an interest in the sustained use of fossil fuels. It is important that this student considers the source of information *before* considering the content.

Such an activity is featured on Digital Inquiry Group (DIG) formerly known as Stanford History Education Group (SHEG). The publicly accessible lessons aim to build skills like sourcing and evidence evaluation for productive civic reasoning. These skills can also be built in history classrooms for successful historical inquiry and transferred to the civic domain. The DIG's civic online reasoning curriculum also features multiple activities to build sourcing skills in historical contexts.

In historical inquiry, sourcing a document is important for at least two reasons: (1) to evaluate the document's perspective, credibility, and reliability; and (2) to resolve disagreements between sources by considering differences in perspectives or purposes (Wineburg, 1991). For instance, when reading about the events leading to the Battle of Lexington in 1775, considering the perspectives of firsthand accounts—whether a colonist or British officer is recounting events from that day—matters as these viewpoints may influence their retelling of events. If two sources disagree—for example, a colonist's account and a British officer's account of a skirmish in the American Revolution—considering source information, time, place, and perspective can help resolve discrepancies that would otherwise leave the historical situation unresolved or incoherent (Rouet et al., 2017). Noting discrepancies between sources can lead to a more effortful evaluation of each source and a search for additional sources of information—critical skills for effective argument writing in history (Monte-Sano, 2012).

Advanced sourcing moves to resolve discrepancies can be particularly important when students feel ambivalent about the truth or who to trust. Consider the following eighth-grade student writing about the events leading to the Boston Massacre:

> This evidence is reliable because it came from a British captain. But it may also be unreliable because maybe the captain was not honest about what happened and lied about what actually happened.

At first, this analysis acknowledges that history is an act of interpretation from documents of varying reliability. But the student concludes their writing, "*sometimes there is no right answer to what happened, and anything can be right or wrong.*" While sourcing helped this student recognize that there are two sides to a story, pushing past subjectivism to find the best, most plausible interpretation given all the facts is important in history. Beliefs about knowledge in history hold there is an objective truth even if we cannot know it in the present moment (Stoel et al., 2017). Sourcing (and corroboration, which is covered in the next chapter) helps students resolve this ambivalence.

How do historians integrate evidence from multiple sources to build arguments?

What Are Historical Sources?

Historical sources are artifacts created in a specific time and place with embedded agendas, viewpoints, and biases.

When working with multiple documents, texts, or sources, noting where evidence comes from—**attribution**—is foundational. This is true in history as it is in civic or social reasoning in the twenty-first century. Inside and outside the classroom, students are increasingly inundated with information from countless sources, each with various perspectives and differing degrees of reliability (Bråten et al., 2017). For example, when reposting or sharing information about a major epidemic, students, and indeed society, are best served when individuals can distinguish between information shared by medical experts and information shared by their distant relative who is most definitely *not* a doctor and is, arguably, *way too* active on social media. In historical inquiry and civic argumentation, noting who says or shares something comes before noting what is said or shared. In history, we think about sources *not* as authoritative accounts that transmit knowledge, but as artifacts created in a specific time and place with embedded agendas, viewpoints, and biases. We must identify and consider the source of information before interpreting the content. Thus, attribution is aligned with the disciplinary norms of history given its purpose of constructing evidence-based interpretations of the past using *multiple* sources that have unique perspectives (Cowgill II & Waring, 2017).

A more advanced skill, **sourcing**, means thinking about how the publisher, creator, or context of a source should influence how we interpret that source: Do they have expertise? Were they present at the event? Are they trying to profit or benefit from how this event is interpreted? Given the prevalence of sources with various motives, purposes, and perspectives, sourcing is also a key skill in historical inquiry and civic life (Monte-Sano, 2010; Wineburg, 1991).

Teachers have a great opportunity and an immense civic responsibility to build students' skills for sourcing to build robust historical, civic, and information literacies (Chinn et al., 2021).

Knowledge about sources includes the context of sources, the relations between sources, and an assessment of sources' usefulness, trustworthiness, and relevance (Wineburg, 1991). Researchers refer to this as an intertextual model (Rouet & Britt, 2011)—how sources and texts relate, agree, or disagree. This is the conceptual base for sound historical reasoning and writing. The intertextual model can change and develop over time as a reader encounters new information. For example, when learning about the results of a national election, individuals update their understanding by aggregating multiple sources of information from news outlets, social media, and conversations with peers. It is crucial for them to evaluate the sources of information as they decide whether to count or discount the information in order to revise their understanding of events. If a particular source, known to peddle misinformation, explicitly disagrees with multiple reputable news sources, an individual can reasonably ignore information from this source. This discounting of information ensures that the student can later advance a factually accurate interpretation of events by sourcing documents and corroborating evidence, all of which are hallmarks of effective historical writing (Monte-Sano, 2012).

Shifting students to think about documents as constructed in specific historical contexts can be difficult if they are accustomed to classrooms where the history textbook is the dominant source of knowledge and pedagogical approaches do not question its authority (Nokes & De La Paz, 2023). Because textbooks tell a relatively straightforward account of events, students may develop an understanding of historical knowledge as fixed, simple, and unassailable and may lack the dispositions to question the authority of sources and documents handed to them by the teacher. Inquiry-based instruction with multiple sources and a classroom that centers students as meaning-makers and that engages students in examining and interrogating sources of information can help build these dispositions.

Teaching students sourcing skills helps them learn to view historical knowledge as *tentative*, evidence-based *interpretations* of the past supported by particular historical lenses and sources of evidence with varying levels of *reliability* and relevance (Wiley et al., 2020). Though it is common for students to resort to writing heuristics like "the text says," such an utterance is unclear in history. Still, many secondary students do not find attribution and sourcing to come naturally. Figure 4 shows sourcing moves observed in student writing at varying levels of specificity. Students can develop sourcing skills when they are provided with guidance and instruction. In history and civic life, documents and

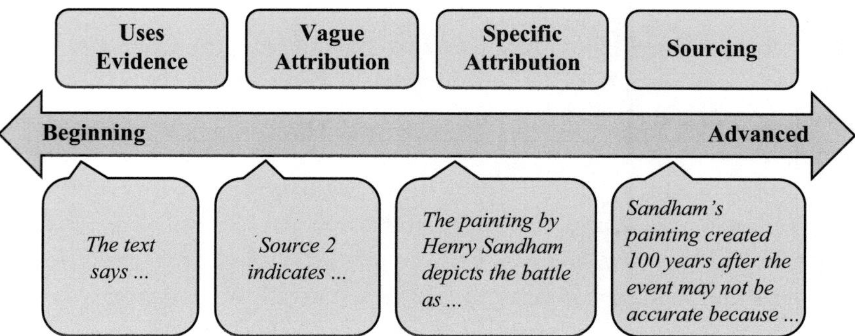

Figure 4. Sourcing Moves Observed in Student Writing

their contents can only be fully understood, evaluated, and used for argumentative purposes when the *source* is assessed and kept in mind. When it comes to presenting an argument, students must be able to attribute evidence to specific sources and develop an ability to distinguish between sources, evaluate sources, and communicate relevant source information to readers.

While noting where specific evidence comes from and whether it is reliable or not is a key first step to using evidence, there are a variety of ways to *present* evidence in argument writing. Understanding these ways both conceptually and linguistically is key for effective communication. First, writers may directly **quote** material from specific texts to support their arguments. They might also **paraphrase** information within sources and across sources. They might even use the sources themselves as evidence.

Choosing between quoting or paraphrasing is often a rhetorical decision, but a few key principles regarding evidence use also guide choices in how evidence is integrated in argument writing in history. Chauncey Monte-Sano (2012) argues that students who use evidence proficiently maintain factual accuracy, select evidence that is persuasive, source evidence (discussed previously), corroborate sources, and contextualize evidence. These concerns align with the purpose of history—describing what is true or really happened after considering multiple pieces of evidence from sources that vary in reliability and relevance.

Directly quoting from sources needs to be purposeful and factually accurate in order to be persuasive. When corroborating evidence, however, paraphrasing might be a clear choice. For example, an eighth-grade student noted that the participation from multiple social and civic organizations was a key factor in the success of the Montgomery Bus Boycott. No source they read explicitly said this, but multiple primary and secondary sources students used in the eleventh-grade unit emphasized the contributions of multiple actors—Jo

Ann Robinson's memoir noting the distribution of flyers and Bayard Rustin's diary discussing the efforts of citizens to organize and carry out a carpool. Some of the most sophisticated claims written by students made a case for collective action, and these claims were supported by paraphrased evidence from multiple sources.

In order to synthesize information from multiple sources, writers first make connections among sources; identify patterns, themes, commonalities, and differences; highlight and summarize what the sources say about the topic being explored; and then strategically select ideas and details from sources to quote, paraphrase, and integrate into their argument writing (Lunsford et al., 2016). Corroboration and contextualization are key skills underlying the process of evidence selection and integration. Attribution and sourcing are still key when synthesizing information across sources. Being specific and accurate about the sources of evidence allows for contestation, as our understanding of the past can be revised when we learn something new (Nokes & De La Paz, 2023).

Finally, evidence does not always come *from* the source. Sometimes, evidence might be the source itself. For example, consider the letter from Cesar Chavez, urging local shoppers to boycott grapes in order to support the strike of Delano grape workers (Figure 5). A student might place this letter into their evolving mental model of the Delano Grape Strike and Boycott, noting it as another example of Chavez's leadership or the role of consumer choices in supporting workers' movements. Either way, the letter itself—who wrote it and who was its audience—can be used as evidence to support a claim about Chavez's role in helping the strike and boycott succeed. A student who can place this document in the past and consider how it may have influenced historical actors and events will be using the source as evidence to advance compelling interpretations.

II. Languaging Practices for Integrating Sources in Argument Writing

Writers strategically use language to communicate *where* information comes from, *how* specific sources are used for evidence to support or counter a claim, and *why* sources are more or less reliable. The use of sources helps writers establish credibility (ethos), avoid plagiarism, and clarify and explain who, and perhaps with what authority, contributes ideas to the topic being explored. To use multiple sources effectively, students need to develop knowledge of the sources they are using, an understanding of the rhetorical purposes behind these sources, and fluency in disciplinary language conventions for attributing and integrating sources into their writing. By focusing on the languaging

Dear Los Angeles Friend:

Another Xmas finds us picketing in the fields and boycotting grapes all over the United States and Canada - instead of celebrating the season as all of you are doing.

This is a season when men pay special attention to the needs of their brothers, and we are grateful for the support that has come from some of our Los Angeles friends.

But we don't want to always have to depend upon the gifts of others. We only want a simple thing: to escape from poverty and suffering by getting the grape-growers to provide decent wages and working conditions. When that Great Day arrives, then we will be able to take care of our own needs, not only at Xmas time, but every day of the year. Meantime, we must continue in the only way open to us to gain our rights - the way of the strike and the boycott.

But we cannot win without your help. During the Holiday Season, please remember the Farm Worker, who harvests your food. DON'T BUY GRAPES! Urge your friends not to buy grapes. Speak to the members of all the organizations you belong to, and urge them not to buy grapes.

Finally, if you really want to make Xmas merrier in Delano this year, and make that Great Day of our victory come sooner, you can do even more. You can join our "all-out, year's end, CONSUMER ACTION CAMPAIGN". You can get together with friends and visit every chain-store manager in your neighborhood and tell them you won't shop there until they remove the grapes.

Merry Xmas

Cesar Chavez

"MIGHT AS WELL MOVE ON.. NOBODY TRADING AT THIS STORE"

Please Don't Buy Grapes

UNITED FARM WORKERS - AFL-CI
$3016\frac{1}{2}$ E. 1st ST., L.A. 63
265-1053 - 265-1584

Figure 5. Cesar Chavez's Letter (Digital Public Library of America)

practices used for attributing evidence to sources, integrating evidence, and sourcing in argument writing in history, teachers can simultaneously foster disciplinary literacy and rhetorical problem-solving skills.

As students are encouraged to think about sources as artifacts created in a specific time and place with embedded agendas, viewpoints, and biases, they need to first build knowledge of the sources they are using to develop their arguments. Several research-based tools exist to help students identify and understand important source information. Literacy organizations, such as the Digital Inquiry Group, feature scaffolded questions and online resources for students to practice analyzing and identifying source information. We have modified and added to the scaffolded questions originally developed by the Digital Inquiry Group and categorized them into four areas: naming the source, contextualizing the source, questioning the source, and evaluating the source. We center the languaging practices of source use in argument writing around these four areas:

- Naming the source: *Who wrote/created this source/artifact? What type of source/artifact is this?*
- Contextualizing the source: *When was this source/artifact written/created/published? Where was this source artifact created?*
- Questioning the source: *What is the author's/creator's perspective or bias? Who is the intended audience for this source/artifact? Why and for what purpose was it created/written?*
- Evaluating the source: *Is this source/artifact reliable or trustworthy? How does it contribute to our understanding of the topic? How does this source contribute to my argument?*

The first two areas, *naming* and *contextualizing*, are a starting place for identifying important source information and making an attribution statement in writing (e.g., in *Jo Ann Robinson's memoir*). The last two areas, *questioning* and *evaluating*, are arguably more complex than source attribution. They are less frequently observed in secondary student writing but can be developed with source-based instruction (Steiss et al., 2024).

How is language used to attribute evidence to sources?

Attribution requires students to name and contextualize sources using precise language that communicates where specific evidence comes from. The languaging practices used for source attribution *vary* depending on the nature of the source and the rhetorical situation that guides the writing. In some cases, the name of the author may be most important; in other cases, the date may be important. Students must be well versed in the different ways one can name a source. We first focus on naming the source.

Naming the Source with the Author. Naming the source using its author's or creator's name is a conventional method of source attribution in academic writing. In fact, the author-page method of in-text citation is a well-established disciplinary convention. When referencing the author, using the full name of the author/creator at first mention and the last name in subsequent references is a common practice. We observe that students who are not familiar with the disciplinary language convention of source attribution tend to use the first name of the author or use vague terms such as "the author" instead of the specific name of the author. We provide examples that illustrate different languaging practices and the conventions used in Table 4.1.

In naming the "who" of the source, writers can make several linguistic choices: placing the name of the author in the subject position often followed by a reporting verb (*Jo Ann Robinson recounts*); using an introductory phrase (*According to Robinson*); and providing the author information in the parenthetical citation (*Robinson 46*). Writers can also provide additional information about the author, such as affiliation, occupation, position, and role, to establish the credibility of the author. A writer can provide these additional details about the author in various grammatical structures:

- Modifying noun phrases (*Women's Political Council President* Jo Ann Robinson . . .)
- Adjective clauses (Jo Ann Robinson, *who was actively involved in the boycott*, . . .)
- Appositives (Bayard Rustin, *a close advisor to Martin Luther King*, . . .).

Table 4.1. Naming the Source with the Author

Naming the Source: Who wrote this source, and what type of source is this?	
Languaging Practices	• **Jo Ann Robinson, the president of the Women's Political Council, recounts** her and her students' involvement in the boycott. • **According to Robinson,** handouts with a boycott message "were dropped off at schools, where both students and staff members helped distribute them further" (46). • Handouts a boycott message "were dropped off at schools, where both students and staff members helped distribute them further" (**Robinson 46**).
Conventions	• Use author's last name or the full name when first mentioned. • Include page number when including a direct quotation. • Use only last name for the parenthetical citation. • Note that MLA Style is used in these examples.

Naming the source with the author embedded in the sentence, rather than given in a parenthetical citation, affords an opportunity to state additional information about the author. This information can communicate the author's perspective, purpose, or credentials. Descriptive information about the author is often provided early in writing. Other details, such as the author's role, perspective, or bias, can be provided later to assess credibility or reliability. Table 4.2 provides examples that highlight various linguistic choices for naming sources with the author.

Naming the Source with the Title. Another way to make an attribution statement is by using the title of the source. Writers may use the title for source attribution when the source has an unknown or anonymous author or when the title of the source is more important than the author. In some contexts, historical documents and sources may lack a clear author, in which case writers need to name the source by referencing other information such as the title and genre. In other cases, writers may also choose to include the title in addition to

Table 4.2. Language Resources for Source Naming with the Author

Linguistic Choices	**Sample Sentences (with grammatical structures underlined)**
Author in the <u>parenthetical citation</u>	The Montgomery bus boycott movement had "all the elements to touch the hearts of men" and "no force on earth" could stop it (<u>Rustin</u>, 10).
Author placed as the <u>subject</u> of the sentence	<u>Bayard Rustin</u> wrote, "As I watched the people walk away, I had a feeling that no force on earth can stop this movement. It has all the elements to touch the hearts of men" (10).
Author introduced in a <u>linking phrase</u>	The Montgomery bus boycott movement, <u>as observed by Rustin</u>, had "all the elements to touch the hearts of men" and "no force on earth" could stop it (10).
Author described with a <u>modifying noun phrase</u>	<u>An African-American civil rights activist</u> Bayard Rustin noted that the Montgomery bus boycott movement had "all the elements to touch the hearts of men" and "no force on earth" could stop it (10).
Author described in an <u>adjective clause</u>	Rustin, <u>who helped organize the March on Washington Movement</u>, noted that the Montgomery bus boycott movement had "all the elements to touch the hearts of men" and "no force on earth" could stop it (10).
Author described in an <u>appositive</u>	Bayard Rustin, <u>one of the most influential organizers of the civil rights movement</u>, noted that the Montgomery bus boycott movement had "all the elements to touch the hearts of men" and "no force on earth" could stop it (10).

author's name. For example, when citing Martin Luther King, Jr., writers may add a title of the specific source (e.g., King's *Stride Toward Freedom*) to indicate which of King's many works the evidence comes from.

Writers can make several language choices when naming a source with its title. When teaching students the options that are available to them, it is important to show these different linguistic choices in full-sentence examples, demonstrating the grammatical structures of naming the source with its title. We show these choices using one of the examples from Table 4.3 (the grammatical structures are underlined).

- Choice 1: "A Timeline of the Montgomery Bus Boycott" published by Beacon Press gives insight into the progression of the boycott until it reached the point where the Supreme Court deemed segregation of city buses illegal.
  (*The title as the subject of the sentence*)
- Choice 2: In "A Timeline of the Montgomery Bus Boycott" published by Beacon Press, the progression of the boycott events from March 1955 to December 1956 was recorded.
  (*The title in a prepositional phrase. Notice the use of comma.*)
- Choice 3: As stated in "A Timeline of the Montgomery Bus Boycott" published by Beacon Press, "The Supreme Court's orders of injunction

Table 4.3. Naming the Source with the Title

Naming the Source: Who wrote this source, and what type of source is this?	
Languaging Practices	• **"A Timeline of the Montgomery Bus Boycott"** published by Beacon Press gives insight into the progression of the boycott until it reached the point where the Supreme Court deemed segregation of city buses illegal. • **In *Stride Toward Freedom: The Montgomery Story,*** Martin Luther King, Jr., stressed the importance of the collective effort of the community. • **A Letter from the Women's Political Council to Mayor Gayle** stated, "There has been talk from twenty-five or more local organizations of planning a city-wide boycott of buses."
Conventions	• Italicize titles of books, plays, films, periodicals, and websites. • Use quotations marks for titles of articles, essays, chapters, poems, web pages, songs, speeches, and letters. • Note that MLA Style is used for naming titles in these examples.

against segregation on city buses are delivered to the Montgomery City Hall."
(*The title in an introductory phrase. Notice the use of comma.*)

- Choice 4: "The Supreme Court's orders of injunction against segregation on city buses are delivered to the Montgomery City Hall" ("A Timeline of the Montgomery Bus Boycott").
(*The title in parentheses. Notice the quotation marks.)*

In the first three examples, the title is expanded by the participle (*published by Beacon Press*) that provides where the timeline was published, making it easier for the readers to locate the evidence.

Naming the Source with the Genre. The genre or type of source (e.g., *memoir, diary, newspaper article, painting, film*) can also be used in source attribution as it can help readers discern whether it is a primary or secondary source. Primary sources include diaries, personal journals, letters, speeches, memoirs, direct interviews, photographs, manuscripts, and other original artifacts. Secondary sources include summaries, critiques, analyses, and textbooks that are written by those who did not have direct involvement in events but may have expertise as a historian or journalist. By indicating that the source is a *memoir* or a *diary* written by a historical actor who was involved in an event, a writer communicates that the source is a direct, firsthand account of an event rather than an interpretation of events from later in time. Firsthand accounts, however, are not always accurate depictions of what happened if sources have agendas or biases. Sophisticated writers consider multiple details when sourcing to assess reliability, which we will discuss later. For now, information about the type of source is often accompanied by naming the author and the title of the source, as shown in Table 4.4.

Table 4.4. Naming the Source with the Genre

Naming the Source: Who wrote this source, and what type of source is this?	
Languaging Practices	• In his **memoir** *Stride Toward Freedom*, Martin Luther King, Jr., emphasized the collective effort of the community members "who learned to fight for their rights with the weapon of love" (9). • Bayard Rustin's **diary** written on February 24, 1956, states that the boycott had "all the elements to touch the hearts of men" (10).
Conventions	• Do not capitalize the genre unless it is part of the title. • Provide other source information such as author and title.

It is a common practice to include the title, author, and genre at the first mention of the source in the text but leave out some information to avoid unnecessary repetition in the subsequent references. To illustrate this point, we share the following student example:

PARAGRAPH 1: In his diary, written in 1956 during the boycott, Bayard Rustin describes the efforts of the carpool to help citizens get to work while boycotting.

PARAGRAPH 2: Rustin describes several key actions by the community . . .

Again, when attributing evidence to sources, decisions about what source information to provide and how to name sources depend on historical reasoning skills and the rhetorical context. For example, a writer might note that the author of a document lived during the historical period. Therefore their perspective as a witness of the event should be considered. Alternatively, a source might be a painting of a battle created one hundred years after the fact to commemorate the event and build a national identity (e.g., *Dawn of Liberty*, painted by Henry Sandham in 1886, depicting the Battle of Lexington). In that case, the relevant source information to include is not the title, but the time in which the artist worked and the fact that the source was created one hundred years after the actual event. This brings us to our next area—contextualizing the source.

Contextualizing the Source. When or where the source was written or created—its context—is important information that communicates the circumstances of time and place that situate the source within a specific historical period (e.g., *Rustin's diary written during the boycott*). In providing contextual information, it is important to be succinct. Contextual information, while important and even necessary in some cases, is often secondary to argument development. Thus, it is much less common to provide contextual information about the source in an independent, stand-alone sentence. Instead, contextual details are packaged efficiently in various ways that include the use of:

- modifying nouns and noun phrases (e.g., *1958* memoir*; the New York Times* article)
- participles (e.g., diary *written in 1956*)
- clausal embedding using a connector that signals time and place (e.g., Rustin's diary written *while the boycott was happening*).

We summarize some key languaging practices used to contextualize sources in Table 4.5.

Table 4.5. Contextualizing the Source

Contextualizing the Source: WHEN and WHERE was this source written/created?	
Languaging Practices WHEN	• Martin Luther King's **1958** memoir *Stride Toward Freedom* chronicles the events in Montgomery before, during, and after the boycott. • Jo Ann Robinson's memoir **published in 1987** recounts her and her students' involvement in the boycott. • Rustin's diary written **a few months after the Montgomery Improvement Association created a carpool system** reports, "two men, one of whom has walked 7 miles and the other 14 miles, every day since December 5."
Languaging Practices WHERE	• "A Timeline of the Montgomery Bus Boycott" **published by Beacon Press** gives insight into the progression of the boycott until it reached the point where the Supreme Court deemed segregation of city buses illegal. • The ***New York Times*** article written on March 26, 1956, reported that 2,500 people were gathered in a Brooklyn church to welcome the boycott leader. • Martin Luther King, Jr., delivered his famous "I Have a Dream" speech to the crowd gathered **around the Lincoln Memorial in Washington, DC.** • **Reporting from Brooklyn, New York,** Rowland stated that King was welcomed by an audience of 2,500 at a local church.
Conventions	• Use nouns and noun phrases that signal time and place. • Use prepositions and prepositional phrase that signal time (*on, in, during, before after, at the time, one hundred years after the event*). • Use prepositions and prepositional phrases that signal place (*by, in, at, around*). • Use clause connectors that signal relationships of time or place (*once, while, when, where, before, after*). • Use participles (*created by/in, published by/in, written by/in*).

What language choices can be made to evaluate sources?

Moving beyond basic source attribution, writers weigh the strength and quality of evidence they use to build their arguments. In fact, a critical examination and evaluation of sources—who created the source and for what audience and purpose, whether the source is reliable and trustworthy, and in what ways it might be biased—can "become part of the argument itself" (Lunsford et al., 2016, p. 412). Consequently, writers go beyond source attribution and use evaluative language, expressing significance, purpose, and judgment and explaining the perspectives and biases of others.

Rhetorical choices of evaluating sources draw on language resources used for analyzing, critiquing, corroborating, and commenting. We highlight (using italics) the use of such evaluative language in the following excerpt from student writing. As you read the excerpt, pay attention to the specific language choices made to evaluate sources.

Excerpt from Student Writing

> The timeline from "The Fight in the Fields: César Chavez and the Farmworkers' Struggle" states that in February 1968, César Chavez spoke on TV and wrote letters in an effort to convince people to stop purchasing California grapes. In the following year on May 10th, Dolores Huerta spoke on international boycott day, asking U.S. supporters for their continued support. *This information, in the form of a timeline, comes from a website designed to inform visitors of the farm workers' movement through books and videos. Therefore, the information is likely credible because it is from individuals who have spent much time learning about and understanding the movement. This evidence is significant as it shows how leaders of the movement used their voices to publicly speak out and gain national attention.* The strategies used by the leaders of the movement contributed greatly to the success of the movement because without this publicity/advertising, it would have been very difficult to spread the word and gather ongoing support.

The writer goes beyond source attribution to comment on the source's purpose (*to inform*), audience (*visitors of the farm workers' movement*), credibility (*the information is likely credible because*), and significance (*This evidence is significant as it shows*). We first focus on the languaging practices employed to question the source.

Questioning the Source. Questioning and interrogating the source can uncover implicit, less obvious, and often hidden meanings and motives by commenting on the purpose, the intended audience, and the perspective/bias of the author. Table 4.6 shows examples of commenting on the source's purpose, motive, and perspective, as well as reasoning and judgment about its reliability.

Evaluating the Source. Source evaluation involves commenting on the reliability and trustworthiness of the source, as well as its significance and contribution to the argument. By doing so, writers acknowledge history as an act of interpretation from documents of varying reliability that need to be compared, corroborated, and evaluated (Goldman et al., 2016). As the effectiveness

Table 4.6. Questioning the Source

Questioning the Source: Who is the intended audience, for what purpose was it created, and what is the author's perspective/bias?	
Languaging Practices	• This account comes from Captain Preston, a British officer on trial for his actions, who may be saying this **in order to persuade the public** of his innocence. • The letter was written by John Smith **to record the events of the battle for his family.** Because he had just experienced the Gallipoli landing on April 25, 1915, **his perspective and his purpose to inform his family** make this source reliable. • Another specific example of this publicity is a letter written by Chavez himself in 1968 **to grocery shoppers, asking them to demand** their grocery stores to stop selling California grapes until workers receive better wages.
Conventions	• Use prepositional phrases to signal for whom and for what purpose the source is created (e.g., *for his family; for the purpose of, in the interest of; in light of, to grocery shoppers; to the audience of*). • Use infinitive structure to indicate purpose and motive (*to record the events of the battle; to inform his family; to persuade, to address, to recount her involvement*). • Use participles (e.g., *asking them to demand*). • Use connectors and linking words to express reasoning (*so that, in order to, in order that, because, as*).

of historical arguments rests on the quality of the sources, writers strategically use language to evaluate sources. The languaging practices for evaluating sources vary depending on historical reasoning (e.g., *corroborating, countering, extending*) and rhetorical purposes (e.g., *to establish credibility, to make logical connections*) that guide the argument development. Language resources that support this thinking include the use of evaluative adjectives that express significance, judgment, and credibility; causal and commentary verbs; and connectors and linking words that make explicit the relationships between ideas. As we can see in the examples provided in Table 4.7, the languaging practices directly respond to the scaffolded questions designed to help students critically evaluate sources to develop historical arguments.

How is language used to integrate sources in support of a claim?

Beyond describing and evaluating sources, students also need language skills to strategically weave evidence from these sources into their arguments. Integrating evidence from multiple sources involves rhetorical moves of

Table 4.7. Evaluating the Source

Evaluating the Source: Is the source reliable and trustworthy, and how does it contribute to my understanding and argument?	
Languaging Practices	• **Since** the writer of this diary was a person involved in the Women's Political Council, she may have **exaggerated** the hardships and work necessary to the process of making and spreading out the flyers. • This source is **credible because** it is an example of a primary source, written by Jo Ann Robinson, president of the Women's Political Council. The WPC played a crucial role in the Boycott and formation of the Montgomery Improvement Association. • **On the other hand,** the diary was written at the time of the event by Bayard Rustin, someone who was directly involved in the boycott and advised Martin Luther King Jr., **indicating that** the source is **more relevant and trustworthy.**
Conventions	• Use evaluative adjectives (e.g., *(un)reliable, credible, convincing, (un) trustworthy, (im)plausible, faithful, (in)accurate, veracious, well-grounded, sound, reputable, well-documented, genuine, authentic, problematic, questionable*). • Use adjectives of value (e.g., *significant, important, consequential, informative, relevant, valuable, essential, pertinent, influential, dominant, effective*). • Use causal verbs (e.g., *influence, affect, contribute, shape, promote, hinder, lead to, cause, help*). • Use commentary verbs (e.g., *convey, matter, signify, emphasize, exaggerate, highlight, skew, reveal, portray, illustrate, demonstrate, indicate, show, suggest, prove*). • Use connectors and linking phrases to express reasoning (e.g., *since, because, as)* to corroborate (e.g., *although, while, even though, on the other hand, however, even so, still, in spite of that*).

summarizing, paraphrasing, and quoting directly from sources. Writers often use a combination of these three rhetorical moves strategically to develop sophisticated arguments. To illustrate this point, we examine the following excerpt from student writing. Notice how summarizing (bold), paraphrasing (italics), and quoting (underlined) are woven together.

> The determination of local leaders during the boycott is one of the most important factors that contributed to the success of the movement. The resolve shown by leaders like Rosa Parks had a substantial effect on the boycott that cannot go unnoticed. **For example, Rosa Parks' biography written by Arlisha Norwood recounted Parks' involvement in and contribution to the boycott, highlighting how her resistance and refusal to give up her seat sparked the Montgomery**

> **Bus Boycott.** *Rosa Parks is portrayed as an extremely determined and strong-willed person who ignited the boycott almost completely on her own.* Norwood explained that *Rosa Parks' efforts and "courageous act" initiated the boycott of the buses and eventually "led to the integration of public transportation in Montgomery."* While it seems rather self-explanatory, it is clear that Parks was a brave woman with a clear and strong determination that led the boycott into motion inspiring and sending hope to those that felt the need to fight back.

We note that the quotations are seamlessly integrated into the writer's paraphrased sentence, and the evidence used to support the claim is attributed to the source (i.e., *Rosa Parks' biography written by Arlisha Norwood*). These language choices make it clear that the writer is using a specific source and drawing on what's stated in the source to support their argument. We now discuss the languaging practices related to the three rhetorical moves: summarizing, paraphrasing, and quoting.

Summarizing. Writers summarize a source or multiple sources to synthesize information about the historical context, to describe what is relevant about the source, or to highlight key facts about historical events. Source summary is often succinct and combined with source attribution. In a way, summary functions as extended attribution and can be categorized as such for teaching purposes. Writers may provide a more extensive summary if it serves an important purpose in argument development. To maintain the flow of their arguments, writers use linking phrases. We highlight the source summary (underlined) in the sample sentences previously used.

A. *This is a valid point as there is evidence from "A Timeline of the Montgomery Bus Boycott" published by Beacon Press, explaining each of the crucial steps in this movement.*
B. *This is evident in multiple sources, including Jo Ann Robinson's memoir and Bayard Rustin's diary, both of which are primary sources that provide first-hand accounts of the events leading to the boycott.*
C. *Similarly, the memoir written by Jo Ann Robinson, the president of the Women's Political Council, recounts her and her students' involvement in the boycott by making thousands of copies of handouts with boycott messages and mapping out to deliver these handouts to black homes.*

In Example A, source summary is added to the main sentence using a participle (*explaining each of the crucial steps in this movement*). In Example B, source summary is given in a relative clause (*that provide first-hand accounts of the events leading to the boycott*), which is embedded into the main sentence. These clausal embedding techniques allow the writer to provide a succinct summary of the sources without disrupting the flow of the argument. Example C, on the other hand, provides a more extensive summary of the source as a whole sentence. The writer uses a reporting verb (*recounts*) and extends the summary by providing key points.

Paraphrasing. Paraphrasing rephrases the relevant information/evidence from sources. Because an accurate depiction of source material is critical when paraphrasing, writers use language carefully to convey the original meaning while changing the words and sentence structure. When paraphrasing, writers often use introductory phrases (e.g., *according to, as stated by*) and reporting verbs (e.g., *state, explain, argue*). Such languaging practices allow writers to communicate that the paraphrased sentences indicate ideas borrowed from sources. We examine language choices writers make when paraphrasing by comparing a paraphrased example and the original version.

Original Statement

> *I wondered what the response of the drivers would be, since 28 of them had just been arrested on charges of conspiring to destroy the bus company. One by one, they pledged that, if necessary, they would be arrested again and again.* (Excerpt from Bayard Rustin's diary)

Paraphrased Sentence

> *Rustin then explains how, even though 28 of the carpool drivers had been arrested, the remaining ones scattered through the city, pledging that they'd risk being arrested until their hard work was paid off.* (Excerpt from student writing)

The original text from Rustin's diary consists of two sentences, but the paraphrased version is a single complex sentence with clauses and phrases embedded through clause connectors (*even though, until*) and a participle (*pledging that*). While less experienced writers tend to plug in new words while retaining the original sentence structure, more experienced writers change both the words and sentence structure to emphasize details that are central to their arguments. The example above keeps the number and figure (e.g., *28 drivers*) and a few key words such as *drivers*, *arrest*, and *pledge*, but changes most of the text. The writer also makes a linguistic choice of changing the first-person pronoun (*I wondered*) to a third-person reference by naming the author (*Rustin*) and using a reporting verb (*explains*).

Writers also integrate introductory phrases used for source attribution into the paraphrased sentence to maintain the overall flow of writing. The following examples show language choices writers make regarding the attribution phrase in a paraphrased sentence.

Original Statement

> *By 2 o'clock, thousands of handouts had been given to many people. Practically every Black man, woman, and child in Montgomery knew the plan and was passing the word along.* (Excerpt from Jo Ann Robinson's memoir)

Paraphrased versions with attribution phrases in different grammatical structures

A. According to Robinson, the community members learned about the boycott plan through the handouts that were delivered to thousands of people.
B. The community members, according to Robinson, learned about the boycott plan through the handouts that were delivered to thousands of people.
C. The community members learned about the boycott plan through the handouts that were delivered to thousands of people, according to Robinson.

When paraphrasing, writers make sure that they express the source's meaning accurately using their own words and sentence structures and also indicate where the idea comes from through attribution.

Quoting. Quoting—using the exact words, phrases, and sentences from sources—is another important rhetorical move. Purposefully selected quotations from sources can strengthen an argument. If the writer borrows exact phrases or sentences from the source, they should place these in quotation marks. While being purposeful is a crucial skill necessary for the effective integration of quoted materials, students also need to make language choices that allow them to seamlessly weave quotations into writing.

Writers may integrate complete sentences from sources into their writing using introductory phrases. In such a case, the quoted sentence functions as an independent grammatical unit that can stand on its own. Experienced writers tend to use introductory phrases to frame the quoted sentence rather than adding it as a floating quotation without attribution. The following examples indicate full-sentence quotations (underlined) with introductory phrases:

- *According to Robinson, "Every Black man, woman, and child in Montgomery knew the plan and was passing the word along."*
- *As stated in "A Timeline of the Montgomery Bus Boycott" published by Beacon Press, "The Supreme Court's orders of injunction against segregation on city buses are delivered to the Montgomery City Hall."*
- *Bayard Rustin wrote, "As I watched the people walk away, I had a feeling that no force on earth can stop this movement. It has all the elements to touch the hearts of men."*

Beyond quoting a complete sentence with an introductory phrase, writers strategically embed quoted phrases into their own sentences. In other words, quotations are not always complete sentences but rather phrases and clauses added to the writers' own sentences. Embedding quotations is a sophisticated way of integrating evidence as writers have to combine elements of paraphrases, quotations, and reasoning to construct their own sentences. The following examples show how writers strategically embed quoted phrases into their own sentences.

A. *For example, in his diary written on February 24, 1956, Rustin states how he was introduced to "two men, one of whom has walked 7 miles and the other 14 miles, every day since December 5."*
B. *In his memoir of the boycott* Stride Toward Freedom, *Martin Luther King Jr. emphasized the collective effort of the community members "who learned to fight for their rights with the weapon of love."*
C. *Norwood explained that Rosa Parks' efforts and "courageous act" initiated the boycott of the buses and eventually "led to the integration of public transportation in Montgomery."*
D. *An African-American civil rights activist Bayard Rustin noted that the Montgomery bus boycott movement had "all the elements to touch the hearts of men" and "no force on earth" could stop it.*

In Example A, the quotation serves as the object of the verb *introduced to.* In Example B, the quotation is embedded into the sentence, elaborating on the noun phrase *the community members.* Example C shows two instances of quotations. First, the quoted noun phrase *"courageous act"* is added, forming a complex noun phrase as the subject of the sentence (*Rosa Parks' effort and "courageous act"*). The quoted phrases are integrated into paraphrased sentences in myriad ways, but all include source attributions and nuanced rhetorical moves. Students who have yet to develop these sophisticated skills tend to use floating quotations that are not well integrated into writing.

Using Introductory Phrases and Reporting Verbs to Frame Sources. Framing source materials using introductory phrases and reporting verbs is a common languaging practice used for source integration. Introductory phrases often feature source attribution, naming the source's author/creator and/or the title/genre of the source. When doing so, writers follow the conventions of capitalization and punctuation, including the use of commas and quotation marks, to indicate where quoted material begins in the sentence. The following examples show a variety of introductory phrases (underlined) used for source integration:

- *According to a letter from the Women's Political Council to Mayor Gayle, "There has been talk from twenty-five or more local organizations of planning a city-wide boycott of buses."*
- *As Rowland noted in the* New York Times *article, thousands of community members gathered at a local church to welcome Martin Luther King.*
- *In the words of Mary Fair Burks, "the nameless cooks and maids who walked endless miles for a year to bring about the breach in the walls of segregation" contributed to the success.*
- *In Martin Luther King's opinion, the power of collective effort shown by the community members was a crucial force of the civil rights movement.*
- *As specified in "A Timeline of the Montgomery Bus Boycott" published by Beacon Press, the Women's Political Council produced and distributed thousands of handouts a few days after the arrest of Rosa Parks.*

Alternatively, reporting verbs like *argue*, *report*, and *state* are commonly used in framing source materials. Writers with limited language resources tend to overuse generic verbs such as *say* and *write* when reporting. Experienced writers, on the other hand, use a variety of reporting verbs and make choices considering their overall rhetorical goals. When used strategically, reporting verbs communicate subtle meaning by characterizing the author's purpose, perspective, or stance. Table 4.8 provides a variety of reporting verbs used for source integration. We categorized them by the rhetorical moves commonly observed in argument writing.

In some cases, writers create complex phrasing with the reporting verbs to convey the author's message and point of view clearly and even, sometimes, to

Table 4.8. Reporting Verbs

	Rhetorical Moves	**Reporting Verbs**
REPORTING VERBS	Claim/Perspective	argue, assert, believe, claim, conclude, concur, contend, debate, declare, explain, insist, maintain, posit, propose
	Agreement/ Concession	acknowledge, admit, advocate, affirm, agree, confirm, corroborate, endorse, prove, reaffirm, recognize, support, verify
	Disagreement/ Critique	challenge, contradict, counter, criticize, deny, disagree, discredit, disprove, dispute, oppose, question, refute, reject, undermine
	Comment/ Interpretation	convey, demonstrate, exemplify, highlight, illustrate, imply, indicate, interpret, offer, point out, reveal, show, specify, suggest
	Report/Response	comment, declare, delineate, discuss, express, list, mention, note, outline, portray, recount, remark, reply, report, respond, state
	Significance/ Urgency	advocate, call for, demand, emphasize, encourage, exhort, implore, insist, plead, press, stress, underscore, urge, warn
	Speculation/ Hypothesis	assume, conjecture, estimate, guess, hypothesize, postulate, predict, reckon, speculate, think, wonder

express their own stance. The following examples show how writers can use reporting verbs (underlined) in complex phrasing:

- *Robinson stressed the importance of distributing handouts with a boycott message by stating, "Practically every Black man, woman, and child in Montgomery knew the plan and was passing the word along."*
- *Martin Luther King acknowledged Rosa Parks' determination as he recalls that "her character was impeccable and her dedication deep-rooted."*

The use of precise and varied reporting verbs goes beyond framing the source material as they create nuanced rhetorical effects.

III. Cultivating Language Skills for Source Integration

How can teachers cultivate language skills for source integration?

Instructional support is integral to build students' language skills for attribution, sourcing, and evidence integration. Effective instructional support not only builds *language skills* but also promotes *metalinguistic knowledge* that allows students to make strategic language choices to achieve the rhetorical goals for developing arguments. In this section, we provide resources and activities that support students in building language skills and knowledge for attribution, sourcing, and evidence integration. We suggest that you modify the resources and activities to fit within the context and the content of your teaching.

Teaching Move 1: Model-Practice-Reflect

To effectively integrate source material into their writing, students need to first build knowledge of sources. Without such knowledge, students will be constrained as the information about the sources is not readily available to them. Using a Model-Practice-Reflect instructional cycle (Graham et al., 2016), you can first model sourcing. Then, students practice independently or with peers. Finally, students reflect on how, when, and why they can use key historical thinking skills. When modeling, you can use a "think-aloud"—describing your thinking process to students so they can see the procedural knowledge an expert uses to source documents.

Model. The instructional goal of modeling is to demystify the cognitive processes involved in sourcing, Then, through practice and reflection, students develop the habits of mind to source documents. You can start with the basic who, what, when, and where, focusing on naming and contextualizing a grade-level source. Once students gather basic information about sources, you can move them to questioning and evaluating the sources. You can show students that the who, what, when, and where information is not limited to just name, genre/type, and year, but can include additional information about the author, time period, and the type of document. For example, when identifying who wrote the source, you can ask questions such as *Who is Jo Ann Robinson? What do we know about her? How was she associated with the boycott?* When exploring the type of source, you can think aloud: *The fact that this is a memoir written by someone who was involved in the boycott tells us that it is a firsthand account and her recount of what happened at that time.* After gathering some information about the particular source, you can model making an attribution statement in writing. This allows students to reflect on what source information is best when they practice including this information in a modifying phrase.

Practice. Modeling is followed by collaborative and independent practice, so students have multiple opportunities to engage in basic sourcing moves. For

Table 4.9. Instructional Scaffolding Using Think-Alouds

Teacher Model		
Source 1: Book *The Montgomery Bus Boycott and the Women Who Started It*	Who wrote this source?	**Jo Ann Robinson:** president of the Women's Political Council; Civil Rights Movement activist
	What type of source is this?	**Memoir:** firsthand account of her involvement in Montgomery Bus Boycott
	When was this source written?	**1987:** written more than thirty years after the boycott ended; buses were officially desegregated in 1956
Collaborative Practice		
Source 2:	Who wrote this source?	
	What type of source is this?	
	When was this source written?	
Independent Practice		
Source 3:	Who wrote this source?	
	What type of source is this?	
	When was this source written?	

collaborative practice, you can strategically choose different types of documents and sources, such as a letter, a diary, a painting/photograph, and a media post, for students to explore. When students move into independent practice, you can ask students to list all the sources that they are using in their argument writing and gather information about these sources. This initial process of sourcing doesn't have to be linear but can rather be an iterative process, as students explore other sources for evidence. A key objective of practice is to foster a habit of mind that looks beyond what is in the source to consider what makes it good evidence.

Reflect. Providing students with an opportunity to reflect on their investigative process and what they learn about the sources can foster critical thinking skills. Students can reflect on their process in dialogic interactions or in quick write-ups. To scaffold reflection, you can use prompts such as: *How did you locate the information? What did you learn about the source? Why is sourcing important in history?* Steve Graham et al. (2016) point out that engaging students in reflective practice "helps [them] discover ways to improve their [learning] and reinforce the use of effective strategies in future tasks" (p. 23). The goal of using the Model-Practice-Reflect approach is to gradually transition students to using sourcing strategies independently.

Teaching Move 2: Explicitly teach language to attribute sources using mentor texts

To support students in making strategic language choices in their argument writing, it is important to draw their attention to language choices writers make to integrate evidence from sources. This can be done using **mentor texts** in which a variety of language markers and choices are highlighted. Various mentor texts showing different linguistic practices can serve as a roadmap or model of how experienced writers integrate source information and materials into their argument writing. You can use Table 4.2 from the previous section to show a variety of language choices made for naming and contextualizing sources. You can create your own mentor texts to highlight different language choices students can make to attribute sources or you can use the following examples:

NAMING THE TITLE: **"A Timeline of the Montgomery Bus Boycott"** gives insight into the progression of the boycott until it reached the point where the Supreme Court deemed segregation of city buses illegal.

EXTENDING THE TITLE: As stated in "A Timeline of the Montgomery Bus Boycott" **published by Beacon Press** the progression of the boycott events from March 1955 to December 1956 was recorded.

NAMING THE AUTHOR: **According to Rustin,** the Montgomery bus boycott movement had "all the elements to touch the hearts of men" and "no force on earth" could stop it (10).

EXTENDING THE AUTHOR: **Bayard Rustin, one of the most influential organizers of the civil rights movement,** noted that the Montgomery bus boycott had "all the elements to touch the hearts of men" (10).

CONTEXTUALIZING: **Jo Ann Robinson's memoir published in 1987** recounts her and her students' involvement in the boycott.

After reviewing mentor texts, students can create their own attribution, sourcing, and integration statements using grade-level sources.

Activity 1: Sentence Combining

Students need ample practice to build language skills. A sentence combining activity provides students with a scaffolded opportunity to attribute evidence to sources and provide contextual information in a clear and concise manner. Sentence combining is an evidence-based practice that improves writing quality (Graham et al., 2015). Such an instructional approach can involve the teacher modeling and students practicing how to combine short, simple sentences into a complex sentence by using clausal embedding and other grammatical structures.

Table 4.10. Sentence Combining

#	**Sentences to Combine**
1	The book is titled *Stride Toward Freedom.*
2	It was written by Martin Luther King, Jr.
3	It is his memoir of the Montgomery Bus Boycott.
4	Martin Luther King, Jr., wrote this book in 1958.
5	The book said that the black community "took to heart the principles of nonviolence" and "learned to fight their rights with the weapon of love" (page 9).
Combined #1	Sentence: **In his 1958 memoir titled *Stride Toward Freedom*, Martin Luther King Jr.** wrote that the black community "took to heart the principles of nonviolence" and "learned to fight their rights with the weapon of love" (p. 9). Explanation: *This version includes the year, genre, and title in a prepositional phrase at the beginning of the sentence and puts the author's name as the main subject of the sentence, placing the author as the key component of the sentence.*
Combined #2	Sentence: **Martin Luther King's 1958 memoir titled *Stride Toward Freedom*** emphasized that the black community "took to heart the principles of nonviolence" and "learned to fight their rights with the weapon of love" (p. 9). Explanation: *This version combines author, year, genre, and the title into a complex noun phrase that functions as the subject of the sentence. The key noun in the subject is memoir, placing more emphasis on what the memoir said.*
Combined #3	[*students write here*]

Teaching Move 3: Engage students in questioning the source using Think-Pair-Share

Table 4.11. Think-Pair-Share

THINK	Why and for what **purpose** was this source written?	Based on your close reading and information you gathered about the source, write what the author's purpose was for writing this document. Explain what information helped you discern this.
	Who is the intended **audience** for this source?	Based on your close reading and information you gathered about the source, write who this source was created for. Explain what information helped you discern this.
	What is the **perspective** and potential bias?	Based on what you know about the author, as well as your close reading of the source, write what the author's perspective is and how it influences the writing.
PAIR	With a partner, discuss your responses.	When discussing your responses with a partner, identify ways your responses are different or similar. Discuss any differences, revise your responses, and come up with similar responses to present to a group or a whole class.
SHARE	Share to a larger group or a whole class.	After hearing other responses, reflect on how your thinking and understanding have changed as a result of sharing. Revise your thinking as you read and learn more about the sources. Share how you revised your thinking to a whole class.

After source *naming*, students can move toward *questioning* sources. Information students gather during the initial process of naming and contextualizing sources will support source questioning later; they will have to note additional source information—the rhetorical purpose, the intended audience, and the embedded perspective or bias. You can facilitate this by engaging students in discussion using a Think-Pair-Share strategy and collaborative problem solving that recognizes the critical capacities many students already bring to the classroom.

Sentence stems can help students get started. You can use the following sentence stems to scaffold students' dialogic interactions and quick writes:

PURPOSE: Based on ____________________, this source was written because/for the purpose of/in order to ________________________. Because this author was ____________________, I think they wrote/created this to ____.

AUDIENCE: I think the source is intended to __________ because ________. I think the audience is __________ because __________________. Because this source is ______________ and intended for ______________, I think ____.

PERSPECTIVE: The author probably believes/contends________________.

The perspective of the author is ________________________________.

The author conveys a viewpoint that suggests ____________________.

BIAS: The author might have been influenced by__________________.

The author appears to favor_______________________________________.

The author's choice of language suggests bias toward ________________.

Evaluating a source is a complex skill as students need to consider the credibility, relevance, and contribution of a source to the larger argument. You can facilitate source evaluation by engaging students in reflective writing and discussion using the Say-Mean-Matter strategy. This strategy advances students' comprehension and interpretation of sources by having students: (1) determine what the text says in connection to their arguments; (2) form interpretations of the message and meaning the author delivers; and (3) draw conclusions on the significance, relevance, and trustworthiness of the source. Through this inquiry process, students build comprehensive knowledge and an in-depth understanding of the sources they are using to develop their arguments.

Teaching Move 4: Engage students in evaluating sources using a variety of strategies

You can use the following sentence stems to provide additional scaffolding to help students evaluate sources:

SIGNIFICANCE: This source is significant/important because __________
____.

This source matters for a reason that ____________________________.

This source added to my understanding of_____________ by____________.

RELEVANCE: This source is relevant to my argument because ___________.

This source contributes to my argument by______________________. The information presented in this source directly relates to _________________.

RELIABILITY: This source is reliable/unreliable because _______________.

I do/don't trust this source for a reason that_____________________.

The credibility of this sources is established through __________________.

Table 4.12. Say-Mean-Matter

S A Y	What does this source **say**?	Summarize the gist of the source, paraphrase an important idea, and/or select an important quotation that you will use as evidence in support of your claim.
M E A N	What does this source **mean**?	Form an interpretation of what the author/source means by reading between the lines to understand the deeper meaning of the source going beyond what it says to understanding what it means.
M A T T E R	Why does this source **matter**?	Draw a conclusion about the significance, relevance, and credibility of the source based on the information you gathered about the source and on your close reading of the source. Consider the how the source contributes to your overall argument and whether it supports or counters your claim about the historical event.

To help students build language skills for source evaluation, you can further engage them in annotating a mentor text for evaluation and sourcing statements. Students may not always know how to express the source's credibility when developing their claims. In our own research, we find that the sophisticated sourcing moves that comment on the credibility of the source were relatively low in student writing compared to other writing skills in the absence of explicit writing instruction (Steiss et al., 2024). Thus, helping students notice and take note of evaluative signposts and sourcing moves in mentor texts can be beneficial to students. This idea is based on *Notice and Note Signposts,* a close reading strategy developed by Kylene Beers and Robert Probst (2013). The goal is to help students examine and identify language moves that signal statements and claims questioning and evaluating a source and its credibility.

Activity 2: Color-Coding

Students can benefit from practice that focuses on how sources are woven together into the fabric of an argument. To support students in building language skills for integrating sources, you can first use a color-coding strategy (Olson et al., 2023). The color-coding technique used here is adapted to highlight sourcing moves: **red** (bolded) for source attribution, *green* (italicized) for paraphrases and quotes from sources, and <u>blue</u> (underlined) for evaluative language. Color-coding helps make the rhetorical moves *visible* and show students how source information and evidence are woven together.

Table 4.13. Notice and Note Signposts

Mentor Text	Notice & Note
The letter was written by John Smith **to record the events of the battle for his family.** Because he had just experienced the Gallipoli landing on April 25, 1915, **his perspective and his purpose to inform his family make this source reliable.**	• names the purpose and the intended audience of the letter • notes the author's perspective/credibility
Another specific example of this publicity is a letter written by Chavez himself in 1968 **to grocery shoppers, asking them to demand their grocery stores to stop selling California grapes** until workers receive better wages. This letter, which **reached thousands of Los Angeles residents, was extremely helpful** in raising awareness of the movement and **convincing bystanders** of its urgency.	• names intended audience of Chavez's letter • infers purpose of the letter • identifies the audience • infers the effect of the letter
On the other hand, the diary was written **at the time of the event by Bayard Rustin, someone who was directly involved in the boycott and advised Martin Luther King, Jr.,** indicating that **the source is more relevant and trustworthy.**	• explains the credibility of the author • evaluates the trustworthiness of the source

Mentor Text

One might think that an important reason the Montgomery Bus Boycott succeeded was because of the strategic planning of the boycott. This is a valid point as there is evidence from **"A Timeline of the Montgomery Bus Boycott" published by Beacon Press**, *explaining each of the crucial steps in this movement.* **This timeline gives insight into** *the progression of the boycott until it reached the point where the Supreme Court deemed segregation of city buses illegal and thus leading to the desegregation of Montgomery buses.* However, even the best plans cannot succeed without the determination, perseverance, and passion of the participants/citizens. This is evident in multiple sources, including **Jo Ann Robinson's memoir** and **Bayard Rustin's diary**, both of which are primary sources that provide first-hand accounts of the events leading to the boycott. For example, **in his diary written on February 24, 1956, Rustin states** how he was introduced to *"two men, one of whom has walked 7 miles and the other 14 miles, every day since December 5."* **He then explains how**, *even though 28 of the carpool drivers had been arrested, the remaining ones scattered through the city, pledging that*

> *they'd risk being arrested until their hard work was paid off.* The carpool system of the boycott provided the Black citizens with a ride to the places they needed to go and was significant during this movement. *To put in all this work, every person was okay with suffering the punishments inflicted by the city officials, like being arrested or harassed.* Similarly, **the memoir written by Jo Ann Robinson**, <u>the president of the Women's Political Council</u>, **recounts** *her and her students' involvement in the boycott by making thousands of copies of handouts with boycott messages and mapping out to deliver these handouts to black homes.* If these people didn't care or had no passion to end segregation, the boycott wouldn't have succeeded. Each of them made huge sacrifices so that their suffering can aid the others. Thus, despite other rational arguments, the Black citizens' dedication helped the boycott succeed.

After color-coding a model text, students can review their own writing to ensure that the evidence they integrated in their writing has a **red attribution** statement and that the *evidence* in *green* is properly integrated into a sentence. They can also check if they have any <u>blue evaluative</u> statements in their writing.

Activity 3: Dialogue with a Text

Along with visualizing the sourcing moves in a sample paragraph using the color-coding technique, you can engage students in discussion using a strategy called "Dialogue with a Text" (Probst, 1988). The original strategy developed by Robert Probst (1988) is adapted here to focus on different elements of sourcing. This activity helps students to interact with the text to understand rhetorical moves and language choices used to construct an argument.

Activity 4: Sentence Expansion

Students can practice integrating evidence into their writing using introductory phrases and reporting verbs. To facilitate this practice, you can use a sentence expansion activity, providing clear instruction and a model to scaffold the process. You can modify the instruction depending on what you would like your students to practice. For example, you can ask students to add contextual and evaluative statements. This scaffolded technique can help students

Table 4.14. Dialogue with a Text

Focus	Guiding Questions	Note
Number and types of sources used	How many sources are used and what sources are used?	3 sources: (1) Timeline; (2) Diary; and (3) Memoir
Attribution	How were the sources attributed?	The title for the timeline, author names for the diary and the memoir
Contextualizing sources	How are the sources contextualized?	• published by Beacon Press • in his diary written on February 24, 1956
Language choices and markers	What signal phrases and verbs are used to integrate sources?	• This is a valid point as there is evidence . . . • This timeline gives insight into . . . • This is evident in multiple sources, . . . • For example, in his diary written on February 24, 1956, Rustin states . . . • He then explained how . . . • Similarly, the memoir written by Jo Ann Robinson, . . . recounts . . .
Rhetorical moves	What rhetorical moves were used to integrate sources?	• Summary • Paraphrases • Embedded quotations
Credibility	What language was used for credibility	• both of which are primary sources that provide first-hand accounts of the events leading to the boycott. • Jo Ann Robinson, the president of the Women's Political Council, recounts

to skillfully use language for evidence integration and attribution simultaneously. We provide the following examples as models:

- Copy the quotation you are integrating:
  "Every Black man, woman, and child in Montgomery knew the plan and was passing the word along" (p. 5).
- Add source attribution:
  According to Robinson, "Every Black man, woman, and child in Montgomery knew the plan and was passing the word along" (p. 5).
- Extend source attribution providing information about the source or its author:
  According to Robinson, a credible author and a civil rights activist, "Every Black man, woman, and child in Montgomery knew the plan and was passing the word along" (p. 5).

Table 4.15. Introductory Phrase and Reporting Verb Bank for Source Integration

Introductory phrases	Reporting verbs
• According to . . ., • As . . . noted/pointed out, • In the words of . . ., • In the opinion of . . ., • As specified in . . ., • As stated by . . ., • This is supported by . . .	• Perspective: argue, assert, claim, contend, declare • Agreement: acknowledge, admit, affirm, agree • Disagreement: challenge, deny, disagree, dispute • Illustration: convey, demonstrate, explain, point out • Report: recount, remark, report, state, mention • Significance: emphasize, implore, press, stress, urge • Speculation: assume, estimate, guess, speculate

You can provide an introductory phrase and reporting verb bank. This will allow students to go beyond vague, readily accessible phrases and verbs such as "In the text" and "The source said" that they tend to overuse. The introductory phrase and verb bank can also help students characterize the source's viewpoint more clearly.

How can teachers build metalinguistic knowledge and awareness?

To support students in building metalinguistic knowledge and awareness, you can engage them in: (1) evaluating sample texts that show more effective and less effective source integration; and (2) examining language choices made in each text. When reading effective and ineffective texts, ask students to pay attention to source attribution, rhetorical moves, and signal phrases used for source integration. Students first decide which of the samples is more effective, and then annotate sourcing moves and language choices, providing explanations for the language and rhetorical features that make them less or more effective.

Activity 5: Evaluating Sourcing and Source Integration

Students evaluate whether the sourcing moves are effective or ineffective in two texts and explain what features make them more or less effective:

Check:	Explain:
__Effective	
__Ineffective	

Example: Clear source attribution using title, author, and genre. This lets the readers know where the evidence is from.

Sample Text 1

The most significant reason the Montgomery bus boycott succeeded was the carpool system set up by Dr. Martin Luther King Jr. and Rufus Lewis, and here is evidence from source 3 that supports my claim: "the success of the carpool is at the heart of the movement, Lewis said at the meeting. It must not be stopped.". This evidence supports my argument that the carpool system most helped the boycott succeed because it clearly states, "the success of the carpool is at the heart of the movement". Other evidence from source 3 supports my argument: "It thus became necessary for the Black leaders to find an alternative—the carpool. They set up 23 locations where people could gather to wait for free transportation." This evidence supports my claim because it states that the only alternative (other than walking) to help the people participating in the boycott get to their jobs was the carpool system. Of course, other people might say that the handouts were the most important reason or the people who helped the handouts get printed, and they're absolutely right! There is no right or wrong answer here but the carpool system is simply the most important reason because in source 3 it clearly says, "the success of the carpool is at the heart of the movement," this suggests that if the carpool had failed the boycott might have failed along with it.

Sample Text 2

One might think that an important reason the Montgomery Bus Boycott succeeded was because of the strategic planning of the boycott. This is a valid point as there is evidence from "A Timeline of the Montgomery Bus Boycott" published by Beacon Press, explaining each of the crucial steps in this movement. This timeline gives insight into the progression of the boycott until it reached the point where the Supreme Court deemed segregation of city buses illegal and thus leading to the desegregation of Montgomery buses. However, even the best

> plans cannot succeed without the determination, perseverance, and passion of the participants/citizens. This is evident in multiple sources, including Jo Ann Robinson's memoir and Bayard Rustin's diary, both of which are primary sources that provide first-hand accounts of the events leading to the boycott. For example, in his diary written on February 24, 1956, Rustin states how he was introduced to "two men, one of whom has walked 7 miles and the other 14 miles, every day since December 5." He then explains how, even though 28 of the carpool drivers had been arrested, the remaining ones scattered through the city, pledging that they'd risk being arrested until their hard work was paid off. The carpool system of the boycott provided the Black citizens with a ride to the places they needed to go and was significant during this movement. To put in all this work, every person was okay with suffering the punishments inflicted by the city officials, like being arrested or harassed. Similarly, the memoir written by Jo Ann Robinson, the president of the Women's Political Council, recounts her and her students' involvement in the boycott by making thousands of copies of handouts with boycott messages and mapping out to deliver these handouts to black homes. If these people didn't care or had no passion to end segregation, the boycott wouldn't have succeeded. Each of them made huge sacrifices so that their suffering can aid the others. Therefore, despite other rational arguments, still, the Black citizens' dedication helped the boycott succeed.

This activity is better facilitated through an *individual → group → whole class* progression. Once students create their own lists of characteristics that indicate more effective and less effective sourcing moves, they can share these in small groups to compare, modify, and add to their lists. You can bring groups together as a whole class to make a more comprehensive list, as shown in Table 4.16.

Following this activity, it is critical for students to closely read and evaluate their own writing. You can first ask students to compare their writing to the two texts they evaluated. Students can then use the characteristics of more effective sourcing moves listed in Table 4.16 as a checklist and rubric to assess their choices. You will foster metalinguistic knowledge and awareness by providing students with opportunities to examine language choices. For example, you can ask students to examine how language is used to name, describe, and evaluate sources clearly. You can help them notice that complex noun phrases and clauses provide additional information about the sources.

Table 4.16. Characteristics of Less and More Effective Sourcing Moves

Less Effective Sourcing Moves	**More Effective Sourcing Moves**
Uses vague words such as "source 3" to attribute the source. It doesn't tell us where exactly the evidence comes from.	⇒ Clearly attributes sources using title, authors' names, and genre. This lets the readers know where the evidence is from.
Uses a single source for evidence.	⇒ Uses multiple sources for evidence.
The source used is not contextualized to help readers understand the time, the origin, and the place the source was created.	⇒ Contextualizes the sources providing information about where the timeline was published and when the diary was written.
Does not provide an evaluative statement about the source to help readers decipher the credibility of the source.	⇒ Provides an evaluative statement about the source to let readers know that this is a firsthand account and primary source.
The author/creator of the source is not identified.	⇒ Provides extended attribution to help readers understand who the author is.

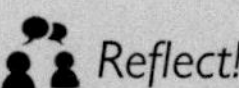

- What language choices did you make for source attribution and integration?
- How effective are your language choices given the rhetorical goals?
- How would you modify your language to improve sourcing moves?

After examining effective and ineffective language choices for sourcing, students can reflect on their choices and examine whether they are effective or not. You provide prompts for quick writes or dialogic interactions in which students reflect on their sourcing moves, their linguistic choices, and the rhetorical effects of their choices.

The pedagogical strategies and activities in this section closely align with the following WIDA standards for English Language Development (ELD) for Social Studies (WIDA, 2020):

ELD-SS.6-8.Explain.Interpretive

Interpret social studies explanations by

- Analyzing sources for logical relationships among contributing factors or causes
- Evaluating experts' points of agreement, along with strengths and weaknesses of explanations

ELD-SS.6-8.Argue.Interpretive

Interpret social studies arguments by

- Evaluating point of view and credibility of source based on relevance and intended use

ELD-SS.9-12.Explain.Interpretive

Interpret social studies explanations by

- Determining multiple types of sources, points of view in sources, and potential uses of sources for answering compelling and supporting questions about phenomena or events

ELD-SS.9-12.Argue.Interpretive

Interpret social studies arguments by

- Evaluating credibility, accuracy, and relevancy of source based on expert perspectives

What should teachers consider for effective instruction?

Is it possible that students in all grades learn to attribute evidence to sources and source documents? We contend that it is, but it is important to be patient with students' development in these skills and to note progress on a developmental spectrum (see Figure 4 in the previous section). Sourcing is a challenging skill for students, especially when there is a discrepancy between sources (Braasch & Bråten, 2017). In our own research, we found that middle school and high school students showed no differences in sourcing capabilities and the quality of sourcing moves was relatively low compared to other writing skills in the absence of explicit writing instruction (Steiss et al., 2024). Such a finding is discouraging at first. But, with instruction, students at each grade level, six through twelve, can improve their sourcing and attribution skills (Moon et al., 2024).

Students can also learn to apply sourcing skills to assess and verify the accuracy and credibility of information shared online about social and civic topics

(McGrew et al., 2018). Given students' potential for development and the civic importance of this skill in a world filled with misinformation, we encourage educators to build students' sourcing capabilities. Because students' sourcing skills and knowledge of conventions for source attribution and integration will vary widely, formative assessment should be used to gauge where students are in their mastery of these skills. Frequent formative assessment allows teachers to monitor student learning and growth (Graham et al., 2016). When planning for instruction, you need to consider the next attainable step for students' writing and note and affirm their progress along the continuum. Given our observations of students' source use in their argument writing, we provide three general developmental stages with specific guides for instruction that these students would benefit from.

Stage 1—Learning to attribute and integrate sources. Students in this stage practice developing clear attribution and integrating evidence. Increasingly, students regulate their writing processes to check that this occurs, but they will need feedback from teachers and peers. Through instructional scaffolding, continued practice, and opportunities for revision, students can learn to attribute and integrate evidence to support their claims more effectively. It may be beneficial to model clear and consistent naming of sources, using basic and succinct attribution statements, introductory phrases, and reporting verbs. At this stage, students might practice at the sentence level, integrating evidence with simple sentences, introduced or followed by attribution statements.

To prompt students to clarify where the evidence comes from and metacognitively check that each piece of evidence is tied to a source, you can use the following questions:

- **What sources does the evidence come from?**
  - Who wrote or created the source?
  - What type of source is it?
- **What evidence did you use from this source to support your claim?**
  - What claim does the author make?
  - What evidence does the author use?
- **How did you integrate the evidence in your writing?**
  - Did you use quotations?
  - Did you paraphrase what the source said?

These questions can also be used as a self-assessment tool to build metalinguistic awareness when students engage in process-based writing. Table 4.17 provides descriptions of the sourcing and language skills that students need to develop, along with the instructional foci necessary to build these skills.

Table 4.17. Learning to Attribute and Integrate Sources

Stage 1	**Descriptions**	**Instructional Foci**
Learning to attribute and integrate sources	**Sourcing Skills:** • Identify the author, genre, and title of the source (*Who created this? What type of document is this?*) • Extract evidence from multiple sources to support a claim (*What claim does the author make? What evidence does the author use?*) **Languaging Practices:** • Name the source using author, title, and genre • Use introductory phrases and reporting verbs to integrate evidence	__Practice clear and consistent source attribution __Practice integrating evidence from multiple sources __Practice integrating quotations and paraphrases as evidence using introductory phrases and reporting verbs

Stage 2—Extending attribution and evidence integration. Students developing their skills in evidence use will practice varied attribution statements and more complex ways of integrating evidence. They pull out specific information from sources, like the date, context, and author's position/perspective. At this stage, students learn to integrate evidence consistently and in varied ways, using both quotations and paraphrasing throughout their writing with a variety of introductory phrases and reporting verbs. As students include specific source information in their attribution statements, they may begin to think about why this source information matters and should be included.

Instruction at this stage can focus on helping students contextualize sources and prompting students to think about the author's perspective and position in relation to their historical context. The following questions, which also can be used as discussion prompts, can serve as instructional guides or self-assessment tools to help students contextualize the sources:

- **What do you know about the context in which the source was created?**
    - When was this source created?
    - Where was this source created?
    - What were the unique circumstances at that time?
    - How might the circumstances and context have affected the content?

- **What do you know about the author/creator?**
  - Who is this author/creator?
  - What are the author's values and beliefs?
  - What is the author's position and perspective?

These questions can engage students in moving beyond just naming sources to critically and analytically examining the context in which the sources were created.

Language support for argument writing can focus on using extended and varied source attribution through complex noun phrase structures that allow students to succinctly communicate important and relevant information about the source's context and author. Students, at this stage, continue practicing various ways of integrating evidence by using a variety of introductory phrases and precise reporting verbs to characterize the source's viewpoint, perspective, and stance. Table 4.18 provides descriptions of the sourcing skills, languaging practices, and instructional foci necessary to build these skills.

Stage 3—Executing purposeful attribution and sourcing. Some students may have mastered evidence integration, clearly weaving evidence into arguments to support claims. They might benefit from additional practice using varied sentence structures to strategically select source information for their attribution statements. For example, the date a document was composed or the audience of the source might really matter for the larger argument. These statements then lead to sourcing statements that explicitly evaluate how the perspective, purpose, audience, or bias of a source might influence its reliability or relevance to the argument. For example, a student might note in the attribution statement that "Captain Preston, an officer in the British Army, wrote his account of what happened at the 'Boston Massacre' as he was awaiting trial for his actions." They then explain that "because he has an interest in portraying himself as innocent so he is not arrested or executed for crimes, he is [understandably] biased and therefore we cannot trust his account completely." These sourcing moves are deployed to contextualize this evidence and help advance the larger argument about what caused the violence at the Boston Massacre.

At this level, students practice questioning and evaluating sources to understand their motives, purposes, significance, relevance, credibility, and trustworthiness. The following questions can prompt students to think critically about the source and engage in dialogic interactions:

- **Why was this source created?**
  - What is the author's motive and purpose of creating this source?
  - To whom was it intended?

Table 4.18. Extending Attribution and Evidence Integration

Stage 2	Descriptions	Instructional Foci
Extending attribution and evidence integration	**Sourcing Skills:** • Identify when and where the source was created and understand how the context influences the content (*When and where was it created? How might the context have affected the content?*) • Understand and identify the author's position and perspective (*Who is the author? What is the author's belief, perspective, and bias?*) **Languaging Practices:** • Contextualize the source by providing time and place, using modifiers, prepositional phrases, and participles • Extend source attribution by providing who the author is and the author's value/belief/perspective, using participles, appositives, and other clause embedding	__Contextualize sources by situating them in historical time and place __Prompt thinking about the author's position and perspective __Practice extending source attribution by providing contextual details and additional information about the author/creator __Practice various ways of integrating evidence by using a variety of signal phrases and verbs

- **What makes this source reliable/unreliable and trustworthy/untrustworthy?**
    - Is this source reliable?
    - Is this source trustworthy?
    - What makes the author/creator credible or not credible?
- **What is the significance and relevance of this source?**
    - How does this source contribute to our understanding of the historical topic?
    - Why is this source significant?
    - How is this source important in building your argument?

The key instructional focus at this stage is to help students deploy complex sourcing moves to advance arguments. Language support can focus on practicing purposeful attribution, integration, and evaluative statements by constructing complex sentences with elaborated noun phrases and clausal embedding. Students practice strategically blending quotations, paraphrases, and evaluative statements to build more nuanced arguments.

In this chapter, we provided a variety of instructional strategies to help students build language skills for integrating sources effectively in their argument writing. A key to effective language support is contextualizing these resources

Table 4.19. Executing Purposeful Attribution and Sourcing

Stage 3	Descriptions	Instructional Foci
Executing purposeful attribution and sourcing	**Sourcing Skills:** • Identify and question the author's purpose, the author's motive, and the source's intended audience (*Why was this source created? To whom was it intended?*) • Evaluate the source's trustworthiness, relevance, and significance, and the author's credibility (*Is this source reliable and trustworthy? What is the significance and relevance of the source? What makes the author/creator credible?*) **Languaging Practices:** • Communicate and comment on the purpose/agenda, motive, and intended audience, using prepositional phrases, infinitive structure, participles, and clauses • Evaluate the source's credibility and relevance, using adjectives of value, causal and commentary verbs, and clause-linking devices	__Evaluate source's credibility, trustworthiness, significance, and relevance __Practice questioning the source to uncover its purpose and intended audience __Practice purposeful attribution and evaluative statements __Practice constructing complex sentences that convey source information succinctly __Practice blending quotations and paraphrases

within grade-level content. We acknowledge that sourcing is a complex skill, and much of the instruction that fosters critical thinking skills for sourcing needs to start before students begin to write. Since our goal is to support students' language development for effective argument writing using sources, we specifically focus on languaging practices used for integrating sources in support of a claim. Integrating multiple sources to build a historical argument requires additional reasoning skills such as corroborating and commenting on how sources support the argument. We address these reasoning skills in the next chapter.

CHAPTER 5

Reasoning to Advance a Historical Argument

Guiding Questions

- How is reasoning used to develop historical argumentation?
- How is language used to present reasoning in argument writing?
- How can teachers help students build language skills for presenting reasoning?

How do students use reasoning when exploring the causes and consequences of an event that happened in the distant past? In a seventh-grade world history class, students focus on "the social, cultural, and technological changes that occurred in Europe, Africa, and Asia" in medieval times (California Department of Education, 2000, p. 27). As part of an inquiry-based unit to understand social change, students work to answer the following question: *What caused the decline of feudalism?* This is a difficult question for seventh graders to grapple with as they will have to use historical reasoning, reading, and writing skills to construct a well-supported argument.

After reading and examining multiple sources, students make claims about what caused the decline of feudalism using evidence from the sources to support their claims. They explain *how* the evidence they have put forth supports their arguments and why their interpretations are valid. Clarifying the *how* and *why* is at the core of developing arguments and is key to reasoning (Kuhn, 2019). Reasoning requires language resources that enable individuals to present their thoughts clearly and effectively. Students who have not developed the language resources necessary for higher-order thinking and abstract ideas may have difficulty conveying their reasoning. The following paragraph written by a student in a seventh-grade class can help us understand the challenge a student faces in articulating their reasoning. As you read Writing Draft 1, pay attention to language choices that convey the causal connection between the Magna Carta and the decline of feudalism.

Writing Draft 1

> Feudalism was in 771 to 1800 AD. The thing that led to decline of feudalism was when the Magna Carta was written and when all of the people died from the plague. The timeline says King John I (England) signed the Magna Carta, a written document that diminished the king's power and strengthened nobles' rights. It placed limits on the King's power. Under feudalism the King had a lot of power. but then after this he had less power. The Black Death also happened at this time of feudalism and it was terrible because it killed ⅓ of the total population of Europe. There were not a lot of workers. "The laborers were so proud and hostile that they took no notice of the King's law. If anyone wanted to employ laborers, he had to pay them what they asked—or lose his fruit and crops." (Source 4).

In writing their initial draft, the student makes a claim and uses sources. However, the language resources used in the sample are more aligned with the linguistic features of recounting genres. Rather than explaining *why* the Magna Carta and the plague led to the decline of feudalism, the student simply enumerates events in additive style, primarily using temporal connectors such as *when, then,* and *after* and action verbs such as *was written, died,* and *signed.*

After instruction that focuses on historical reasoning and languaging practices for argumentation, the student writes the following draft. As you read Writing Draft 2, notice how the language choices in this revised draft differ from those in the previous section.

Writing Draft 2

> Feudalism, a social system in Europe from 771-1800, came to an end because of multiple factors, including the Black Death plague and the Magna Carta which significantly contributed to the deterioration of the system. First of all, the Black Death plague was consequential for the decline of feudalism because it took out a large number of the peasants who were the backbone of feudalism in Europe. According to the Timeline of the Decline of Feudalism, the Black Death killed about

one third of the population in Europe, making people afraid to leave their homes and causing the loss of the labor force. Without people working, the land crops rotted and people didn't get food. The Black Death had a hard hit on the economy. The historical account of the Black Death by Henry Knigton states, "Lords who had lent land in return for yearly labor service were forced to change these services. They either had to let the serfs off the services, or else accept money instead." This quotation suggests because there were no people to work, those who did stay behind demanded to be paid better. This led to a change in the feudal system.

The second draft exhibits more explicit reasoning with clear explanations of *why* the Black Death should be considered as a plausible reason for the decline of feudalism. The use of causal phrases (e.g., *because of, contributed to, consequential for*), nominalization and complex noun phrase structures (e.g., *deterioration of the system, decline of feudalism, the loss of the labor forces*), and causal verbs (e.g., *contribute to, causing, led to*) enables the student to establish causal links between ideas. The student goes beyond recounting what happened in the past to build an interpretive argument.

For secondary students, providing reasoning or warrants for how evidence supports a claim can be especially challenging (Olson et al., 2023). Specific rhetorical moves emblematic of *historical* reasoning are also particularly challenging for secondary students (Steiss et al., 2024). However, with explicit instruction in disciplinary writing and frequent opportunities to practice source-based inquiry, secondary students can improve their historical reasoning and argument writing skills (Monte-Sano, 2008). In this chapter, we provide instructional guidance and resources for teachers to better support their students to present reasoning for argument writing in history. We make visible the languaging practices used for historical reasoning, which involves interpreting evidence, corroborating, explaining causes and consequences, and posing counterfactuals. The three main sections of the chapter are outlined below:

I. **Conceptual Overview:** Reasoning Involved in Historical Argumentation
   - What is the role of reasoning in historical argumentation?
   - What types of reasoning support historical knowledge?

II. **Language Focus:** Languaging Practices for Reasoning in Argument Writing
   - How is language used to explain causes, consequences, and counterfactuals?

- How is language used to corroborate evidence from multiple sources?
- How is language used to interpret and comment on evidence?

III. **Instructional Support:** Cultivating Language Skills for Presenting Reasoning

- How can teachers cultivate language skills for expressing reasoning?
- How can teachers build metalinguistic knowledge and awareness?
- What should teachers consider for effective instruction?

I. Reasoning Involved in Historical Argumentation

What is the role of reasoning in historical argumentation?

Argument writing in history is *interpretive*. Because interpretations are not unassailable truths, we need to support claims with evidence and *reasoning*. Whether we are writing or voicing our claims, we need to convince our reader or conversation partner *why* they should believe our interpretation and why the evidence we have put forth supports our claim. In his framework for argumentation, Stephen Toulmin (1958) defines *warrants* (which we presently refer to as reasoning) as one of three key argumentative elements next to evidence and claims. He notes that when we engage in arguments dialogically, our reasons are usually provided, especially when we are presented with a warrant-generating question: *Why do you think so? So what? What does this mean or show? I get that vegetables are good for me, Mom, but why does that mean I have to eat them?* Indeed, most of us can provide reasoning to support our claims when pressed.

Reasoning is defined as a form of thinking to reach *justifiable* and *defensible* conclusions (Moshman, 2013). We justify and defend our claims to or from someone, real or imagined. This is why Carla Van Boxtel and Jannet van Drie (2018) describe historical reasoning as a *socially situated activity*. This is also why dialogue with peers in a discourse community is a key practice to build students' argumentation skills (Schleppegrell et al., 2023). Because historical argumentation is fundamentally dialogic, the best historical arguments implicitly or explicitly acknowledge other interpretations when advancing an argument (Monte-Sano & Allen, 2019).

Students who acknowledge alternative interpretations in their writing typically engage in more reasoning (Steiss et al., 2024). We contend these students understand the dialogic nature of argumentation. By imagining themselves arguing with someone else, they work to assert their interpretations in a sea of countless other claims and, therefore, engage in more reasoning. In short, thinking about the other side gives a reason to reason. Ignoring other perspectives, students may engage in one-sided explanations that typically substitute reasoning for recall or summarization of events (Coffin, 2004). The difference between dialogic argumentation and one-sided explanation is best illustrated in the following examples.

<u>One-sided Explanation</u>

> The Black Death also happened at this time of feudalism and it was terrible because it killed 1/3 of the total population of Europe. The Black Death was terrible and affected feudalism. There were not a lot of workers. Source 4 says, "The laborers were so proud and hostile that they took no notice of the King's law. If anyone wanted to employ laborers, he had to pay them what they asked—or lose his fruit and crops." The black death led to the decline of feudalism.

<u>Two-sided Argument (emphasis added)</u>

> The Black Death was the *most significant factor* that led to the decline of feudalism. According to the timeline, the Black Death killed about 1/3 of the population of Europe, making people afraid to leave their homes and work (Source 1). *Without* people working, the land crops rotted and people didn't get food, *which* had a hard hit on the economy. The text titled Black Death says "Lords who had lent land in return for yearly labor service were forced to change these services. They either had to let the serfs off the services, or else accept money instead" (Source 4). *Because* there were no people to work, those who did stay behind demanded to be paid better. T*his led to* a change in feudalism.

In the second example, the student appears to be convincing someone else why their interpretation is valid. They create causal links between the black death, fewer workers, and a change in feudalism using causal language. Making explicit how evidence supports a claim often distinguishes experts from novice writers, whose reasons remain implicit (Crammond, 1998). Reasoning also makes the argument more transparent. We can question the reasons or accept them based on other evidence and understanding. Reasoning, therefore, helps us in our pursuit to know what really happened in the past. It is fundamental to historical inquiry.

Because argument writing in history is *interpretive*, students benefit from viewing historical knowledge as constructed, tentative interpretations of the past supported by evidence and substantiated through reasoning. However, the predominance of textbook-based instruction and a lack of writing assignments that ask students to transform knowledge or engage in interpretive reasoning can hinder the development of this view (Wiley et al., 2020). A lack of inquiry and argumentation can lead students to think of history as a static collection of facts that must simply be known. Consequently, many students may not include reasoning in historical argumentation because they don't think it is necessary—they don't see historical interpretations as needing substantiation; the past is simply known.

Moving away from the predominance of textbook-centric instruction toward document-based inquiry where students construct meaning using sources is intended to build literacy skills and promote a fundamental epistemological shift that history is knowledge construction, not the memorization of unassailable facts (Alston et al., 2021). Such a shift not only centers reasoning with evidence as the very foundation of history as a discipline but also prioritizes student voice. Thus, students need linguistic resources to argue and reason with evidence. Before turning to language features, however, we discuss various types of reasoning involved in argumentation.

What types of reasoning support historical knowledge?

Although reasoning is a key part of argumentation in all disciplines, it is adapted to the norms, standards for knowledge creation, and sources of evidence used within a disciplinary community (Goldman et al., 2016). *Historical* argumentation involves reasoning with multiple sources, and Sam Wineburg's (1991) historical reasoning heuristics central to knowledge creation in history: sourcing, contextualizing, and corroborating.

Examining how expert historians analyze sources, Wineburg (1991) notes how they consistently: (1) attend to who wrote documents and for what purposes (i.e., sourcing); (2) analyze the context of events and peoples to make causal inferences or establish the significance of actions (i.e., contextualization); and (3) consider how accounts agree and disagree (i.e., corroboration). Such reasoning moves are present in effective argument writing with sources. We discussed sourcing in the previous chapter, so in this chapter we describe languaging practices for contextualization, corroboration, and other reasoning moves like commenting on significance, establishing causal links, and considering multiple causes and perspectives.

First, we consider *contextualization*—placing sources, actors, and events within their social and political contexts (both temporally and geographically) to better understand the relations between events, actors, and historical context (Seixas & Morton, 2013; Wineburg, 1991). When students answer historical questions using multiple sources, they utilize knowledge of historical context to construct a model of the situation, including how events, actors, forces, and consequences relate (Rouet et al., 2017). To illustrate, in explaining the key role of the carpool in the Montgomery Bus Boycott, students consider why, in that specific time and place, carpools were so important. The time and place indicate a single year in Montgomery, Alabama, but it is also the United States and the Jim Crow South. Knowledge of these contexts, both from the sources and from prior knowledge, will help students better understand the complexities of historical topics and how events relate and matter (Cowgill II, & Waring, 2017).

Importantly, contextualization is key for *causal* and *consequential thinking* as it allows students to put events in order and evaluate the relative contributions or effects of historical events (Seixas & Morton, 2013). This can be seen in the following student writing about the success of the Delano Grape Strike and Boycott:

> The march to Sacramento was another reason the boycott and strike succeeded because it raised awareness about the unfair treatment that the farm workers endured. In an interview with Roberto Bustos, a participant of the boycott and strike, he stated that, "We stopped at 53 towns and explained why we were marching." This march was important because it raised awareness of low pay and poor working conditions. It led to the success of the strike and boycott because once people were informed of the farm workers' situation, they could join in the boycott and help their cause. Therefore, they could gain more attention from the media and more supporters.

This student places the march within the larger context of the Delano Grape Strike and Boycott, showing the role of contextualization in substantiating causal arguments with multiple potential causes.

Contextualization is also intricately linked to *counterfactual reasoning*. Experts consider historical events and consequences as neither predetermined nor inevitable, underscoring the value of thinking in counterfactuals—what might have happened without some key factor. For example, consider the following student writing about the factors leading to the success of the Montgomery Bus Boycott:

> Without [Jo Ann Robinson's] distribution and hard work of the WPC, many people wouldn't have known about the boycott, and it may not have succeeded. Since many people of color didn't have access to the same resources as white people (aka radios, television, live and public speaking, etc.), the best way to get the word out was manually and word of mouth.

The student, responding to the implicit question—*Just how important was the distribution of letters?*—poses a counterfactual (*Without the letters*) situated in the historical context to emphasize Robinson's role.

Another type of historical reasoning involved in argumentation is *corroboration*—the process of comparing information across sources to determine whether two sources agree or disagree on some key point. During inquiry, students weigh multiple accounts or explanations of the past as they pursue the truth (Stoel et al., 2017). Sometimes, accounts disagree. In these cases, corroboration is key in creating an accurate model of the historical situation as it enables students to resolve apparent discrepancies between sources (Rouet et al., 2017). Instead of ignoring disagreements, historians weigh the validity of competing claims by considering which and how much evidence confirms or challenges different interpretations (Bråten et al., 2017). Thus, helping students resolve discrepancies through valid methods of inquiry is critical for them to develop sound argumentation.

In our own examination of student writing, we find that students do not consistently use corroboration as a strategy when engaging in argument writing (Steiss et al., 2024). This indicates that they often need support in this skill both conceptually and linguistically. Still, with scaffolded inquiry-based instruction, students can improve in this area (Moon et al., 2024). For example, consider the following student writing about the causes of the Battle of Lexington:

> A couple days after the violence had erupted, Amos Doolittle, a silverman that was part of the militia, made an image. This image showed the redcoats (British soldiers) moving further into the county. This may seem like an unreasonable source but he made this image after speaking to individuals that were involved in the battle. Henry Sandham created an image of the battle as well but did it roughly 100 years later and did not mention his involvement with anyone who was present. Doolittle's image is more credible because the individuals that described the events in the image were witnesses and were there when the battle was

> happening. Unlike Sandham's image made 100 years later with no sense of evidence or witnesses of what happened during that time.

By directly comparing sources and their claims, students can work to better understand sources, the historical context, and the subject for inquiry. With an emerging understanding of historical reasoning, we now turn to the linguistic resources students need to engage in reasoning with historical evidence.

II. Languaging Practices for Reasoning in Argument Writing

Reasoning for historical argumentation requires higher-order thinking, including analysis and synthesis of sources, contextualization of historical actors and events, interpretation of evidence, and explanation of causes and effects (van Drie & Van Boxtel, 2008). Because thinking is externalized through language, understanding how language is used in various ways to present reasoning when developing an argument in history can help students expand their linguistic resources and "make agentive language choices" (Schleppegrell et al., 2023, p. 8).

To see how a student presents reasoning when building an argument, we examine an excerpt from a student essay about the women's suffrage movement. As you read the following passage, pay attention to how language is used to express reasoning (in italics).

> *Because* there was still work to do, the National Women's Party staged a number of public demonstrations *to pressure the President and others in Congress to change* their stances on suffrage. The protests by the NWP *are documented in* the 1918 NYTimes article and 1974 interview with Alice Paul. These protests, including picketing and hunger strikes, *applied pressure needed for* the movement to progress. Alice Paul, a leader of these demonstrations and the NWP, *underscores* the progress of the movement by noting, "President Wilson made a magnificent speech calling for the amendment as a war measure." In fact, this speech came *after* these protests. *Without* action on a national stage in the form of pickets, protests, and the accompanying press, the President *would not have appealed* to the Congress calling for the passage of the amendment and the Congress *may not have ever passed* the 19th amendment. The National Parks Service article *also confirms the impact of* the NWP's picketing on the President and Congress' changing perspective on women's suffrage.

In this writing, the reasoning is clearly presented through the use of: (1) causal language (*because, to pressure, applied pressure needed for*) to explain the causes and consequences, elucidating why and to what end the NWP staged public demonstrations; (2) chronological sequence (*the speech came after the protests*) to contextualize historical events; (3) nominalization and complex noun phrases (*movement to progress; passage of the amendment*) to name events; (4) signal verbs (*are documented, underscores, confirms*) to integrate, interpret, and corroborate evidence; and (5) conditional statements (*without, would not have appealed, may not have ever passed*) to offer counterfactual explanations. These language resources enable the writer to effectively communicate their reasoning.

While a wide range of language resources is used to express the reasoning for historical argumentation, we focus on key languaging practices used for three reasoning moves crucial to interpreting evidence and defending claims: (1) explaining *causes, consequences*, and *counterfactuals*; (2) *corroborating* sources; and (3) *commenting on* (or interpreting) evidence. Our goal is to provide guidance so teachers can better support their students to strategically use language to present reasoning in argument writing.

How is language used to explain causes, consequences, and counterfactuals?

To unpack how language is used to explain the causes and consequences of events, we first turn to Peter Seixas and Tom Morton's (2013) historical thinking concepts concerning cause and consequence, which include the following five guideposts:

GUIDEPOST 1: Change is driven by multiple causes, and results in multiple consequences.
GUIDEPOST 2: The causes that lead to a particular historical event vary in their influence.
GUIDEPOST 3: Events result from the interplay of two types of factors: (1) historical actors and (2) social, political, economic, and cultural conditions within which the actors operate.
GUIDEPOST 4: Historical actors cannot always predict the effect of conditions, opposing actions, and unforeseen reactions.
GUIDEPOST 5: The events of history were not inevitable, any more than those of the future are. (p. 11)

The guideposts emphasize the importance of examining multiple forces and the complex interconnections between causes, consequences, and historical contexts. To express this complex thinking in argument writing, students draw on language resources to: (1) clearly name the causes and consequences of events and situate them in their historical contexts; (2) establish causal links between events and actors; and (3) present counterfactual reasoning. We discuss the language resources under each of these three reasoning moves.

Naming Causes and Consequences

Reasoning in history necessarily requires writers to frame concrete actions and actors into *nameable* abstract things, events, groups, moments, and concepts. For example, instead of reporting what happened and describing an action (*Rosa Parks was arrested on December 1, 1955*), writers turn the action into a single moment—*the arrest of Rosa Parks*. This way of abstracting allows writers to elaborate on and explain how the abstract thing/event is causally linked to other related events (*the arrest of Rosa Parks galvanized local political groups*). The abstraction is done through particular linguistic choices to package historical events into a causal chain. To illustrate this point, we use a sample sentence from the summary of the Montgomery Bus Boycott from the Martin Luther King, Jr. Research and Education Institute at Stanford University, highlighting the information that names events (italics).

> Sparked by *the arrest of Rosa Parks* on 1 December 1955, *the Montgomery Bus Boycott* was *a 13-month mass protest* that ended with *the U.S. Supreme Court ruling* that *segregation on public buses* is unconstitutional.

The highlighted phrases in the sentence are nominal groups that name short-term and long-term events that are interrelated to one another. By naming the events, rather than focusing on the actions, the writer is able to efficiently establish the causal link between the actor/action and the boycott. Table 5.1 shows how focus on actions expressed in complete sentences can shift to the abstract thing/event expressed in phrases.

Students who understand the causal relations between events but are still developing language resources for reasoning may focus on actions rather than naming events as causes and consequences. For example, a student with developing language skills may write the following:

Table 5.1. Turning Actions into Abstract Concepts/Events

Action: What happened?	**Abstract Concept/Event:** What is?
Rosa Parks was arrested on 1 December 1955.	⇒ the arrest of Rosa Parks on 1 December 1955
People boycotted buses in Montgomery.	⇒ the Montgomery Bus Boycott
The protest involved a large number of people and continued for 13 months.	⇒ a 13-month mass protest
The U.S. Supreme court ruled that segregation on public buses is unconstitutional.	⇒ the U.S. Supreme court ruling that segregation on public buses is unconstitutional

> Rosa Parks was arrested on 1 December 1955. This made a lot of people protest and boycott the buses in Montgomery. The protest involved a large number of people and continued for 13 months. So, the U.S. Supreme Court ruled that segregation on public buses is unconstitutional.

This rewritten version conveys similar ideas expressed in the original sentence, but the language use is noticeably different. Differences in linguistic choices and their rhetorical effects can be made visible to students by focusing on key language features that include contextualization, nominalization, and abstraction.

Contextualization. Contextualization is key to reasoning because understanding the causes and consequences of historical events necessarily requires an understanding of how historical contexts influence actors and events. Contextualizing historical actors and events is realized through various language resources used for expressing time (e.g., *on 1 December 1955*) and place (e.g., *Montgomery*). One subtle way of using language is packaging relevant contextual facts and details to efficiently name causes and consequences. This is done through the construction of complex noun phrases. For example, the complex noun phrase *the arrest of Rosa Parks on 1 December 1955* packages the details about time when naming the event, specifying not just the what (*the arrest*) but also the who (*of Rosa Parks*) and when (*on 1 December 1955*). Similarly, the noun phrase *a 13-month mass protest* packages information about the duration (*a 13-month*) and the magnitude (*mass*) of the protest. Because complex noun phrases package descriptive and contextual details, they tend to be abstract and dense. Unpacking these dense noun phrases can help students see how information is packaged when naming

Table 5.2. Use of Modifiers in Naming Abstract Concepts and Events

Modifier before Noun	Head Noun	Modifiers after Noun
Rosa Parks'	arrest	on December 1, 1955
the Montgomery Bus	Boycott	x
a 13-month mass	protest	x
The U.S. Supreme Court	ruling	that segregation on public buses is unconstitutional

events, causes, and consequences. In a complex noun phrase, a head noun is expanded to include contextual and descriptive details using modifiers (i.e., word and phrases that describe and modify) that come before or after the head noun. To show these constituents, we unpack several complex noun phrases in Table 5.2.

The head noun, often a key word, is not specific when used alone, but becomes specified through modifiers that add precise meaning, specificity, clarity, and contextualization in writing. Therefore, modifiers have an important function in the naming of events, causes, and consequences, as well as actors and groups. Deconstructing a complex noun phrase to show what the key word/head noun is and how it is modified to clearly name and situate events in their historical contexts can help students construct meaning with clarity and precision.

Nominalization. Another key language resource used for naming causes and consequences is nominalization—the process of transforming adjectives, verbs, and clauses into nouns and noun phrases. Nominalization is a crucial language resource that "enables writers to construct worlds of logic and abstraction" from actions and happenings (Derewianka & Jones, 2023, p. 294). Because nominalization repackages attributes (typically expressed by adjectives) and actions (typically expressed by verbs) into events and abstract concepts, it allows writers to "develop a chain of reasoning that at the time embeds interpretation and judgment" (Fang & Schleppegrell, 2010, p. 590). Table 5.3 shows how adjectives, verbs, and clauses are nominalized in examples commonly used for causal expressions.

We examine the use and function of nominalization in the following excerpt from an eleventh-grade student writing about Prohibition. Notice that the nominalized noun phrases (italicized) denote abstract concepts and events.

> The Volstead Act was passed by the U.S. Congress in 1919, leading to *the criminalization of the buying and selling of alcohol.* Such a law was

Table 5.3. Nominalization

Nominalization of Adjectives	Nominalization of Verbs	Nominalization of Clauses
difficult → difficulty effective → effectiveness ineffective → ineffectiveness important → importance significant → significance possible → possibility present → presence resilient → resilience	contribute → contribution establish → establishment expand → expansion develop → development justify → justification treat → treatment pass → passage enforce → enforcement	The Nineteenth Amendment to the U.S. Constitution was ratified on August 18, 1920. ↓ The ratification of the Nineteenth Amendment to the U.S. Constitution on August 18, 1920

> created to decrease *the presence of alcoholic beverages in U.S. society* which many saw as a problem. After 15 years though, Prohibition failed, and the law was repealed by the 21st Amendment. Although some may see *the failure of Prohibition* as due to *a loss of tax revenue*, the main reason it failed was *the difficulty in enforcing Prohibition*. Following *the passage of the Volstead Act*, enforcing the law was difficult, which weakened its resolve and power. For example, an excerpt from the 1923 book by Haskin, describes *the ineffectiveness of enforcing prohibition nationally*.

The nominalized phrases denote abstract concepts and events that are linked to one another. For example, the nominalized phrase *the criminalization of the buying and selling of alcohol* is an abstract concept linked to another abstract concept, *the Volstead Act*, through the causal verb *leading to*, making causes and consequences more explicit in the argument.

Abstract Nouns. Causes, consequences, and change in history are often abstract notions—things we cannot see and touch—that are expressed in abstract nouns. The abstract nouns used to present causes (e.g., *reason, contribution, role*), consequences (e.g., *effect, result, outcome*), and change (e.g., *growth, decline, diffusion*) are combined with nouns and noun phrases that name historical events and concepts to create causal links. Table 5.4 provides a list of abstract nouns that encapsulate causes, consequences, and changes. Organizing these language resources based on historical thinking concepts can help students make thematic mapping between abstract concepts.

These language resources enable writers to clearly name events and frame them as causes and consequences. For instructional purposes, teachers can identify noun phrases and nominal groups in mentor texts and unpack complex noun phrases by deconstructing them into their components. This

Table 5.4. Abstract Nouns for Causes, Consequences, and Change

Abstract nouns for CAUSES	basis, cause, contribution, excuse, factor, force, grounds, impetus, influence, justification, origin, rationale, reason, role, root
Abstract nouns for CONSEQUENCES	aftermath, backlash, byproduct, effect, emphasis, end result, consequence, failure, impact, importance, outcome, prominence, ramification, repercussion, result, significance, success
Abstract nouns for CHANGE	advance, advancement, change, expansion, establishment, fall, development, decline, deterioration, diffusion, growth, rise, spread

deconstruction will help students construct and convey meaning with clarity and precision. Strategies and activities that help students build these language resources will be discussed in section III, which focuses on instructional support.

Establishing Causal Connections

While naming causes and consequences is important, students also need to understand how causal links between historical events, actors, and contexts are established through language. Causal links are built through several language resources including causal verbs, prepositional phrases, and connectors. Causal verbs (e.g., *lead to, result in, stem from*) and prepositional phrases (e.g., *due to, as a result of, because of*) typically make causal connections between noun phrases (e.g., *the difficulty in enforcing Prohibition resulted in its failure; the failure of Prohibition is due to a loss of tax revenue*). Connectors establish causal links between clauses and sentences (e.g., *It was difficult to enforce prohibition. Therefore, prohibition failed. Prohibition failed because it was difficult to enforce it*). These resources enable writers to make a variety of language choices necessary for demonstrating causality. Recognizing varied and nuanced ways of constructing causality will enhance students' strategic use of language to present reasoning. Next, we discuss several key language resources writers draw on to construct causality. We focus on three key areas: causal verbs, prepositional phrases, and connectors.

Causal Verbs. Causal verbs are commonly used in argument writing to establish causal links between ideas in a more efficient way. In fact, "reasoning within a clause through verbs rather than between clauses through conjunctions" is a prominent linguistic feature of historical argumentation (Schleppegrell et al., 2004, p. 75). To illustrate this point, we examine two versions of a sentence from eleventh-grade student writing drafts.

- Draft 1: *The Prohibition forbade the sale of alcohol, so the revenue from it decreased.*
- Draft 2: *Prohibiting the sale of alcohol led to the decrease in revenue.*

In Draft 1, two clauses are combined using the coordinating conjunction *so*. In Draft 2, the student revised their sentence, making it more efficient through the use of the causal verb *led to* to link the two ideas—*prohibiting the sale of alcohol* and *decrease in revenue*—expressed in abstract noun phrases.

Some verbs make direct causal links between actors and events (e.g., *Women played crucial roles in the success of the boycott*). We illustrate this point using an excerpt from the summary of the Montgomery Bus Boycott from the Martin Luther King, Jr. Research and Education Institute at Stanford University (italics added):

> Although most of the publicity about the protest was centered on the actions of black ministers, women *played crucial roles in* the success of the boycott. Women such as Robinson, Johnnie Carr, and Irene West sustained the MIA committees and volunteer networks. Mary Fair Burks of the WPC also *attributed* the success of the boycott *to* "the nameless cooks and maids who walked endless miles for a year *to bring about* the breach in the walls of segregation" (Burks 82).

In this excerpt, causal links are established between historical actors and events through verbs and verb phrases such as *played crucial roles in, attributed the success of the boycott to,* and *to bring about.*

Verbs used to construct causality are wide-ranging and have different connotations and functions. For example, verbs such as *hinder* and *inhibit* have negative connotations and encapsulate negative change, while verbs such as *foster* and *cultivate* have positive connotations and capture positive change. Thus, causality can be constructed through various verbs with shades of meanings that express change, progression, and continuity from different angles. Table 5.5 provides a list of verbs commonly used to establish causal links between actors, events, and concepts.

Causal verbs take different grammatical forms in a sentence depending on their roles. They can function as the main verb of the sentence, making a direct causal link between two events or concepts. They are also commonly used in passive construction and participle forms making causal links between and among actors, events, and concepts. These three common forms and functions of causal verbs are illustrated in the following examples.

Table 5.5. Causal Verbs Chart

Verbs that encapsulate CAUSES/REASONS	cause, contribute to, determine, give rise to, induce, play a role in, produce, prompt, result in, stem from, trigger
Verbs that encapsulate EFFECTS/RESULTS	affect, bring about, engender, generate, impact, influence, lead to, precipitate, shape
Verbs that encapsulate POSITIVE CHANGE	advance, boost, cultivate, enhance, facilitate, foster, further, promote, stimulate, strengthen
Verbs that encapsulate NEGATIVE CHANGE	cripple, curtail, discourage, hamper, hinder, impede, inhibit, obstruct, prevent, restrain, stymie, thwart
Verbs that encapsulate CONTINUITY	block, delay, deter, grow/decline, halt, hold back, progress/disrupt, spark/end, start/stop

- Causal verbs functioning as <u>main verbs</u>:
    - *The Black Death Plague <u>contributed to</u> the decline of feudalism.*
    - *The arrest of Rosa Parks <u>prompted</u> the mobilization of black community.*
- Causal verbs in <u>passive constructions</u>:
    - *Both sources suggest that the labor shortage <u>was caused by</u> a large number of deaths.*
    - *The mobilization of Montgomery's black community <u>was triggered by</u> Rosa Parks' arrest.*
- Causal verbs in <u>participles</u> (present and past participle forms):
    - *The Black Death killed about 1/3 of the population in Europe, <u>causing</u> labor shortage in the region* (<u>present participle</u>).
    - *<u>Sparked by</u> the arrest of Rosa Parks on 1 December 1955, the Montgomery Bus Boycott was a 13-month mass protest that ended with the U.S. Supreme Court ruling that segregation on public buses is unconstitutional* (<u>past participle</u>).

Mariana Achugar and Mary Schleppegrell (2005) point out that causal reasoning in history is presented through a wide range of linguistic resources that go beyond connectors such as *because, so, therefore*, and so on. Causal verbs are among these wide-ranging language resources used to establish causal links. Learning the nuances of causal verbs can expand students' linguistic repertoires, allowing them to make more strategic language choices.

Prepositions and Prepositional Phrases. Another way of establishing a causal connection is through prepositions and prepositional phrases (i.e., phrase linkers) of causality. Single-word prepositions, such as *through* and *via*, and multi-word prepositional phrases, such as *due to* and *as a result of*,

Table 5.6. Prepositions and Prepositional Phrases for Causality

Prepositions	Examples
via through because of due to owing to thanks to by means of as a result of on account of on the grounds of with the help of	• *Through march to Sacramento and the use of media*, the Delano Grape Strike succeeded, giving farm workers better wages and suitable working conditions. • One of the most important reasons why the Delano grape boycott and strike succeeded was *because of the publicity and the attention that Cesar Chavez received from the media.* • The United Farm Workers Union was created *as a result of a series of strikes led by labor activities and civil rights advocates such as Cesar Chavez, Dolores Huerta, and Larry Itliong.*

are used with nouns and noun phrases to build causal links. Pointing out how prepositions and prepositional phrases are used to build causal links can help students recognize that there are multiple ways to construct causality. Students who have more expansive language resources will be able to present their reasoning effectively when developing their arguments. Table 5.6 summarizes prepositions and prepositional phrases commonly used to construct causality.

Causal Connectors. Causal connectors, such as *because, as,* and *therefore,* are commonly used to build causal relationships between clauses and sentences. There are two types of connectors: conjunctions (e.g., *since, as, because*) and sentence connectors (e.g., *therefore, thus, as a result*). While conjunctions are used to combine two or more clauses into a single sentence to establish causal links, sentence connectors signal a transition from one sentence to another to establish a causal link. To see how a student uses causal connectors, we examine an excerpt from a tenth-grade student's essay about the Salt March (italics added).

> In March of 1930, Mahatma Gandhi led a nonviolent protest with a 240-mile march known as the Salt March to protest the British monopoly on salt. The Salt March was successful *because thousands of people joined the march along the way* despite the fact that the peaceful protest was met by harsh violence from the British. While the Salt March was a slow walk on foot, Gandhi and his followers quickly made an impact. In 24 days, Gandhi would stop in the villages along the way to speak and denounce the British and the salt monopoly. *As a result*, the procession grew from 78 people to thousands, showing how Gandhi's message had such broad appeal that people would lay down what they were doing to

> join the march. A timeline of the Salt March states, "Stopping in each village along the route, they gained thousands of supporters" enough to form a "miles-long procession." This source is reliable *as it draws from eyewitness accounts of a news reporter following Gandhi.*

The student uses several connectors (italicized) to establish causal links between clauses and sentences. Causal conjunctions (*because; as*) are used to combine clauses, adding reasoning into the main clauses, and the sentence connector *as a result* establishes a cause-effect relationship between two sentences.

Conjunctions and sentence connectors commonly used to build causal links are summarized in Table 5.7. To show their functions, we use sample sentences from student writing about the Salt March. As these two types of connectors have distinct functions in their use, the punctuation rules vary based on how they are positioned within a sentence. Notice that the examples we use show different positions and punctuation patterns.

A dependent clause with a causal conjunction can be placed either before or after the main clause. While there is no *semantic* difference between two versions of the same clause in different positions, discourse flow and patterns change. The writer's choice of position is dependent on a number of discourse-level considerations, such as the flow of ideas and sentence variety. The change in discourse patterns prompts a change in punctuation. A common

Table 5.7. Causal Connectors

Linking Devices	Connectors	Examples
Conjunctions (establish causal links by combining two or more sentences into one)	*as* *because* *given that* *since* *so* *so that*	• Some might say that Gandhi was successful with his Salt March *because the British opened up negotiations in an attempt to avoid more violent protests.* • *Since the harsh response from the British was shown on the world stage*, the nonviolent resistance led by Gandhi gained worldwide attention.
Sentence Connectors (signal causal links between sentences)	*as a result* *consequently* *hence* *thereby* *therefore* *thus*	• Thousands of supporters joined the peaceful march as Gandhi stopped at villages along the way to speak. ***Consequently,*** a miles-long procession was formed. • Gandhi's commitment to nonviolent resistance mobilized significant support. The protest, ***therefore***, was successful in uniting Indians against British rule.

practice is that the dependent clause that precedes the main clause is followed by a comma (illustrated in Example A), but the comma is removed when the dependent clause comes after the main clause (Example B). It is important to note the exceptions to this punctuation rule. For example, when a dependent clause with the contrastive conjunction of *whereas* or *while* are in sentence-final position, we use a comma after the sentence-initial main clause (Example C).

- Example A: *Since the harsh response from the British was shown on the world stage*, the nonviolent resistance led by Gandhi gained worldwide attention.
- Example B: The nonviolent resistance led by Gandhi gained worldwide attention *since* the harsh response from the British was shown on the world stage.
- Example C: The Salt March was a pivotal act of civil disobedience in India, *whereas* the British government responded with harsh repression to suppress it.

The punctuation pattern for sentence connectors is such that they commonly appear either at the beginning of the sentence followed by a comma (*Consequently, a miles-long process was formed*) or in subject-verb split position (*The protest, therefore, was successful*). Recognizing these patterns of constructing causality allows students to use language strategically to explain causes, consequences, and continuity.

Counterfactual Reasoning. Reasoning in history also involves considering counterfactuals or possible alternatives to historical events. Counterfactual reasoning involves imagining *what if* and reasoning about what could have or might have happened and how things could have turned out differently. In argument writing, counterfactual reasoning is expressed through language that presents alternative possibilities contrary to what actually happened. To illustrate how a student uses counterfactual reasoning to develop their argument, we examine an excerpt from student writing (italics added):

> Cesar Chavez, a civil rights advocate who fought for farmworkers' rights, made an important contribution to the success of the Delano Grape strike and boycott because he publicized the cause and gained popularity and recognition through the media. For example, the timeline stated, "Cèsar Chavez speaks on television and writes letters asking people to stop buying all California grapes." Many people watch television, so it is a convenient way to inform others of what the grape

> boycott and strikes stood for. *If he hadn't spoken on television, the boycott and the strikes wouldn't have gained a lot of publicity. Without publicity, it would have been harder to raise public awareness of the low pay and mediocre work environments that the farmers experienced.*

In this passage, counterfactual reasoning is expressed through *conditionals* that explain how things might have turned out in the absence of specific actions taken by the historical actor.

A common form of counterfactual conditionals is the use of an *if-clause* that presents a plausible alternative condition (*if he hadn't spoken on television*), which is added to the main clause that presents the potential alternative outcome (*the boycott and strikes wouldn't have gained a lot of publicity*). The counterfactual conditional is syntactically complex—it combines clauses and uses a complex verb tense system (*wouldn't have gained*). Like other dependent clauses, the *if-clause* can be placed either before or after the main clause. The following examples illustrate the sentence-initial and sentence-final positions of the *if-clause*. The complex verb systems are underlined.

- <u>Example 1</u>: The boycott and the strikes <u>wouldn't have gained</u> a lot of publicity *if Chavez <u>hadn't spoken</u> on television.*
- <u>Example 2</u>: *If Clark and Lewis <u>refused</u> help from the Native Americans or <u>were</u> hostile towards them*, many members of the team <u>would not have returned</u> safely from the expedition.

Other language resources used to present counterfactual reasoning include prepositions (*without*) and prepositional phrases (*in case; in the absence of*). The following examples highlight these language features:

- <u>Example 3</u>: Although the actions and tactics of the NWP were important, *there <u>would have been</u> no political action <u>without</u> the advocacy of early suffragists like Susan B. Anthony.*
- <u>Example 4</u>: The state level efforts of the NAWSA slowly changed opinions across the country eventually leading to the passage of the 19th Amendment. *<u>In the absence of</u> these state level victories, <u>not</u> enough states <u>would have ratified</u> the amendment in 1920.*

Making explicit these language resources used to express counterfactuals will help students explore alternative conditions and potential consequences—an essential reasoning move in argument development.

How is language used to corroborate evidence from multiple sources?

Corroboration is a historical thinking skill necessary to construct credible interpretations of historical events. Evidence comes from multiple sources that may provide similar or different accounts of the past. Thus, sources need to be compared and evidence needs to be verified. Corroboration involves weighing evidence by considering how sources confirm and challenge a historical interpretation. In argument writing, corroborating evidence is done through languaging practices that compare sources and determine points of agreement and disagreement. To show how a student uses corroboration, we revisit the excerpt we presented earlier (italics added). As you read the passage, pay attention to the specific language resources used to corroborate.

> Because there was still work to do, the National Women's Party staged a number of public demonstrations to pressure the President and others in Congress to change their stances on suffrage. The protests by the NWP are *documented in the 1918 NY Times article and 1974 interview with Alice Paul.* These protests, including picketing and hunger strikes, applied pressure needed for the movement to progress. Alice Paul, a leader of these demonstrations and the NWP, underscores the progress of the movement by noting, "President Wilson made a magnificent speech calling for the amendment as a war measure." In fact, this speech came after these protests. Without action on a national stage in the form of pickets, protests, and the accompanying press, the President would not have appealed to the Congress calling for the passage of the amendment and the Congress may not have ever passed the 19th amendment. *The National Parks Service article also confirms the impact of the NWP's picketing on the President and Congress' changing perspective on women's suffrage.*

The two italicized sentences in the excerpt verify the evidence across multiple sources to strengthen the argument. Corroboration draws on compare-contrast language resources that (1) express agreements or consistencies across sources and (2) express disagreements or discrepancies between sources.

Expressing Agreements or Consistencies across Sources. Experienced writers use a combination of language resources to express agreements and consistencies across sources. These language resources include connectors used for comparison (e.g., *similarly*; *in addition*), linking words and phrases that connect two sources (e.g., *both . . . and; neither . . . nor*), and verbs that signal agreement (e.g., *acknowledge, confirm*). Table 5.8 summarizes language resources commonly used to corroborate sources for agreements and consistencies.

In argument writing, these language resources are commonly used with source names to compare and verify information in two or more sources (e.g., *both the NY Times article and the interview with Alice Paul*). For example, verbs of agreement can be used with the source's author, title, genre, or a combination of these to attribute evidence to specific sources. Connectors that signal comparison often indicate a reference to another source (e.g., *also, similar to, as well*). In short, corroborating evidence across multiple sources requires language resources to explain how and where sources agree and what evidence is consistent across multiple sources. Highlighting these language resources can be beneficial as it helps build corroboration skills.

Expressing Disagreements/Discrepancies between Sources. Sources do not always agree, and expressing the discrepancies between sources draws

Table 5.8. Language Resources for Expressing Agreements across Sources

Language	Resources	Examples
Sentence connectors used to contrast sources	*additionally, all, also, in addition to, likewise, similarly, similar to*	• *In addition to the Sacagawea biography, the Lewis and Clark Timeline* acknowledges the help of Native Americans. • *Similar to Bayard Rustin, Jo Ann Robinson* affirms the determination of the community members in Montgomery in her memoir.
Clause-linking phrases used to connect two or more sources (examples of correlative conjunctions)	*both . . . and . . . not only . . . but also . . . neither . . . nor . . . either . . . or . . .*	• Labor shortage caused by a large number of deaths was mentioned *both in the Timeline of the Decline of Feudalism and the summary of the Hundred Years' War.* • *Neither the Women's Suffrage overview nor the NY Times article* indicates that Susan B. Anthony's speech was effective in moving public opinion or producing legislation to the 19th amendment.
Verbs that signal agreements	*acknowledge, affirm, confirm, corroborate, support, verify*	• *The Lewis and Clark Timeline and Sacagawea Biography confirm each other as they both acknowledge* the help of Native Americans. • *The National Parks Service article also confirms* the impact of the NWP's picketing on the President and Congress' changing perspective on women's suffrage.

on language resources that encapsulate adversativity, contrast, and disagreement. These language resources include clause connectors or conjunctions with contrastive meanings (e.g., *but, although, even though*), sentence connectors that signal a change in direction (e.g., *however, in contrast*), and verbs that express disagreement (e.g., *contradict, refute*). Table 5.9 summarizes language resources commonly used to corroborate sources for disagreements and discrepancies.

Clause-linking devices that present discrepancies between accounts make it explicit that what is said in the main clause is *contrary* to what is said in the dependent clauses. Clause connectors or conjunctions convey "Yes, but . . ." meaning where the writer acknowledges "the truth of one proposition while asserting the truth of another proposition in such a way as to make the first proposition seem of lesser importance" (Celce-Murcia & Larsen-Freeman, 1999, p. 529). Verbs of disagreement, on the other hand, show how a source disagrees with another source (e.g., *contradicts, denies, refutes*). Similar to verbs that indicate agreements, these verbs can be used with the source's title, author, and genre in corroboration statements. Knowing these different ways of expressing disagreement between sources allows students to make strategic language choices to accomplish the rhetorical purposes and goals of their writing.

Table 5.9. Language Resources for Expressing Disagreements between Sources

Language	Resources	Examples
Sentence connectors used to compare sources	*alternatively* *conversely* *however* *in contrast* *on the contrary* *on the other hand*	• *The British Lieutenant John Barker's diary* states that American colonists "fired one or two shots." *In contrast, the testimony given by Nathaniel Mulliken and Philip Russel*, two of the 34 American colonial soldiers, refutes this account.
Clause connectors used to express contrast and adversativity	*although, but, even though, whereas, while*	• *Whereas the British Lieutenant John Barker's diary* states that American colonists "fired one or two shots," *the testimony given by Nathaniel Mulliken and Philip Russel*, two of the 34 American colonial soldiers, refutes this account.
Verbs that signal disagreements	*contradict, counter, deny, disagree, refute, reject*	• *The testimony given by the two American colonial soldiers refutes the British Lieutenant John Barker's account* of what happened.

How is language used to interpret and comment on evidence?

Another essential type of reasoning in argument writing involves *interpreting* evidence and explaining how the evidence supports the claim. In this section, we discuss the language resources used to interpret evidence, explaining its relevance and significance. To illustrate how this is executed in argument writing, we examine an excerpt about the passage of the Nineteenth Amendment. Notice how the writer uses language to interpret the evidence (italics added).

> In her interview with Richard Gallagher, Alice Paul comments, "I always feel the movement is sort of a mosaic. Each of us puts in one little stone, and then you get a great mosaic in the end." *What Paul is suggesting here is that no one person is responsible for accomplishing the goal of passing the 19th Amendment. Rather, each person contributes a "stone" to build a movement that succeeds. As someone who was close to the movement, part of the NAWSA and NWP* she can attest to the collective effort of individuals and organizations coming together for a common cause.

In this excerpt, the writer interprets the evidence (*what Paul is suggesting here*) and then connects it to the main claim about the collective effort of individuals and organizations as instrumental in the passage of the Nineteenth Amendment. Signal verbs such as *suggest* and *attest to* are employed when interpreting evidence. In what follows, we discuss the language resources used for interpreting evidence and ascribing significance.

Interpreting evidence. Interpreting evidence in argument writing often focuses on what the evidence shows and how it supports the claim. Language resources include the use of commenting verbs (e.g., *suggest, imply, indicate*) and other linking expressions (e.g., *in other words, to put it another way . . .*) as seen in the following examples:

- Jo Ann Robinson, a credible author, who lived through these times states that "every Black man, woman, and child in Montgomery knew the plan and was passing the word along" (p. 5). *This statement <u>illustrates</u> how the black community interacted with each other and <u>highlights</u> the importance of teamwork and cooperation during this time.*
- In the article, Dr. Howard Anna Shaw claims, "Suffrage is no longer a local question because the National House of Representatives has

discussed suffrage." *As demonstrated in this quotation, the movement made progress towards national attention, progress that had not yet been seen since the Seneca Fall Convention 60 years ago.*

- The 1923 book describes how bootleggers and distillers escaped the notice of local police and states, "Smuggling from Mexico and Canada has been successful on a large scale because it is impossible to patrol the thousands of miles of border." *This suggests that the enforcement of prohibition was ineffective and that people were already aware of this situation in 1923.*

The italicized sentences comment on and interpret the evidence, linking it to the claims and reinforcing the main argument.

Ascribing Significance. In some cases, writers present reasoning for why particular evidence is used in support of a claim by explicitly explaining the significance of the evidence. In the following excerpt, the italicized reasoning illustrates a more explicit explanation of why the evidence is important.

> The march to Sacramento was another reason the boycott and strike succeeded because it raised awareness about the unfair treatment that the farm workers endured. In an interview with Roberto Bustos, a participant of the boycott and strike, he stated that, "We stopped at 53 towns and explained why we were marching." *This statement is important as it reveals how the march raised awareness of low pay and poor working conditions.*

Ascribing significance to evidence is often conveyed through the use of adjectives that express value judgments (e.g., *consequential, important, significant*) and causal connectors (e.g., *as, because, since*). Typically, when indicating the significance of evidence, elaboration follows to provide a reason for why it is deemed important. For instructional purposes, we summarize common language resources used to interpret evidence and ascribe significance in Table. 5.10.

Students who have expansive language resources and are familiar with those used to present reasoning are able to develop their arguments by making strategic language choices to achieve their rhetorical goals. Thus, it is important for teachers to provide guidance and scaffolding to build language skills for reasoning. In the following section, we provide instructional guidance to build students' language skills and knowledge for presenting reasoning.

Table 5.10. Language Resources for Interpreting Evidence

Language	Resources	Examples
Commenting verbs	*demonstrate, emphasize, highlight, illustrate, imply, indicate, offer, reveal, specify, stress, suggest*	• *This implies* the labor shortage and the demand to be paid better led to a change in feudalism. • *The evidence suggests that* the congressional amendments failed multiple times and these failures occurred years after Susan B. Anthony's speeches, *indicating* her speeches were not pivotal to the passage of the 19th amendment.
Linking phrases	*as it implies, as shown in, in essence, in other words, it is clear that*	• *It is clear that* enforcing prohibition nationally proved ineffective and this led to its failure. • *As shown in the sworn testimony* of the two American colonial soldiers, the militia wasn't the one that started shooting.
Adjectives of significance	*consequential, critical, crucial, essential, important, key, pivotal, valuable, vital*	• Gandhi's letter to Lord Irwin is *consequential* because it lays out the reasons for civil disobedience and grievances against the British. • This evidence is *significant* for revealing the government's own admission of corruption as a result of prohibition.

III. Cultivating Language Skills for Presenting Reasoning

How can teachers cultivate language skills for expressing reasoning?

You can support students to expand their language resources for reasoning through explicit instruction that helps them notice how language is used for rhetorical purposes and effects. To guide you in this effort, we provide instructional resources and activities that you can easily modify to meet your students' linguistic needs for argument writing. We begin with instructional strategies and activities designed to cultivate language skills for presenting reasoning. We then focus on building students' metalinguistic knowledge and awareness. We end this chapter by providing guidance on how you can differentiate instruction based on your students' needs.

Teaching Move 1: Integrating reading and writing to analyze an exemplar text

Instruction can start with helping students notice and examine language choices in exemplar texts. This strategy involves combining close reading of a model text with writing about key language features of the text. According to Steve Graham et al. (2016), this evidence-based practice familiarizes students with salient features of an exemplar text so they can emulate these features in their writing. It is important to select a text that is contextualized within the learning content and shows a variety of linguistic choices. You can choose an effective piece of student writing, or you can write your own model text. To engage students in close reading of the exemplar text, you can use cognitive strategies such as *analyzing the author's craft*, *asking questions*, and *evaluating* to scaffold their reading (Olson et al., 2023). The cognitive strategies approach is found to be effective in improving students' argument writing in multiple disciplines, including their reasoning and language skills (Olson et al., 2023). You can then have students annotate the text highlighting the language used for reasoning. Students can rewrite sections of text in their own words. Consider using the following sequence to scaffold instruction:

- Read: Choose an exemplar text that is contextualized within learning content and shows a variety of language resources used for various reasoning moves.
- Annotate: Engage students in close reading using cognitive strategies of analyzing author's craft, asking questions, and clarifying.
- Write: Provide options to write about the text, to rewrite the text in their own words, or to emulate the reasoning presented in the text.

The instructional scaffolding using cognitive strategies to closely read, analyze, and annotate a mentor text is shown in Table 5.11.

Table 5.11. Using Cognitive Strategies for Close Reading

Exemplar Text	**Cognitive Strategies**
The Volstead Act was passed by the U.S. Congress in 1919, leading to the criminalization of the buying and selling of alcohol. Such a law was created to decrease the presence of alcoholic beverages in U.S. society which many saw as a problem. After 15 years though, Prohibition failed, and the law was repealed by the 21st Amendment. Although some may see the failure of Prohibition as due to a loss of tax revenue, the main reason it failed was the difficulty in enforcing Prohibition. Following the passage of the Volstead Act, enforcing the law was difficult, which weakened its resolve and power. For example, an excerpt from the 1923 book by Haskin, describes the ineffectiveness of enforcing prohibition nationally.	**Analyze author's craft:** • The author uses . . . language in order to . . . • Words and phrases used to present reasoning are . . . **Ask questions:** • I wonder why they used this language . . . **Evaluate:** • The language use is effective/ineffective because . . .

Activity 1: Read and Annotate

This activity engages students in close reading of an exemplar text, annotating reasoning moves and commenting on language choices. Students use cognitive strategies to guide their annotations.

After students closely read the exemplar text using cognitive strategies, they can then write a paragraph summarizing, analyzing, and forming interpretations of the text and its language features. Students can use the cognitive strategies sentence starters provided in the cognitive strategies column in Table 5.11 for their writing. Students can also rewrite the paragraph in their own words. You can provide them with a writing template with sentence starters. The template is particularly beneficial for students who need support to get started.

Activity 2: Write with Sentence Stems

You can start this activity by asking students to review the sentence stems. You can then prompt students to notice how reasoning is presented in the sample passage. Students then write a paragraph summarizing, analyzing, and evaluating the text using the following sentence stems:

The main idea of this excerpt is/This excerpt talks about____________.
The writer argues that ____________________. To present their reasoning, the writer used ____________________. For example, the phrase _________________ helped me understand ____________________. The writer also uses ______________ language in order to __________________.
The use of language is effective/ineffective because ________________________________.

While this writing practice fosters analytical skills and language awareness, you can also have students practice paraphrasing. This allows students to leverage their existing linguistic resources to rewrite the text.

Activity 3: Rewriting the Text

As an alternative writing practice, students rewrite the text in their own words and then evaluate their own language choices.

Table 5.12. Rewriting the Text

<table>
<tr><td colspan="2">Writing Practice: Rewrite the text in your own words</td></tr>
<tr><td colspan="2">Rewrite the text in your own words, using precise language to present the reasoning clearly.</td></tr>
<tr><td>Language choices made in the original excerpt to present reasoning:</td><td>Language choices to present reasoning in my rewrite:</td></tr>
<tr><td>•
•
•</td><td>•
•
•</td></tr>
</table>

To build metalinguistic awareness, students can work in groups or pairs to share their rewrites, evaluate their language use, and provide feedback to each other. They can compare their versions with the original exemplar text, highlighting the differences in language choices made to present reasoning.

The construction of complex noun phrases is an essential languaging practice used for naming causes and consequences. A deconstruct-to-construct approach shows how key nouns are used and specified with modifiers to more clearly link causes, consequences, and change. You can use Table 5.2 from the previous section that deconstructs complex noun phrases into head nouns and modifiers that come before or after the nouns. You can also use examples of complex noun phrases from the passage students read and analyzed. We show this in the following examples from the passage about Prohibition, in which the head noun is underlined and the modifying words and phrases are italicized.

NOUN PHRASE 1: *the* criminalization *of buying and selling of alcohol*
NOUN PHRASE 2: *the ineffective* enforcement *of prohibition at a national level*
NOUN PHRASE 3: *the sworn* testimony *of U.S. representative in congress*

You can highlight how some of these noun phrases use nominalization, providing a few examples from the exemplar text before asking students to add more examples of nominalization they might use to talk about causes and consequences.

Activity 3: Sentence Transformation

The sentence transformation activity scaffolds the construction of complex noun phrases, turning an action into an abstract thing. This activity can be introduced before students rewrite a model paragraph.

Table 5.13. Nominalization

Nominalization of Adjectives	**Nominalization of Verbs**	**Nominalization of Clauses**
difficult → difficulty ineffective → effectiveness present → presence	criminalize → criminalization enforce → enforcement pass → passage	Prohibition failed. ↓ The failure of Prohibition
Provide three more examples of nominalization under each of the three categories		

Table 5.14. Sentence Transformation Activity

Clause (simple sentence)	**Phrase (complex noun phrase)**
The U.S. Congress passed the Volstead Act in 1919.	• the Volstead Act passed by the U.S. congress in 1919
The Volstead Act passed.	• the passage of the Volstead Act
The buying and selling of alcohol were criminalized.	• the criminalization of the buying and selling of alcohol
Alcoholic beverages were present in U.S. society.	• the presence of alcoholic beverages in U.S. society
The prohibition failed.	• the failure of prohibition
The Government lost tax revenue.	• the loss of tax revenue
It was difficult to enforce Prohibition.	• the difficulty of enforcing prohibition
Enforcing prohibition nationally proved ineffective.	• the ineffectiveness of enforcing prohibition nationally

When engaging students in the sentence transformation activity, you can incorporate language instruction focusing on two important language features for naming: nominalization and construction of a complex noun phrase.

Teaching Move 2: Constructing and deconstructing complex noun phrases

You can show and teach various ways of building causal connections using model/example sentences. After showing various ways of expressing causal relationships between ideas using model sentences, you can engage students in close reading of a model paragraph. The move from sentence to paragraph is crucial because students need to see how writers construct causality in various ways to build arguments. First, you can present students with a chart that

Table 5.15. Building Causal Connections

Language	Resources	Examples
Clause connectors (combine clauses establishing causal links)	*as, because, given that, since, so, so that*	• Some might say that Gandhi was successful with his Salt March *because* the British opened up negotiations in an attempt to avoid more violent protests. • *Since* the harsh response from the British was shown on the world stage, the nonviolent resistance led by Gandhi gained worldwide attention.
Sentence connectors (signal causal links between sentences)	*as a result, consequently, hence, thereby, therefore, thus*	• Thousands of supporters joined the peaceful march as Gandhi stopped at villages along the way to speak. *Consequently*, a miles-long procession was formed. • Gandhi's commitment to nonviolent resistance mobilized significant support. The protest, *therefore*, was successful in uniting Indians against British rule.
Prepositions and prepositional phrases (build causal links to nouns and noun phrases)	*as a result of, because of, due to, thanks to, through*	• *Through* march to Sacramento and the use of media, the Delano Grape strike succeeded, giving farm workers better wages and suitable working conditions. • The United Farm Workers Union was created *as a result of* a series of strikes led by civil rights advocates such as Cesar Chavez, Dolores Huerta, and Larry Itliong.
Causal verbs (establish causal links between ideas, concepts, events, actors)	*cause, contribute to, give rise to, lead to, result in, stem from*	• The Black Death Plague *contributed to* the decline of feudalism. • Both sources suggest that the labor shortage *was caused* by a large number of deaths. • The Black Death killed about one-third of the population in Europe, *resulting in* labor shortage in the region.

summarizes language resources with example sentences. We model this in Table 5.15 using examples on various kinds of historical topics, but you might modify these based on the topics from your class.

Teaching Move 3: Teach various ways of building causal connections using models

Activity 4: Analyzing a Text for Causal Reasoning

After presenting students with various ways of expressing causality using the chart, you can engage them in reading and annotating a model text for causal links. We show how this can be done using the same passage about Prohibition.

Table 5.16. Analyzing a Text for Causal Reasoning

Model Paragraph	Annotate
The Volstead Act was passed by the U.S. Congress in 1919, **leading to** the criminalization of the buying and selling of alcohol. Such a law was **created to decrease** the presence of alcoholic beverages in U.S. society which many saw as a problem. After 15 years though, Prohibition failed, and the law was repealed by the 21st Amendment. Although some may see the failure of Prohibition as **due to** a loss of tax revenue, **the main reason** it failed was the difficulty in enforcing Prohibition. Following the passage of the Volstead Act, enforcing the law was difficult, which **weakened** its resolve and power. For example, an excerpt from the 1923 book by Haskin, describes the ineffectiveness of enforcing prohibition nationally.	• Causal verb explains the effect of the Act • Causal verbs explain why the law was created • Prepositional phrase explains why it failed • Noun phrase states the reason • Causal verb explains negative effect or change

Activity 5: "Beyond Because" Sentence Combining

Most students are familiar with and use connectors like *because* and *so* to build causal connections between ideas. This activity can move students beyond the use of *because* and *so* to show how causal links are built in different ways. The sentence combining activity is an opportunity to practice using various language resources. You can first model using a think-aloud strategy and then have students combine two simple sentences on their own or in groups.

SENTENCES TO COMBINE: *It was difficult to enforce Prohibition at a national level. Prohibition failed.*

COMBINED VERSION 1: *It was difficult to enforce Prohibition at a national level, so it failed.*

COMBINED VERSION 2: *Prohibition failed because it was difficult to enforce it at a national level.*

COMBINED VERSION 3: *The main reason Prohibition failed was the difficulty of enforcing the law at a national level.*

COMBINED VERSION 4: *Prohibition failed due to the difficulty of enforcing it at a national level.*

COMBINED VERSION 5: *The difficulty of enforcing Prohibition at a national level led to its eventual failure.*

COMBINED VERSION 6: *Enforcing Prohibition at a national level proved difficult, and as a result, Prohibition eventually failed.*

This activity can scaffold students' use of a variety of language resources. You can ask students to work in groups and combine sentences in several different ways. Each group can then share their combined sentences with other groups or with the whole class.

Teaching Move 4: Practice counterfactual reasoning through dialogic interactions

To help students practice presenting counterfactual reasoning, you can engage them in a "Think-Write-Pair-Share" (TWPS) activity, which promotes both individual and collaborative learning. It provides students with (1) time and structure for thinking about possible alternatives, counterfactuals, or "what if" scenarios, and (2) opportunities to engage in dialogic interactions, sharing their counterfactual reasoning with others. It is important to guide students through each step. You can develop questions/prompts or model creating "what if" alternatives to provide additional scaffolding.

Activity 6: Think, Write, Pair, Share

- THINK: Students imagine a "what if" scenario related to the historical event/s.
  What would have happened if Cesar Chavez hadn't used the media to publicize the boycott?
- WRITE: Students write responses explaining the alternative conditions or consequences using counterfactual reasoning. Teachers scaffold students' writing by showing a model and highlighting language resources used to present counterfactual reasoning.
  If he hadn't spoken on television, the boycott and the strikes wouldn't have gained a lot of publicity. Without publicity, it would have been harder to raise public awareness of the low pay and mediocre work environments that the farmers experienced.
- PAIR: Each student is paired with another student to share what they have written. They compare responses, discuss their reasoning, and evaluate the language used to express the reasoning.
- SHARE: Students share their responses in a larger group, highlighting similarities and differences in their responses. Then they present their counterfactual reasoning to a whole class.

Teaching Move 5: Practice corroboration skills using an Inquiry Chart

Using an Inquiry Chart (I-Chart), you can engage students in corroborating evidence across multiple sources and writing corroboration statements. The I-Chart is a post-reading and pre-writing strategy and graphic organizer designed to help students gather information from multiple sources. For effective use of the I-Chart, you need to have students (1) closely read the sources to identify agreements and disagreements; (2) record their answers in the I-Chart; and (3) synthesize and write corroboration statements.

Activity 7: I-Chart for Corroborating Sources

The first step is to identify whether or where multiple sources agree or disagree. To do this, students need to closely read the sources. You can provide an I-Chart with guiding questions and sentence stems.

The next step in this activity is to summarize and synthesize whether the sources agree or disagree and then write a corroboration statement. Using the information gathered in their I-Chart, students practice writing. To scaffold their writing, you can provide them with sentence stems and examples.

- Summary and Synthesis:

  These sources all agree/disagree about ______________________.

  Some sources agree, but others disagree. For example, ____________.

- Corroboration Statement:

  The diary of British Lieutenant John Barker states that the American colonists fired the first shots. However, the sworn testimony of two American colonial soldiers indicates that it was the British soldiers who fired behind their backs.

You can provide language resources commonly used for agreement and disagreement. Table 5.18 can be used for instructional purposes and given to students as a handout.

Teaching Move 6: Practice interpreting evidence with "Staking My Claim"

Table 5.17. I-Chart for Corroborating Sources

Questions	**Source 1**	**Source 2**	**Source 3**
What does the source say about your topic?	*This source states . . .*	*This source states . . .*	*This source states . . .*
Do the sources agree or disagree?	*This source agrees/ disagrees with . . .*	*This source agrees/ disagrees with . . .*	*This source agrees/ disagrees with . . .*
Does the source confirm or refute the evidence?	*This source confirms/ refutes . . .*	*This source confirms/ refutes . . .*	*This source confirms/ refutes . . .*

Table 5.18. Language Resources for Expressing Agreement and Disagreement

	Examples of Corroboration Statements	**Language Resources**
A G R E E	• *Both* the Lewis *and* Clark Timeline and Sacagawea Biography report Native Americans going out their way to help the travelers by providing horses and supplies. • *In addition to* the Sacagawea biography, the Lewis and Clark Timeline acknowledges the help of Native Americans.	**Connectors:** *also, likewise, in addition to, similarly, both . . . and . . .; not only . . ., but also . . .; neither . . . nor . . .* **Verbs:** *affirm, acknowledge, confirm, corroborate, verify*
D I S A G R E E	• *Whereas* the British Lieutenant John Barker's diary states that American colonists "fired one or two shots," the testimony given by Nathaniel Mulliken and Philip Russel, two of the 34 American colonial soldiers, refutes this account. • The testimony given by the two American colonial soldiers *refutes* the British Lieutenant John Barker's account of what happened.	**Connectors:** *although, but, even though, while, whereas, alternatively, however, in contrast, on the contrary, on the other hand* **Verbs:** *contradict, deny, counter, disagree, refute, reject, contradict, oppose, dispute, differ, contrast, challenge*

In argument writing, students need to interpret/comment on evidence and present their reasoning by explaining how the evidence supports their claims. You can provide instructional support to students through an activity called "Staking My Claim." This activity helps students interpret evidence, connect their evidence and claims, and provide reasoning. It can be completed in two stages. First, you provide a sample claim and evidence and leave the "Reasoning" column blank. Then, ask students to provide reasoning by interpreting the evidence and explaining why the evidence is significant and how it supports the

Table 5.19. Staking My Claim Model

Claim	Evidence	Reasoning
Although early suffragists generated interest in the cause of women's suffrage, the actions and tactics of the NWP were most directly responsible for the passage of the 19th amendment because they put crucial pressure on national political figures.	The 1915 NY Times article describes a suffrage amendment being voted on in Congress but being defeated by a "vote of 174 to 204."	While at first this seems negative, it does show progress in changing national lawmakers' opinions on the issue of suffrage in 1915.
	In the article, Dr. Howard Anna Shaw claims, "Suffrage is no longer a local question because the National House of Representatives has discussed suffrage . . ."	This shows that the movement is finally making progress toward a national amendment, progress that had not yet been seen since the Seneca Fall Convention 60 years ago.
	In her interview with Richard Gallagher, Alice Paul comments, "I always feel the movement is sort of a mosaic. Each of us puts in one little stone, and then you get a great mosaic in the end."	What Paul is suggesting here is that no one person is responsible for accomplishing the goal of passing the 19th Amendment. Paul's sentiment acknowledges the contributions of individuals and organizations

claim. To scaffold their writing, you can use Table 5.10 to highlight language resources and provide sentence stems that will help them get started.

<u>Sentence stems for interpreting and commenting on evidence</u>

- This means/suggests/implies that____________________________.
- This quotation demonstrates/implies/indicates that______________.
- This evidence/source is relevant because_________________________.
- This evidence suggests that______ because ____________________.

After students practice writing reasoning statements using a model, they can work on their own writing. For this stage, students create their own "Claim, Evidence, Reasoning" graphic organizer.

How can teachers build metalinguistic knowledge and awareness?

The activities and strategies we offer in the previous section provide students with opportunities to practice their language skills and expand their linguistic repertoires. The instructional strategies integrate teacher modeling, student practice, collaboration, and dialogic interactions. Effective implementation of these activities will help students develop metalinguistic knowledge and awareness. However, students can deepen their understanding of how language is used to meet various rhetorical purposes by engaging in evaluative activities. In this section, we provide several evaluative activities that promote students' metalinguistic awareness.

Activity 8: Evaluating a Paragraph for Reasoning

This activity can promote metalinguistic knowledge and awareness by engaging students in evaluating how language is used to establish causal links between ideas. You can choose or write three different versions of a paragraph on the same topic or historical event. Students read these different versions and evaluate how causal links are established in each version. They rank the paragraphs based on how effectively they establish causal links between ideas and historical events. Then, they explain their reasoning.

Table 5.20. Paragraph Evaluation Activity

Sample Texts	**Ranking**
Rosa Parks was arrested on 1 December 1955, so people boycotted the buses in Montgomery as a protest. The protest involved a large number of people and continued for 13 months. The U.S. Supreme Court ruled that segregation on public buses is unconstitutional	_Beginning _Developing _Advanced
Rosa Parks was arrested on 1 December 1955. This caused people to boycott the buses in Montgomery as a protest. The protest involved a large number of people and continued for 13 months. At the end of the protest, the U.S. The Supreme Court ruled that segregation on public buses is unconstitutional.	_Beginning _Developing _Advanced
Sparked by the arrest of Rosa Parks on 1 December 1955, the Montgomery bus boycott was a 13-month mass protest that ended with the U.S. Supreme Court ruling that segregation on public buses is unconstitutional.	_Beginning _Developing _Advanced
Explain your reasoning: • *What language choices are made to establish causal links in these paragraphs?* • *What language choices are effective and why do you consider them effective?*	
Write your own version:	

Following this activity, students can closely read their drafts and evaluate the language resources they drew on to establish causal links. You can ask students to highlight the causal language (e.g., *causal connectors, prepositional phrases, causal verbs*) and evaluate whether they are making effective choices. Based on their evaluations, students revise their writing to more effectively present their reasoning.

Activity 9: Sentence Variety

Students enhance their writing styles by engaging in activities that help them craft sentences using a variety of structures. To build sentence fluency and stylistic variety, students are provided with a paragraph that consists of simple sentences. They revise the paragraph by combining or expanding sentences, adding variety, creating cohesion, and establishing logical connections between ideas. They are encouraged to make intentional language choices, which promotes metalinguistic awareness.

- <u>A Paragraph to Revise</u>:

    The U.S. Congress passed the Volstead Act. This act criminalized and prohibited the buying and selling of alcohol. The consumption of alcohol was widespread in U.S. society. This was a problem. The law was created to decrease the consumption of alcohol. This act of prohibiting alcohol failed. The law was repealed by the Twenty-first Amendment after fifteen years. Some people think Prohibition failed due to loss of tax revenue. The loss of tax revenue is not the main reason. It was difficult to enforce the law. It was difficult to enforce the law at a national level. And this weakened its resolve and power.

- <u>Revision Guidelines</u>:

    Notice that the paragraph above consists mainly of simple sentences. Revise the paragraph by making connections between sentences, using causal language to explain causes and consequences, presenting reasoning, and creating cohesion.

Activity 10: Evaluating Reasoning

You can engage students in thinking more broadly about ways of presenting reasoning by evaluating how reasoning is presented in sample writing. Students read two sample paragraphs, examining the types of reasoning presented in order to evaluate whether they are effective or ineffective in presenting reasoning. Ask students to analyze language features in each paragraph. You can first present them with the following prompts and checklist to evaluate the sample paragraphs:

- What types of reasoning are presented?

__ Explains causes	__ Explains consequences
__ Presents counterfactuals	__ Connects evidence and claim
__ Contextualizes	__ Explains how the evidence is important
__ Corroborates evidence	__ Interprets evidence

- Does this paragraph present reasoning effectively?

Sample Passage 1

Feudalism was in 771 to 1800 AD. The thing that led to decline of feudalism was when the Magna Carta was written and when all of the people died from the plague. The timeline says King John I (England) signed the Magna Carta, a written document that diminished the king's power and strengthened nobles' rights. It placed limits on the King's power. Under feudalism the King had a lot of power. but then after this he had less power. The Black Death also happened at this time of feudalism and it was terrible because it killed 1/3 of the total population of Europe. There were not a lot of workers. "The laborers were so proud and hostile that they took no notice of the King's law. If anyone wanted to employ laborers, he had to pay them what they asked—or lose his fruit and crops" (Source 4).

Sample Passage 2

Feudalism, a social system in Europe from 771-1800, came to an end because of multiple factors, including the Black Death plague and the Magna Carta which significantly contributed to the deterioration of the system. First of all, the Black Death plague was consequential for the decline of feudalism because it took out a large number of the peasants who were the backbone of feudalism in Europe. According to the Timeline of the Decline of Feudalism, the Black Death killed about one third of the population in Europe, making people afraid to leave their homes and causing the loss of the labor force. Without people working,

> the land crops rotted and people didn't get food. The Black Death had a hard hit on the economy. The historical account of the Black Death by Henry Knighton states, "Lords who had lent land in return for yearly labor service were forced to change these services. They either had to let the serfs off the services, or else accept money instead." This quotation suggests because there were no people to work, those who did stay behind demanded to be paid better. This led to a change in the feudal system.

These activities are designed to help students notice a variety of language resources that are used to present reasoning. For example, they can notice how nominalization and abstraction are essential in explaining causes and consequences, and how contextualization, corroboration, and counterfactual reasoning are expressed through complex noun phrases and causal verbs.

Another key practice that helps build language awareness is engaging students in reflection. Students can reflect on their own writing to see whether their language choices are aligned with the rhetorical goals of argument writing. You can provide guiding questions that can be used as prompts for reflective writing or dialogic interactions.

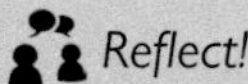

- What language choices did you make to present reasoning?
- How effective are your language choices given the rhetorical goals?
- How would you modify your language to effectively present reasoning?

The pedagogical strategies and activities we suggest closely align with the following WIDA standards for English Language Development (ELD) for Social Studies (WIDA, 2020):

ELD-SS.6-8.Explain.Interpretive and ELD-SS.9-12.
Explain.Interpretive

Interpret social studies explanations by

- Evaluating experts' points of agreement, along with strengths and weaknesses of explanations

- Evaluating experts' points of agreement and disagreement based on their consistency with explanation given its purpose

ELD-SS.6-8.Explain.Expressive & ELD-SS.9-12.Explain.Expressive

Construct social studies explanations that

- Introduce and contextualize phenomena or events
- Establish perspectives for communicating outcomes, consequences, or documentation
- Develop reasoning, sequences with linear and nonlinear relationships, evidence, and details, acknowledging strengths and weaknesses
- Generalize multiple causes and effects of developments or events
- Generalize experts' points of agreement and disagreement about multiple, complex causes and effects of development or events

ELD-SS.6-8.Argue.Expressive & ELD-SS.9-12.Argue.Expressive

Construct social studies arguments that

- Introduce and contextualize topic
- Show relationships between claim and counterclaims, differences in perspectives, and evidence and reasoning

What should teachers consider for effective instruction?

Building students' reasoning is a challenging yet attainable goal for teachers working with diverse learners. Many students may still present writing as "knowledge telling" (Bereiter & Scardamalia, 1987). This could be due to viewing the task as retelling—as opposed to an interpretative argument—and a lack of analytical thinking around source materials. Further, due to the "unnaturalness" of historical thinking, many students will not engage in corroboration and contextualization without explicit instruction first, regardless of their current language skills (Wineburg, 2001). Therefore, teachers play a key role in modeling and guiding students to reason with multiple sources and to interpret them using disciplinary thinking.

We argue that students across all grade levels can develop skills in reasoning and present these in writing. Yet, these aspects of writing are generally slower to develop than students' abilities to integrate evidence or articulate claims. Given this, we suggest moving through the following three "stages" when providing targeted instruction to students: *commenting* on evidence, *interpreting* evidence using historical thinking, and *synthesizing* evidence across sources. Each one of these stages represents students gradually moving from knowledge telling to knowledge transformation and increasingly engaging in disciplinary thinking.

Commenting on evidence. Many students will comment on evidence by simply restating or summarizing it. These students need a push to *interpret* evidence or *justify* why evidence supports their claims. This might involve describing the purpose of argument writing more clearly: to present and justify a claim and not to merely summarize what happened. As mentioned earlier in this chapter, a shift toward classroom discourse where students advance and defend their thinking with peers is one way to help students build an understanding of argumentation.

One activity that engenders reasoning is "Ranking the Evidence." With a collection of student samples or teacher-curated evidence, have students rank the evidence from weakest to strongest in support of a specific claim. As students work together, they have to explain or justify their rankings. The point of the activity is not to correctly rank evidence but to prompt students to *justify* and *explain* their thinking about why specific pieces of evidence support the claim. After this activity, students can practice providing reasoning for a specific piece of evidence in writing.

When giving individual feedback to students who are mostly commenting on evidence, you can ask questions such as: *What does this evidence show?* and *How or why does this evidence support your main claim?* When revising writing or transitioning from a discourse-centric activity like ranking evidence, some of the language moves described in this chapter will be helpful to students. For example, you can ask students to revise their writing to include more reasoning and provide them with language resources presented in Table 5.10.

Interpreting evidence using historical thinking. If students are already using interpretive language to reason with evidence, helping them develop more disciplinary thinking is a reasonable next step. Contextualization is a key aspect of historical reasoning you can emphasize with discourse-centric activities and language support. For example, you can encourage students to consider the following historical reasoning moves when "countering" someone else's claim:

- Compare *contributions*: Why is one person/event more influential than another?

- Think about the *order* of events: Were early factors more important than things that occurred later or closer to the moment of change?
- Think about *context* for each cause: Did the context or conditions make one cause more or less influential?

After discussing how students integrated knowledge about context in their reasoning, you can have students write a paragraph countering their peer's claim. You can provide language resources for building causal links presented in Table 5.15.

Synthesizing evidence across sources. Students who are consistently displaying reasoning can likely still improve in corroboration, a relatively complex skill compared to other aspects of reasoning (Steiss et al., 2024). One way to help students move toward corroboration is by asking them to construct an intertextual model (Rouet et al., 2017). This means mapping where sources agree and disagree using a graphic organizer. You can also help students identify evidence from specific sources that support each potential response to the historical question. Then, students can intentionally practice corroboration. You can provide students with language resources used for corroboration, as well as example sentences to scaffold this process.

Overall, we see revision as an ideal place to intentionally practice key reasoning and language use. We acknowledge that reasoning is a complex skill, and much of the instruction that fosters critical thinking skills for historical reasoning needs to start *before* students start writing. Through instruction and scaffolding, you can help students develop reasoning for historical argumentation and express their reasoning clearly and effectively. Regardless of students' proficiency in argument writing, any student can improve their writing. This chapter offers ways to present reasoning to advance a historical argument.

CHAPTER 6

Presenting and Addressing Counterarguments

Guiding Questions

- What is the role of a counterargument in historical argumentation?
- How is language used to present and address a counterargument?
- How can teachers help students build language skills for countering?

In a tenth-grade history class that focuses on the culture, geography, and history of the modern world, students engage in a lively discussion about the Salt March as part of a source-based inquiry unit. The essential question that guides the inquiry is: *To what extent was the Salt March successful in bringing Indians together against British rule?* This is not an easy question to answer as students try to make sense of this geographically and temporally distant event. To write an argument in response to this essential question, students read multiple primary and secondary sources to learn what happened, analyze various factors that contributed to the success of the march, and form their own interpretations based on evidence.

Importantly, students must consider alternative interpretations and other perspectives, which will help them refine their own thinking and strengthen their arguments. The following excerpt from a tenth-grade student's essay shows how they strengthen their argument by addressing a counterargument. As you read the passage, notice how language is used to present and address a counterargument (italics added):

> The success of the Salt March was not predetermined. The ideas of non-violence taught by Gandhi were always met with violence from the British. *Some might say that Gandhi was successful with his Salt March*

because the British opened up negotiations in an attempt to avoid more violent protests. However, this claim misses the fact that Gandhi and his followers had been practicing their civil disobedience peacefully for many years before the Salt March and had always been met with violence. With the Salt March, non-violent resistance was ultimately successful because of the harsh response from the British being shown on the world stage, which led to negotiations on reforming the salt laws.

In this excerpt, the student presents a counterargument (*Some might say that . . .*), addresses it through rebuttal (*However, this claim misses . . .*), and reinforces their original claim (*With the Salt March, . . .*). The student recognizes that there is not one but many answers to historical questions and that multiple factors contribute to the success of an event like the Salt March. Thinking about how others might have different interpretations and how they might see things differently also helped this student strengthen their argument through more elaborative reasoning.

Although presenting and addressing a counterargument is not routine for secondary writing in history, students across all grade levels can incorporate counterarguments when provided with explicit instruction, clear guidance, and opportunities to practice. This chapter provides guidance and resources to support teachers in helping their students consider multiple perspectives, present alternative claims, and respond to them to strengthen their arguments. Countering is a key disciplinary practice in history and an essential rhetorical component for developing argumentation. The goal of the chapter is not only to foster an understanding of the role of counterarguments in historical argumentation but also to make visible the languaging practices used for integrating counterarguments in argument writing. The chapter is organized around three main sections outlined below:

I. **Conceptual Overview:** The Role of Counterargument in Historical Argumentation
  - Why do historians counter and challenge alternative perspectives?
  - How do beginners and experts differ in addressing counterarguments?

II. **Language Focus:** Languaging Practices for Presenting a Counterargument
  - How is language used to present a counterargument?
  - How is language used to respond to and refute a counterargument?

III. **Instructional Support:** Cultivating Language Skills for Countering
   - How can teachers cultivate language skills for countering?
   - How can teachers build metalinguistic knowledge and awareness?
   - What should teachers consider for effective instruction?

I. The Role of Counterargument in Historical Argumentation

Why do historians counter and challenge alternative perspectives?

To understand the foundational role of counterarguments, claims that oppose the main claim of an argument, we return to our chapter on making a claim (chapter 3), where we first explained why historians make claims. Phrased most succinctly, historians make evidence-based interpretations about the past (De La Paz et al., 2017). In substantiating claims, historians eventually enter into *dialogue* with other historians to voice their interpretive claims (Nokes, 2017). This means arguments are dialogic (Erduran, 2007).

Viewing argumentation as *dialogic* means one's argument is always in conversation with those of others in a discourse community. Whether you are in a heated conversation with your friend about the role of charismatic leaders in the Delano Grape Strike and Boycott or you are writing an interpretation in class, your claims are liable to be challenged because that is part of what doing history entails.

Chauncey Monte-Sano and Amina Allen (2019) make a simple but illustrative point when they note that a one-sided (historical) argument is not an argument at all—it is an explanation. They also note that a failure to see historical arguments as two-sided and dialogic can result in students writing summaries instead of interpretive accounts. Thus, whether in writing or in conversation, recognizing an argument as dialogic is crucial to historical understanding, good writing, and developed reasoning.

Deanna Kuhn (2019) notes that the process of making one's thinking and reasoning public (e.g., in writing) can be considered dialogic argumentation by its very nature. Including counterarguments in writing then can encourage students to be more dialogic when composing and allows them to participate in disciplinary discourse. When students address counterarguments, they enter an ongoing disciplinary conversation, an existing network of claims and counterclaims about a particular topic as they acknowledge, build upon, or challenge the ideas of others.

Finally, representing counterarguments not only positions students as disciplinary discourse participants but is also *practically* important in history. Because historical writing constructs meaning from facts with no clear answers, disciplinary norms require writers to position their interpretations of events as tentative, unconfirmed, and liable to be disproved with countervailing evidence (Breakstone et al., 2013; Wineburg, 1991). In order to develop interpretations of the past, historians are expected to alter their claims to account for available evidence. Rather than ignoring contradictory evidence, historians reconsider or revise their claims (Monte-Sano, 2010). Therefore, acknowledging the validity of counterclaims is a crucial part of source-based arguments in history that writing instruction must address (Nokes & De La Paz, 2023). It is also a central disciplinary practice of history that allows us to get closer to the most plausible and accurate interpretation of the past (Monte-Sano & Allen, 2019).

Activities featuring listening, considering alternative viewpoints, weighing competing evidence, and drawing conclusions offer opportunities for teachers to position students as authentic disciplinary participants in a community that values understanding and diverse perspectives. While students craft evidence-based arguments in conversation with their peers, they develop an understanding that their interpretations are part of a larger conversation. Students also learn that knowledge production requires conversation, consensus, and countering as we collectively strive to make sense of our world. In argument writing, counterarguments may seem like an add-on to an essay, but they are fundamental to the meaning-making practices of historians as they seek a true understanding of the past.

How do beginners and experts differ in addressing counterarguments?

Presenting and addressing counterarguments in written discourse may be difficult for students due to their views of how knowledge is constructed in history. As discussed earlier, the prevalence of textbook-based instruction may lead students to perceive history as a simple and straightforward collection of facts that one simply memorizes (Bain, 2006; Van Boxtel, & van Drie, 2018). Based on what he observed in his high school classroom, Bob Bain (2006) noted that most students saw history as fixed, selecting one interpretation of the past as true and others as false. In these novice conceptions of history, counterarguments play no role because history is not seen as interpretive.

In contrast to novices, more experienced learners view history as resolving competing interpretations of the past through evidence-based reasoning and dialogue with others (Monte-Sano & Allen, 2019). For these students, addressing other potential interpretations of events through disciplinary reasoning is an essential practice that makes their arguments more effective and better reasoned (Kuhn, 2019). Thus, viewing historical knowledge as constructed through dialogue both requires and *inspires* reasoning and historical thinking. In our work, we find students' abilities to present historical thinking and reasoning in writing to be highly correlated with the inclusion of a counterargument (Steiss et al., 2024). The counterargument often gives the writer a reason to reason.

Sam Wineburg offers a useful metaphor for the importance of multiple perspectives and claims in the process of historical reasoning. In *Historical Thinking and Other Unnatural Acts*, Sam Wineburg (2001) describes the sophisticated process of expert readers and thinkers in history as they synthesize information across texts. He describes an individual's thinking as a meeting in a boardroom with several executives and company leaders. This emphasizes that historical thinking is not directed by a single leader but by an "executive board where members clamor, shout and wrangle over controversial points" (p. 72). This representation is an apt metaphor to share with students who may be new to thinking about the creation of historical knowledge as dialogic, tentative, and, at times, unruly! Emphasizing the need to address counterarguments is one key way students can develop an adaptive view of how knowledge is constructed through dialogue and reasoning with others.

Finally, it is important to note that in this executive board, where members seem opposed, they are actually working together to reach the best conclusion. Thus, students should not present superficial or weak counterarguments only to quickly "take them down." Instead, evidence and reasoning for the opposing interpretations of events should be genuinely and honestly put forth. Again, recognizing counterclaims, other perspectives, or counterarguments is not a mere add-on to an essay; it is fundamental to doing the work of history. Recognizing argumentation as dialogic, we now turn to the language that helps students present and address counterarguments so they can flourish as disciplinary meaning-makers.

II. Languaging Practices for Presenting a Counterargument

Given the important role of counterarguments in the argumentation process, students need to understand how language is used to present and address counterarguments in writing. First, there is no fixed place for a counterargument in argument writing. In fact, where a counterargument is placed and how it is presented and addressed are guided by the overall rhetorical purpose and structure of the writing. Understanding the dynamics of integrating a counterargument for argument development is critical for students to flourish as skilled communicators.

Rhetorically, a counterargument can be presented in several different ways in argument writing. In some instances, an entire argument can be positioned as a counterargument. Some may set up their writing as a counterargument by first articulating a position with evidence and analysis that they are going to directly argue against. The argument is then constructed as a direct response to an alternative interpretation or claim. For example, a student might construct an argument against the claim that Reconstruction had a positive impact on African Americans given the effects of Jim Crow laws in the South. A different student might begin their writing by stating that there is a common belief that the women's suffrage movement successfully granted women the right to vote. Then, they introduce their counterargument that the movement was not successful in 1920 given the persistent disenfranchisement women of color faced.

In other instances, a counterargument can be presented as an acknowledgment of an alternative claim or view that challenges the writer's argument. Students may introduce their main claim first with some hedging language or an embedded counterclaim, as discussed in chapter 3. Then, they reserve space for discussion and refutation of that counterclaim to show why their argument is stronger or more convincing than the alternative. For example, a student might make a claim that the difficulty of enforcing Prohibition was the most important reason for its failure, but they acknowledge that others might challenge the claim by stating that the loss of tax revenue was a more significant factor that contributed to this failure.

Alternatively, writers may present two contrasting interpretations and then advance an argument explaining which of the two interpretations is more plausible based on evidence. In this case, students may introduce both claims in contrast to one another, discussing each, and then evaluating and choosing the most plausible claim. For example, one student structured their writing with the following claim:

> Although one might argue that the most significant reason for the success of this boycott was its publicity/advertising, the most significant reason for its victory was the inspiration and initiative taken from powerful and experienced leaders.

They then write body paragraphs providing evidence and reasoning for each of the perspectives listed in their claim. In a final paragraph, they offer additional evidence for their main claim—that powerful and experienced leaders were the most significant reasons the strike succeeded:

> However, while the use of publicity/advertising was extremely important, the most significant reason the Delano strike succeeded was the initiative and inspiration taken from powerful and experienced leaders. According to an interview with Roberto Bustos, . . .

Because varied rhetorical purposes and structures necessitate varied language choices, a student who has both the language skills and the rhetorical awareness will be able to integrate counterarguments effectively in their writing. Using the following excerpt from a student's essay on the women's suffrage movement, we highlight the language choices made to present and address a counterargument (italics added). As you read the passage, notice how the language presents and addresses a counterargument.

> *Others may argue* that there would have been *no political action without the advocacy of early suffragists* like Susan B. Anthony. Anthony references the Constitution and citizenship rights in her speech given in 1872: "it was we, the people; nor we the white male citizens; nor yet, we the male citizens; but we, the whole people who formed this union." *However, none of the documents indicate her speech was effective in moving public opinion* or producing legislation leading to the 19th amendment. There is actually much evidence her words were ineffective. *The timeline* of the Women's Suffrage movement *notes* that congressional amendments failed multiple times in the 19th and 20th centuries; these failures occurred years after her speeches and writings and years after her death indicating that her speeches were not pivotal to the passage of the 19th Amendment.

In this excerpt, the student first presents a counterargument by stating a potential opposing claim/position with distancing language (e.g., *others may argue that*). Then, they refute the counterclaim using evaluative language (e.g., *none of the documents indicate her speech was effective . . . much evidence her words were ineffective*) that contextualizes and provides evidence to justify the rebuttal. The student also uses a sentence connector (e.g., *however*) to signal the transition from the statement of position to rebuttal. These intentional choices of language make explicit the rhetorical moves (e.g., a statement of counterclaim, concession, refutation) involved in presenting and addressing a counterargument.

Table 6.1. Rhetorical Moves of Presenting and Responding to a Counterargument

Counterargument	Rhetorical Moves	Examples
Present an alternative or opposing position as a counterargument	**State** an alternative viewpoint	Others might argue the loss of government revenue was a big reason prohibition failed.
	Concede and explain its validity	Source 2 indicates that hundreds of millions of government revenue were lost due to prohibition.
Responding to a counterargument	**Refute** and provide rebuttal to the counterargument explaining its weakness/flaw	However, they might not have anticipated that alcohol consumption would continue and that the laws would be so ineffective. Source 2 even shows alcohol consumption increasing during these decades.
	Reinforce one's claim explaining why it is more convincing	Therefore, the ineffective enforcement of laws and corruption are more likely reasons prohibition would fail and politicians would begin to argue to end it.

We organize the languaging practices used for presenting and addressing a counterargument by the rhetorical moves of (1) stating an opposing claim/position; (2) conceding; (3) refuting the counterargument; and (4) reinforcing a claim. We deconstruct a sample counterargument based on the rhetorical moves in Table 6.1. As shown in the example, the writer first presents a counterargument by clearly stating an alternative view and providing a concession that acknowledges its validity. Then, the writer addresses the counterargument by refuting and providing a rebuttal that points out its weaknesses and reinforces their own claim. Deconstructing a counterargument by explicitly identifying the rhetorical moves and describing the language resources used for these moves can help build an understanding of how language functions in context.

In the following sections, we discuss the language resources for addressing counterarguments so teachers can build the linguistic knowledge needed to support their students. At the end of the chapter, we provide instructional activities designed to help students develop linguistic awareness for presenting and addressing counterarguments.

How is language used to present a counterargument?

Stating an Alternative Claim. The first step in presenting a counterargument is introducing an alternative position on the topic and stating it as a counterclaim

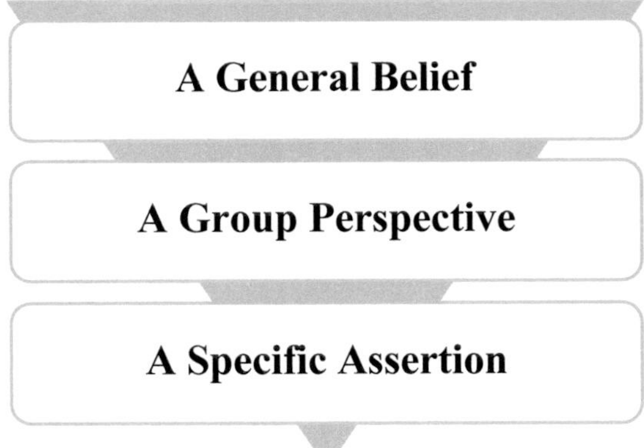

Figure 6. Framing a Perspective

to one's own argument. An alternative interpretation or opposing view can be framed as a general belief without naming a specific source, actor, or group (e.g., *some people might argue*). To do this, students need to consider possible objections to their claim or other reasonable ideas that might challenge their argument. A counterargument can also be framed as the perspective of a certain group with shared values and beliefs (e.g., *the opponents/supporters/critics argue that*). Alternatively, a counterargument can be a specific assertion by a specific author or actor (e.g., *the British officer named Captain Thomas Preston asserted*) in a specific source (e.g., *Captain Thomas Preston's testimony*).

We provide the language resources used for these different ways of framing counterarguments, along with a few examples, in Table 6.2. The examples provided in the table are typical cases of stating a counterargument in argument writing. When deconstructing the sentences that express the statement of counterargument, we see that there are two major components: (1) framing the counterargument using distancing language and (2) the alternative claim to counter. The language resources used for framing counterarguments help writers distance themselves from a potential alternative claim. Such distancing language is an integral part of introducing and presenting a counterargument.

Making a Concession. Once an alternative claim is stated, writers may choose to make a concession that points out some truth and validity of the counterclaim before they refute it. Experienced writers recognize that there are no single, clear-cut answer to complex issues and topics; counterclaims may hold some truth and validity. By acknowledging some validity in counter-arguments, writers show that they have considered a historical issue/topic from multiple perspectives without invalidating their own arguments.

Table 6.2. Language Resources for Framing a Counterargument

Framing	Language Resources	Examples
General Belief	Using generic phrases: *One might argue (that)...* *Others may suggest/say...* *Some might argue/contend/feel...* *One common belief about...is...* *Some people argue/believe/say...* *A common concern about...is...* *It is true that...*	*Some might say that* Gandhi was successful with his Salt March because the British opened up negotiations in an attempt to avoid more violent protests. *It is true that* the team's personal and navigational skills were integral in the success of the Lewis and Clark Expedition.
Group Perspective	Using specific phrases for groups: *The opponents (of...) argue (that)...* *The supporters (of...) believe...* *The advocates (of...) maintain...* *The proponents (of...) claim...* *The critics/naysayers contend...* *The WPC members declared...* *The Federalists opposed...*	*The naysayers might argue that* the Bill of Rights was simply added to appease some states who feared a strong central government. *The supporters of the Montgomery Bus Boycott might suggest that* the reason for the immense achievement is the community coming together.
Specific Assertion	Attributing the counterclaim to a specific author or source: *Captain Thomas Preston asserted...* *The NY Times article suggests...*	*The British officer Captain Thomas Preston asserted that* the colonists' assaults of the British soldiers led to the soldiers' firing into the crowd.

The languaging practices for making a concession can be varied but often indicate some agreement with and/or elaboration on the counterargument. A concession can be a short statement such as *While this might be true.* In some cases, however, more extensive elaboration is given to acknowledge the limited validity of the counterargument and concede that the counterargument gets something right. These various moves are illustrated in the following examples:

- Example 1: *What contributes to the success of the Lewis and Clark Expedition?*

COUNTERCLAIM: It is true that the team's personal and navigational skills were integral in the success of the Lewis and Clark Expedition.

CONCESSION: An account of Lewis's preparation says that the explorer strengthened his exploration skills by studying cartography, botany, animals, medicine, and astronomy, and then enlisted experienced military geographer Clark for his trek. *These skills were definitely important* as they explored new territories with unknown places, plants, and animals. *Without this preparation, they might not have made it* over hundreds of miles.

In Example 1, the student acknowledges the validity of the counterargument by pointing to evidence that indicates the importance of navigational skills, which is the main point of the counterargument. This is to concede that the counterargument "gets this part right." This acknowledgment is explicitly expressed through evaluative language (*These skills were definitely important*) and counterfactual reasoning (*Without this preparation, they might not have made it*). This elaborated concession adds nuance by recognizing the multiple causes and consequences of a historical event. By not refuting the counterargument outright, the writer can later argue that their proposed cause was simply *more* influential.

- Example 2: *What led to the success of the Montgomery Bus Boycott?*

COUNTERCLAIM: The supporters of the Montgomery Bus Boycott might suggest that the reason for the immense achievement is the community coming together.

CONCESSION: *Admittedly, that may be the case* as the boycott *wouldn't have happened without* the collective effort and dedication of the community members.

The concession statement in Example 2 is less elaborated compared to the one in the previous example. Using hedging language (*that may be the case*) and counterfactual reasoning (*the boycott wouldn't have happened without*), the student shows agreement and acknowledges some validity in the counterargument.

The language choices for making a concession are guided by the rhetorical structures of presenting a counterargument. While some rhetorical situations necessitate more elaborate concessions, as in the first example, the concession statements can be short and combined with refutation in other cases. The following sentence stems indicate language resources commonly used to externalize the rhetorical move of making a concession.

- The argument makes a valid point about ______________________.
- This view seems convincing/plausible at first/given that___________.
- This might be the case in [*describe a specific situation*]_____________.
- The point about _______________ is true, but ________________.
- It is reasonable to think that ______________ ; however, __________.
- While this position/view is popular/widely accepted, _____________.
- Although part of the claim is valid, __________________________.

To sum up, stating an alternative claim and making a concession are two important rhetorical moves involved in presenting a counterargument. After this, writers must respond to the counterclaim by providing rebuttal and reinforcing one's claim. We now discuss the language resources used to execute these rhetorical moves.

How is language used to respond to and refute a counterargument?

Refuting a Counterargument. When addressing and responding to a counterargument, writers provide backing, evidence, and warrants to refute and challenge the counterargument. They provide a rebuttal to establish that their own argument is more convincing in light of this potential alternative claim. How writers refute a counterclaim and what language choices they make are dependent upon what aspects of the counterargument—lack of evidence, underlying assumptions, faulty reasoning, or fallacy—they are challenging. For example, writers can refute the counterargument by explaining what it misses, how it is irrelevant, or why it doesn't apply in a particular context. Thus, refutation involves complex reasoning, often including counterfactuals, contextualization, or corroboration.

The languaging practices for refuting a counterargument depend on the approach to challenge the counterargument. Typically, writers use language resources to express disagreement, discrepancy, critique, and evaluation of the counterclaim. Using clause connectors (e.g., *while, although*) and sentence connectors (e.g., *however, still*) is a common practice that signals transition from concession to refutation of a counterclaim to backing one's own claim. We highlight these language features in the following examples from student writing.

- Example 3: *To what extent was the Salt March successful in bringing Indians together against British Rule?*

COUNTERCLAIM: Some might say that Gandhi was successful with his Salt March because the British opened up negotiations in an attempt to avoid more violent protests.

REFUTATION: This claim *seems convincing at first, but it misses the fact that* Gandhi and his followers had been practicing their civil disobedience peacefully for many years before the Salt March and had always been met with violence.

In Example 3, the writer uses evaluative language to express judgment (*seems convincing at first*) before pointing out the weakness of the claim (*it misses the fact that*).

- Example 4: *Why did Prohibition fail?*

COUNTERCLAIM: Others might argue the loss of government revenue was a big reason prohibition failed. Source 2 indicates that hundreds of millions of government revenue were lost due to prohibition.

REFUTATION: *However, they might not have anticipated that* alcohol consumption would continue and that the laws would be so ineffective. Source 2 even shows that alcohol consumption increased during these decades.

In Example 4, the student uses a sentence connector (*however*) to signal the transition to refuting the counterargument (*they might not have anticipated*).

As stating, conceding, and refuting a counterargument involve subjective judgment, writers use hedging language to qualify their stance and express reservations. The use of qualifiers (*some, others*), modal auxiliary verbs (*may, might*), introductory verbs (*seem, appear*), qualifying adverbs (*probably, likely*), the anticipatory "it" (*It is likely that; It might be the case*), clause connectors (*even though, although*), and prepositions (*despite, in spite of*) allow writers to hedge while presenting and refuting a counterargument.

Reinforcing One's Claim. In response to a counterargument, a writer reinforces their argument, explaining why their stance is more convincing and why the reader should believe it considering the alternative position. They provide further backing, evidence, warrants, and explanations to establish the strength of their positions. Because a counterargument stands in contrast to one's own argument, reinforcing one's argument is an important rhetorical move. We highlight this move in the following examples:

- Example 5: *What contributes to the success of the Lewis and Clark Expedition?*

<u>Counterclaim</u>

It is true that the team's personal and navigational skills were integral in the success of the Lewis and Clark Expedition. An account of Lewis's preparation says that the explorer strengthened his exploration skills by studying cartography, botany, animals, medicine, and astronomy, and then enlisted experienced military geographer Clark for his trek. These skills were definitely important as they explored new territories with unknown places, plants, and animals. Without this preparation, they might not have made it over hundreds of miles.

Reinforcing One's Claim

> *But more important for Lewis and Clark was the help from Native Americans.* Multiple sources describe the role of Native Americans. For example, it is noted in Sacagawea Biography that "The travelers came across a group of Shoshone which happened to be led by Sacagawea's brother, Chief Cameahwait. Sacagawea's translations led to her brother giving horses, a guide, and other supplies to the travelers." *The help of Sacagawea was crucial in providing aid to the expedition in the form of additional horses and supplies for travel and shelter.*

In this example, the student returns to their argument after making a concession that acknowledges some validity in the counterargument. Then, the use of a comparative adjective (*more important*) reinforces the significance of the help from Native American people to the success of Lewis and Clark's expedition. To reinforce their argument, the student corroborates and provides additional evidence and reasoning. Example 6 below shows a different rhetorical structure compared to Example 5.

- Example 6: *To what extent was the Salt March successful in bringing Indians together against British Rule?*

COUNTERCLAIM: Some might say that Gandhi was successful with his Salt March because the British opened up negotiations in an attempt to avoid more violent protests.

REFUTATION: This claim seems convincing at first, but it misses the fact that Gandhi and his followers had been practicing their civil disobedience peacefully for many years before the Salt March and had always been met with violence.

REINFORCEMENT: With the Salt March, *the nonviolent resistance was ultimately successful because the harsh response from the British was shown on the world stage,* which led to negotiations on reforming the salt laws.

After refuting the counterargument, the student reinforces their claim (italics) that establishes the publicity of the march on the world stage as the factor that led to the negotiation and to the ultimate success of the nonviolent resistance. This is done through causal language including a causal connector (*because)* and a causal verb (*led to*).

Effective integration of a counterargument strengthens and adds nuance to one's argument. Students with an understanding of the role of counterarguments and knowledge of language resources used to present and respond to an alternative position can integrate counterarguments effectively when developing their arguments. Teachers can provide explicit instruction to guide students to make effective rhetorical and language choices. The following section offers instructional guidance and resources to support students in presenting and responding to counterarguments.

III. Cultivating Language Skills for Countering

How can teachers cultivate language skills for countering?

Instructional support is integral to helping students imagine, anticipate, and address counterarguments. The resources and activities we provide in this section can help students to first think about alternative perspectives and then present and respond to one when building their own arguments. Considering alternative views allows students to think critically about a historical event and reflect on the limitations of their own views—maybe they overlooked something, maybe they are missing some key factor or evidence, or maybe they need to revise their initial claims. Further, if students have to defend their arguments about a historical event while someone else is advancing a different argument, they need to reason more and show more evidence to prove their claim.

Teaching Move 1: Facilitate dialogic interactions using the "Four Corners" activity

Key to building the knowledge and skill of countering an alternative viewpoint is engaging students in dialogic interactions. Dialogic evaluation of competing claims can help students realize that they are entering an ongoing conversation with others who have different interpretations and viewpoints. This dialogic interaction can be facilitated through the "Four Corners" activity.

Activity 1: The Four Corners

In the "Four Corners" activity, students are presented with four different claims that could be made in response to a historical question. These claims are posted in each of the four corners of the classroom. After reviewing the four different claims, the teacher asks students to (1) select the claim that they feel is most convincing; (2) go to the corner where their chosen claim is posted; and (3) discuss with others in the same corner why this claim is most convincing. Students take notes of the reasons and evidence in support of their claims to get ready for the next step, which involves countering. To model this, we provide four different claims made about the passage of the Nineteenth Amendment.

CLAIM 1: The protests and demonstrations in the 1910s put increased pressure on national political figures and most directly led to the passage of a constitutional amendment. Therefore, the tactics of the NWP were the most significant reason for the passage of the Nineteenth Amendment.

CLAIM 2: Although the actions and tactics of the NWP were important, there would have been no political action in the 1910s without the advocacy of early suffragists like Susan B. Anthony.

CLAIM 3: The state level efforts of the NAWSA slowly changed opinions across the country eventually leading to the passage of the Nineteenth Amendment. Without these state level victories, not enough states would have ratified the amendment in 1920.

CLAIM 4: President Wilson's timely appeal to Congress was the reason that led to the passage of the Nineteenth Amendment.

Next, students pair up with a classmate from a different corner. In pairs, they share their competing claims and engage in countering each other's claims. Students will have to imagine all the possible reasons they might offer to counter the alternative claim presented by their peers. To prepare students to challenge each other's claims, you can prompt them to:

- <u>Compare contributions</u>: Why is one event/factor more influential than another?
- <u>Think about the order of events</u>: Were early moments/ideas more important than things that occurred later or close to the moment of change?
- <u>Consider the context for each cause</u>: Did the context or conditions make one cause more or less influential?

After countering each other's claims, the student who presented first can acknowledge the counterargument presented by their peer and refute it with logical, convincing reasoning. Next, their peer does the same.

Activity 2: Quiet Countering

An alternative approach to this activity is "Quiet Countering," in which students respond to different claims in writing. After selecting or writing a claim, students rotate around the room to write counterarguments, concessions, and refutations to claims they encounter. Students could also simply pair with someone who has a different claim and then engage in a silent exchange, addressing and refuting their partner's claim. Finally, they return to their own claim, which now has a robust counterargument, and respond to it. To facilitate this silent exchange, you can first model the process using a think-aloud strategy. The key focus of this activity is to break down presenting and responding to counterarguments in specific steps as a form of cognitive and linguistic *scaffolding*. Table 6.3 provides a teacher model and student practice using a sample claim.

Table 6.3. Teacher Model and Student Practice

Sample Claim	**Teacher Response/Counterclaim**
The protests and demonstrations in the 1910s put increased pressure on national political figures and most directly led to the passage of a constitutional amendment. Therefore, the tactics of the NWP were the most significant reason for the passage of the 19th Amendment.	Yes, it is true that the protests and demonstrations were essential tactics the NWP used to command the attention of the politicians and the public. However, there would not have been any political actions in the 1910s without the advocacy of early suffragists like Susan B. Anthony.
My Claim	**My Peer's Response/Counterclaim**
Write your claim	*Yes, but* *OR* *No, because*

The "Four Corners" and "Quiet Countering" activities engage students in dialogic interactions in either oral or written forms. The dialogue with peers helps students prepare for writing through oral rehearsal. To scaffold the process even further, you can provide sentence stems for various rhetorical moves. Sentence stems can be particularly beneficial to students who need language support for both oral and written communication. The following sentence frames can help students get started.

Sentence stems for presenting and responding to a counterargument:

- Some people might argue that [*state the counterclaim*] ____________. However, [*provide a reason to refute*] ____________________.
- Despite the argument that [*state the counterclaim*] ______________ their evidence is not convincing because [*provide a reason to refute*] ____________________.
- Although [*state the counterclaim*] ________ is significant, a more compelling reason for _______ is _________ because [*provide a reason to refute*] ______________________________.
- Admittedly, [*state the counterclaim*] was one reason ______________ succeeded/failed. Nevertheless, [*reinforce your claim*] _____________ is a more convincing reason because [*provide a reason to refute*] ______________________________.

Finally, after these activities, students should be encouraged to revise their original claims if they have encountered evidence and reasoning that has convinced them to do so.

Teaching Move 2: Engage students in close reading to identify a counterargument

A natural next step following the dialogic interactions in the Four Corners and Quiet Countering activities is to engage students in close reading of an exemplar text to identify and analyze how a counterargument is presented and addressed. Integrating a counterargument effectively in writing can be challenging for many students. They may not know where to add a counterargument, how to connect it with their own argument, or how to use language to introduce and respond to it. There is not one single place or way to integrate counterarguments in argument writing. A counterargument can be presented and addressed before the conclusion, after the introduction, before a claim, or anywhere in the body of the essay. Thus, showing students how to present and address a counterargument using exemplar texts is critical.

To model this, we use a sample essay about the women's suffrage movement. In the following essay, the counterargument and the writer's response to it are italicized while the writer's own claim and the reinforcement of the claim are underlined. You can replace the italics and underlining with color-coding in your classroom (e.g., coding the claim and its reinforcement in blue and the counterargument in pink). The sample essay exemplifies one of many different ways a counterargument is integrated into writing. You may need to consider using shorter exemplar texts depending on your grade level or a variety of texts that show different ways to present a counterargument.

Activity 3: Identifying a Counterargument

Sample Essay with a Counterargument

> The women's suffrage movement was a decades-long struggle that eventually led to the passage of the 19th amendment granting American women the right to vote. Many contributed to the movement, including state-level suffrage organizers, national protests by the National Women's Party (NWP), and early suffragists who laid the foundation for the larger women's rights movement. *Although early suffragists generated interest in the cause of women's suffrage,* the actions and tactics of the NWP were most directly responsible for the passage of the 19th amendment because they put crucial pressure on national political figures.
>
> The protests and demonstrations of the National Women's Party were a critical contributor for passing of the 19th amendment. We first see evidence of their progress in the 1915 NY Times article. The article describes a suffrage amendment being voted on in Congress, but being defeated by a "vote of 174 to 204." While at first this seems negative, it does show progress in changing national lawmakers' opinions on the issue of suffrage in 1915. In the article, Dr. Howard Anna Shaw claims, "Suffrage is no longer a local question because the National House of Representatives has discussed suffrage . . ." This shows that the movement is finally making progress towards a national amendment, progress that had not yet been seen since the Seneca Fall Convention 60 years ago.
>
> Because there was still work to do, the NWP staged a number of public demonstrations over the next five years so that the President and others in Congress began to change their stances on suffrage. We see protests by the NWP in the NPS article (Source 6), the 1918 NYTimes article (Source 5), and the Women's suffrage overview (Source 1). These protests, including picketing and hunger strikes, applied pressure needed

for the movement to progress. Alice Paul, leader of these demonstrations and the NWP, notes the progress of the movement: "President Wilson made a magnificent speech calling for the amendment as a war measure Without action on a national stage in the form of pickets, protests, and the accompanying press, the President and then Congress may not have ever passed the amendment. The NPS article (Source 6) also confirms the impact of the NWP's picketing on the President and Congress' changing perspective on women's suffrage.

Others may argue that there would have been no political action without the advocacy of early suffragists like Susan B. Anthony. Anthony references the Constitution and citizenship rights in her speech given in 1872: "it was we, the people; not we the white male citizens; nor yet, we the male citizens; but we, the whole people who formed this union." However, none of the documents indicate her speech was effective in moving public opinion or producing legislation leading to the 19th amendment. There is actually much evidence her words were ineffective. The timeline of the Women's Suffrage movement notes that congressional amendments failed multiple times in the 19th and 20th centuries: these failures occurred years after her speeches and writings and years after her death indicating that her speeches were not pivotal to the passage of the 19th amendment.

As leader of the NWP, Alice Paul ends her interview noting, "I always feel . . . the movement is a sort of mosaic. Each of us puts in one little stone, and then you get a great mosaic at the end." *Although the contributions of early leaders in the Women's Suffrage Movement were important,* it was Paul's leadership and the catalyzing efforts that were the cornerstone in the mosaic, without which the 19th amendment may not have been passed.

How can teachers build metalinguistic knowledge and awareness?

Students need to learn how to make various linguistic choices to advance rhetorical and communicative goals. Students who have developed metalinguistic knowledge and awareness can make strategic and intentional language choices considering the audience, purpose, and context for writing. Instructional activities that engage students in close reading, analyzing, and evaluating various types of counterarguments for rhetorical moves and linguistic choices can build students' metalinguistic awareness. Such activities show how language choices matter for writing.

Teaching Move 3: Teach counterargument using the model-practice-evaluate cycle

You can use a deconstruction activity to annotate and make visible the rhetorical moves in stating a counterargument, making a concession, adding a refutational rebuttal, and reinforcing one's claim. The use of a model-practice-evaluate instructional cycle helps students gradually develop mastery and internalize the features of effective writing (Graham et al., 2016). First, model annotating a sample counterargument to help students notice the thinking and language moves of an experienced writer. Students then emulate the features of the model text before they evaluate their own writing to see whether or how well they presented and responded to a counterargument.

Following teacher modeling, students practice presenting and responding to counterarguments collaboratively and independently. You can present students with several claims to counter. As an example, we demonstrate three different claims made in response to the same question.

Table 6.4. Modeling an Annotation

Model: Teacher models annotating a sample claim	
Others might argue the loss of government revenue was a big reason prohibition failed. Source 2 indicates that hundreds of millions of government revenue were lost due to prohibition.	This part states and acknowledges an alternative view or a counterargument
However, they might not have anticipated that alcohol consumption would continue and that the laws would be so ineffective. Source 2 even shows alcohol consumption increasing during these decades.	This part refutes the counterargument with reasoning and evidence.
Therefore, the ineffective enforcement of laws and corruption are more likely reasons prohibition would fail and politicians would begin to argue to end it.	This part reinforces the writer's claim in light of the counterargument

Activity 4: Practice Countering

CLAIM 1: The protests and demonstrations in the 1910s put increased pressure on national political figures and most directly led to the passage of a constitutional amendment. Therefore, the tactics of the NWP were the most significant reason for the passage of the Nineteenth Amendment.

COUNTER: ____

CLAIM 2: Although the actions and tactics of the NWP were important, there would have been no political action in the 1910s without the advocacy of early suffragists like Susan B. Anthony.

COUNTER: ____

CLAIM 3: The state level efforts of the NAWSA slowly changed opinions across the country eventually leading to the passage of the Nineteenth Amendment. Without these state level victories, not enough states would have ratified the amendment in 1920.

COUNTER: ____

Activity 5: Evaluate Counterarguments

This activity engages students in evaluating and ranking counterarguments. Students explain their reasoning for their ranking by answering the question: *What makes them more or less effective?*

Evaluation:

___Effective

___ Ineffective

What language choices are made to present and address the counterargument?

Claim 1:

It's clear she lit the fire which inspired others to take a chance. Without her, the movement wouldn't have likely happened as there wouldn't have been anyone to inspire the Black community to hold their ground, making her the reason for the boycott's success.

Counterargument:

> Others may suggest the reason for this immense achievement being the whole community coming together overall, and of course that may be the case as it clearly wouldn't have happened without it. But according to source 4, "Her resistance set in motion one of the largest social movements in history, the Montgomery Bus Boycott." It's clear she paved the way for the entire boycott, in turn assisting everyone in coming together. Without her, they most likely wouldn't have even held the protest at all until maybe later years. This makes her the biggest reason for the success of the whole event.

Claim 2:

> The Montgomery Bus Boycott succeeded through Rosa Parks and MLK Jr.'s courageous action in getting the Montgomery Bus Boycott to be successful and open to Africans.

Counterargument:

> Someone else might say that the Montgomery Bus Boycott succeeded with the help of many things such as carpools. The carpools helped African Americans get free transport safely which helped the boycott succeed. My argument is convincing because almost everyone that has lived in the U.S. knows about her or her name. Rosa Parks made a great impact on society and took one for the team.

The activities and instructional resources included in this chapter are designed to help students understand how language is used to present and respond to counterarguments. For example, students notice that a variety of language resources are used to present, concede, and refute a counterargument. They build an understanding that acknowledging and addressing an alternative view or position can strengthen their arguments.

Another key practice that helps build language awareness is engaging students in reflection. The following guiding questions can be used as prompts for reflective writing or dialogic interactions.

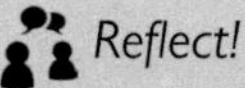

- What language choices did you make to present a counterargument?
- How effective are your language choices given the rhetorical goals?
- How would you modify your language to present, acknowledge, and respond to a counterargument?

The pedagogical strategies and activities presented in this chapter align with the following WIDA standards for English Language Development (ELD) for Social Studies (WIDA 2020):

ELD-SS.6-8.Explain.Interpretive and ELD-SS.9-12.Explain.Interpretive

Interpret social studies explanations by

- Evaluating experts' points of agreement, along with strengths and weakness of explanations
- Evaluating experts' points of agreement and disagreement based on their consistency with explanation given its purpose

ELD-SS.6-8.Explain.Expressive and ELD-SS.9-12.Explain.Expressive

Construct social studies explanations that

- Develop reasoning, sequences with linear and nonlinear relationships, evidence, and details, acknowledging strengths and weaknesses
- Develop sound reasoning, sequences with linear and nonlinear relationships, evidence, and details with significant and pertinent information, acknowledging strengths and weaknesses

ELD-SS.6-8.Argue.Interpretive and ELD-SS.9-12.Argue.Interpretive

Interpret social studies arguments by

- Evaluating point of view and credibility of source based on relevance and intended use
- Identifying topic and purpose (argue in favor of or against a position, present a balanced interpretation, challenge perspective)

ELD-SS.6-8.Argue.Expressive and ELD-SS.9-12.Argue.Expressive

Construct social studies arguments that

- Show relationships between claims and counterclaims, differences in perspectives, and evidence and reasoning

What should teachers consider for effective instruction?

Presenting and addressing counterarguments is a cognitively and linguistically demanding skill. However, both middle and high school students improve substantially in addressing counterarguments in their argument writing in history when receiving instruction in disciplinary literacy (Moon et al., 2024). Still, because of the high cognitive demand of acknowledging, countering, and challenging an alternative view, there are several steps teachers can take to scaffold the process to build this multifaceted skill over time.

Articulating Multiple Claims. First, to present a counterargument, students need to acknowledge and imagine alternative responses to the inquiry question. Some writers, because they are so singularly focused on their claim or view historical explanations as simple and one-sided, omit or ignore other interpretations altogether. Some students even perceive that including a counterargument weakens their writing (Christensen-Branum et al., 2019). Thus, we return to instructional moves we discussed at the beginning of this chapter: help students view argumentation as dialogic and historical inquiry as resolving competing interpretations of the past.

One activity you can use to promote views of argumentation as dialogic is called "Weighing the Evidence." In this activity, students are given *different* pieces of evidence. Then, they separately generate *tentative* claims for the inquiry question. The claims will be different as the pieces of evidence that students receive vary. Next, students meet with someone else, and together they write a new claim that accounts for both pieces of evidence. This step can be repeated again. The point is for students to (1) understand how claims are built on available evidence and (2) imagine multiple responses to the inquiry question. Once students can articulate more than one claim in response to the inquiry question, they are ready to imagine and present a counterclaim in writing and address it.

Presenting and Addressing Counterarguments. Once students understand that a counterargument is a key component of strong argumentation in history, they can present and respond to counterarguments in writing. Many students will be in this stage of writing with varying degrees of proficiency in presenting and responding to counterarguments. As a starting point, graphic organizers and explicit language instruction can ensure that students address counterarguments at least minimally.

The following graphic organizer from the WRITE Center (Table 6.5) provides space for students to present and address a counterargument while planning for writing. You can also have students create their own graphic organizers after providing a model. Having students create their own graphic organizers

Table 6.5. Argument Writing Essay Graphic Organizer

Context		
I will provide the following as context for the historical question:		
The **claim** I want to make in response to the essential question [*insert question here*] is:		
Evidence in support of the claim		
Source information (title, author, genre)	Evidence (quote/ paraphrase)	Reasoning (How does this evidence support your claim?)
• • •	• • •	• • •
Counterargument		
An alternative claim or point of view	Evidence and reasoning for opposing claim	Additional evidence/reasoning to refute the counterclaim
•	•	•

will allow them to think about the different rhetorical decisions they can make to integrate and address counterarguments in their writing.

In addition to planning, scaffolding the use of language can also help students. You can consider guiding students in using the sentence stems shared earlier in this chapter. With opportunities for dialogue, planning, and scaffolding of the specific language moves needed to communicate counterarguments, students will improve their writing over time. Supporting the language for presenting and addressing counterarguments will certainly aid students in constructing effective arguments. A final pedagogical touch is to have students try structuring their writing in different ways for rhetorical effects. This includes using a hedging statement in the claim or devoting the first body paragraph to the counterargument. Having students reflect on the impact of these different moves can help develop their rhetorical problem-solving abilities, as well as their language skills.

Conclusion

In writing this book, we hoped that more students would be better prepared to communicate written arguments effectively, clearly, and confidently. Now, this hope rests in the hands of teachers, teacher educators, school leaders, and others who dedicate themselves to the important and tireless task of helping students grow each day. While we did our best to share the pedagogical language knowledge teachers need for building students' language skills for historical thinking and argumentation, the instruction still needs to happen. To conclude, we now offer a few ideas for how educators can take what they learned in this book and answer the perennial question in teaching: *How can I bring this into my classroom?*

In each chapter, we offered several instructional activities to solve persistent problems of practice related to argumentation in history. These practices can be seen as tools in an educator's ever evolving pedagogical tool kit. One way to begin using this expanding tool kit is by assessing what particular communication problems are most pressing in one's classroom and choosing an activity that aims to solve that problem. The persistent communication problems we focused on, which are well-supported by extant research, are making claims, integrating and sourcing evidence, reasoning, and addressing counterarguments. Determining which one of these problems to focus on first, based on students' needs and curricular pacing, is something teachers are experts in.

However, if it isn't clear what students need to work on first, assigning writing, even just a paragraph, and noticing what students do well and find challenging is a good place to start. After students write, note specific aspects of writing you want to target in that lesson—not all at once, because developing writing takes time. For example, you might start with attribution statements and integrating evidence in an exit ticket where students do document analysis. Alternatively, after much discussion around an inquiry question, students might be ready for explicit instruction in forming claims. Starting small can be beneficial for students who need instruction "chunked" in order to develop mastery. Starting small can also be beneficial for teachers so they can focus on specific skills, one or two at a time.

Eventually, you can move to longer pieces of writing so students can show sustained inquiry skills. When this happens, acknowledging writing as a *process*—and teaching it as such—is key. For example, giving students opportunities to revise after reviewing the specific language instruction and activities offered in this book is one way writing can be taught as a process. The activities that are designed to build students' metacognition about language choices are best facilitated in a classroom where students have multiple sustained opportunities to practice their new skills, revise their thinking and language, and apply their skills to new prompts and topics.

One question that might remain for readers of this book is: How do we balance the demands of "language" instruction with reading or thinking instruction? For us, we don't see this dichotomy as that helpful or reflected in the reality of students' development as writers. In chapter 3, we explained how language is the conduit through which higher-order disciplinary thinking is carried out. Language and thinking are inextricably bound. In many of the examples of student writing growth we share, we can see the language, the writing, and the communication of ideas improved *alongside* the students' historical thinking.

When looking at students who might be challenged by writing assignments in your classrooms, it could be that they have the thinking, but they need the language to externalize their thinking. Or it could be that the language and thinking need to develop concurrently because the language to express historical thinking supports and aids this thinking. We believe the latter has more empirical and theoretical support. In any case, helping students intentionally and reflectively cultivate language skills will enable them to communicate effectively.

In short, we think your existing pedagogies should be used alongside your new and expanding tool kits that include knowledge about language and how to teach students to use language effectively. Both are needed as we teach students the complex but achievable skills required to become effective writers. Finally, while the work of a teacher is challenging, it is also deeply worthwhile and civically important work we hope to support. Teachers who help students learn about the past and cultivate reasoning skills for disciplinary inquiry and for answering vital civic questions are also reading, writing, and language teachers. It is quite a task, but we have the utmost confidence in teachers' abilities to make the best pedagogical decisions for their students.

Glossary of Terms

Abstract Nouns: Nouns that denote intangible ideas, groups, or states, such as causes (e.g., *reason, contribution, role*), consequences (e.g., *effect, result, outcome*), and changes (e.g., *growth, decline, diffusion*).

Academic Language: A language variety that is commonly used in disciplinary and academic discourse. It is characterized by technical, precise, and abstract words, complex syntactic and grammatical structure, and formal register.

Academic Languaging: The term academic languaging has been suggested as a way to move away from prescriptive and exclusionary framing to a more holistic view of language use in response to the problematization of and contentions toward academic language (see Sembiante & Tian, 2021).

Apprenticeship Model of Learning: Rooted in Vygotskian sociocultural theory, the apprenticeship model of learning is based on cognitive apprenticeship (Rogoff, 1990). The apprenticeship model of learning in literacy development focuses on making the thinking processes involved in reading, writing, and disciplinary literacy practices visible through modeling, think-alouds, coaching, and reflection.

Argument vs. Argumentation: According to the *Stanford Encyclopedia of Philosophy*, argument is defined as "a complex symbolic structure where some parts, known as the premises, offer support to another part, the conclusion" (para. 1). Argumentation, on the other hand, refers to "the communicative activity of producing and exchanging reasons in order to support claims or defend/challenge positions" (para. 3).

Attribution: Explicitly naming and crediting the source where evidence is found and information is shared.

Civic Writing: Civic writing fosters youth participation in public debates, discourse, and dialogue through writing on issues and topics that matter to them and their communities. The National Writing Project (NWP) developed the Civically Engaged Writing Analysis Continuum (CEWAC) as a rubric for assessing youth writing about civic issues.

Claim: A claim is the point, the arrowhead, of an argument that communicates a stance, informed by evidence-based reasoning. Claims are bounded by the scope of inquiry, available evidence, and other plausible interpretations.

Clause: A sentence within a sentence that contains at least a subject and a verb. A clause is either independent or dependent. An independent or main clause in a sentence can stand alone as a complete sentence, while a dependent clause is added to the main clause and cannot stand alone as a complete sentence.

Clause Connectors: Words or phrases that link or combine clauses, explicitly showing the logical relations (e.g., *even though, until, because*) between the clauses.

Colloquial Language: A casual and conversational language that is often used in informal and everyday conversations. In writing, colloquial style conveys the effect of informal, spoken language.

Concession: The acknowledgment of a valid point in an opposing argument. It demonstrates fairness and credibility by recognizing other perspectives while still maintaining the strength of the writer's position by focusing on the points of the argument that have not been conceded.

Conditional Statement: A statement that expresses a hypothetical and a possible outcome, often structured as an "if-then" statement to offer a counterfactual explanation.

Contextualization: Understanding of how historical contexts influence actors and events. It involves placing events, actors, or actions within the broader circumstances or conditions of their times and places to deepen understanding.

Corroboration: The process of comparing multiple sources or pieces of evidence to confirm the accuracy, consistency, and reliability of a claim, a statement, or information.

Counterfactual Reasoning: Reasoning about alternatives to past events, actions, and states. It responds to questions like *What would we have seen or what would have happened if something else had happened?* Counterfactual reasoning uses the factual state of affairs to create an imagined alternative.

Credibility of Sources: The trustworthiness of a source; determined by assessing a source's purpose, perspective, and/or expertise.

Critical Language Awareness: Critical language awareness (CLA) refers to knowledge about and understanding of the social, cultural, political, and ideological aspects of language use and linguistic variations. CLA pedagogy strives to promote knowledge about and awareness of language and languaging practices.

Culturally Sustaining Systemic Functional Linguistics (CSSFL): A pedagogical approach that draws on Culturally Sustaining Pedagogy (Paris & Alim, 2014; 2017) and Systemic Functional Linguistics (Halliday, 1978). It centers the dynamic cultural and linguistic practices of diverse learners while supporting their academic, civic, and disciplinary literacy skills in their new cultural context.

Dialogic: Communication that is built upon interaction and the exchange of ideas and perspectives. In argumentation, a dialogic approach acknowledges opposing views to build a more nuanced and comprehensive argument.

Disciplinary Discourse: Disciplinary discourse refers to a written and spoken communication, discussion, and debate within a specific discipline. It represents the complex system of representations, tools, and activities that shape the discourse as they guide the knowledge construction, language convention, and literacy practice of the discipline.

Disciplinary Literacy: Disciplinary literacy refers to the specific literacy practices in a discipline (e.g., history, science), including reading, writing, and other multimodal ways of communicating using symbols and visuals. Disciplinary literacy development entails learning the ways of thinking and building skills that are specific to the discipline, as well as learning to use tools and language that are used by experts in the discipline (Shanahan & Shanahan, 2012).

Discourse Community: Discourse community refers to a community of people who share common goals and use a specific language used within the community to achieve their goals.

Discourse Domains: Discourse domain broadly refers to the context in which communication, either written or verbal, takes place. As language choices and rhetorical moves are shaped by the context in which communication occurs, different discourse domains (e.g., academic written discourse, historical discourse, political speech) exhibit distinct styles, language features, and persuasion techniques.

Functional Language Analysis: Functional language analysis is an approach used to analyze and deconstruct a text to make visible the language patterns and structures to show how language is used and what language choices are made for meaning making. Functional language analysis is grounded in the functional-semantic approach of Systemic Functional Linguistics (SFL).

Functional-Semantic Approach: Functional-semantic approach to language is a theoretical framework grounded in Systemic Functional Linguistics (SFL) that sees language as social semiotic (Halliday, 1978). The framework is used to describe and interpret how language is used in different contexts and how context shapes the language structures and patterns.

Genre-Based Pedagogy: An instructional approach designed to guide students to recognize and understand the language patterns and text structures of different genres. It is a language-centered framework that has been widely used for writing instruction to help students understand how writers make choices to communicate meaning to a given audience, considering the genre conventions and norms.

Hedging: Language that qualifies or limits one's claim. Hedging devices help writers avoid overgeneralization or make a necessary concession before stating their argument more precisely.

Historical Argumentation: Communicative activity of producing and exchanging reasons in order to support claims and defend or challenge positions about people, places, events, phenomena from the past and explaining how they interact across time and place, why and how an event happened in the past, and why it matters.

Historical Inquiry: Historical inquiry is a method of questioning, researching, sourcing, and weighing evidence to form an interpretation about the past. College, Career, and Civic Life (C3) Framework for Social Studies (NCSS, 2013) prioritizes inquiry-based learning for social studies instruction.

Historical Reasoning: Charles Perfetti et al. (1995) define historical reasoning as an ability to "reason about historical topics—to place them in more than one context, to question the source of a historical statement, to realize that more information is needed to reach a conclusion" (p. 5). Carla Van Boxtel and Jannet van Drie (2018) conceptualize historical reasoning as a way "to reach justifiable conclusions about processes of continuity and change, causes and consequences, and/or differences and similarities between historical phenomena or periods" (p. 151).

Intertextual Model: A thinker's evolving mental model of (1) information about individual sources/texts; (2) information *within* these sources/texts; and (3) information about how sources/texts relate. See Tobias Richter and Johanna Maier (2017) for more information.

Introductory Phrase: Words and phrases commonly used with quotations and source materials to provide context or to identify a speaker or source (e.g., *according to, as stated in*).

Knowledge Telling vs. Knowledge Transformation: First introduced by Carl Bereiter and Marlene Scardamalia (1987), these terms refer to two distinct models of composing processes. Knowledge telling involves simpler processing of text construction based on recalling and retelling, while knowledge transformation involves a process of discovery and problem solving as writers go beyond mere retelling and engage in generating knowledge.

Metalinguistic Knowledge/Awareness: Metalinguistic knowledge or awareness refers to knowledge of language for talking about language, as well as an understanding of language forms and functions. According to Ulrike Jessner (2008), metalinguistic awareness is "the ability to focus on linguistic form and to switch focus between form and meaning" (p. 277).

Modifier: A word or phrase (e.g., adjectives, nouns, and clauses used attributively) that modify and specify the meaning of another word or phrase.

Modal Verbs: Auxiliary verbs that express various meanings such as possibility, intent, ability, or necessity. Examples of modal verbs are *can, should, must*, and *might.*

Multilingual Learners of English: The term Multilingual Learners of English is rooted in multilingualism as an asset and is more inclusive in that it highlights students' language assets and existing linguistic repertoire while recognizing that they are learning English as an additional or new language.

Nominalization: Turning a verb, adjective, or clause into a noun form, often to create a more formal tone or to link causes, actors, events, and consequences (e.g., *they passed the amendment → the passage of the amendment*).

Oral Rehearsal: Speaking aloud, with oneself or with a partner, before formalizing thoughts into writing.

Paraphrasing: Restating text/evidence in one's own words while preserving the original meaning.

Pedagogical Language Knowledge: A construct introduced by Tomas Galguera (2011) as a variation of Lee Shulman's (1987) pedagogical content knowledge. Pedagogical language knowledge is essential for developing students' language skills and critical language awareness.

Phrase: A small group of words that stand together as a conceptual unit. A phrase typically forms a grammatical component of a clause.

Raciolinguistic Ideology: The raciolinguistic ideology (Flores & Rosa, 2015) challenges a deficit view toward multilingual and multidialectal students' languaging practices and denounces the systematic stigmatization of the linguistic practices of minoritized populations.

Rebuttal: Response to a counterargument or counterclaim that aims to refute, weaken, challenge, or counter it.

Recording Genres: According to Caroline Coffin (1997, 2006), recording genres include autobiographical recount, biographical recount, historical account, and historical recounts. The overall purpose of recording genres is to retell events and record events in a particular sequence.

Reporting Verbs: Verbs used to convey how information is communicated in speech and discourse, clarifying the speaker's attitude (e.g., *state, explain, argue, exclaim*).

Semiotic System: Semiotic system refers to the mechanism of meaning making using various semiotic tools and modalities, including linguistic, audio, gestural, visual, and spatial signs and symbols. Based on the theory of Systemic Functional Linguistics (SFL), language is considered as part of a semiotic system used for meaning making within a social context.

Signal Verbs: Verbs that indicate how a source is used in writing or to attribute ideas, opinions, or information to specific sources (e.g., *are documented, underscores, confirms*).

Sourcing: Thinking about a source's origin and context to assess its relevance and reliability; questioning who created a source and for what purpose (for a more detailed summary, see Wineburg, 1991, 2001).

Stance: "The speaker's or the writer's feeling, attitude, perspective, position as enacted in discourse" (Strauss & Feiz, 2014, p. 103).

Substantiation: Supporting claims and arguments with appropriate and accurate evidence and reasoning.

Systemic Functional Linguistics: Systemic Functional Linguistics (SFL), initially developed by Michael Halliday (1978), is often used as an analytical approach of text linguistics and deals with language use and patterns within a text in relation to the context in which it appears.

Warrant: The underlying principles or reasoning that connect evidence to claims (for a detailed review, see Toulmin, 1958).

References

Accurso, K., & Gebhard, M. (2021). SFL praxis in U.S. teacher education: A critical literature review. *Language and Education, 35*(5), 402–428.

Achugar, M., & Schleppegrell, M. J. (2005). Beyond connectors: The construction of cause in history textbooks. *Linguistics and Education, 16*(3), 298–318.

Alston, C. L., Monte-Sano, C., Schleppegrell, M., & Harn, K. (2021). Teaching models of disciplinary argumentation in middle school social studies: A framework for supporting writing development. *Journal of Writing Research, 13*(2), 285–321.

Bain, R. (2006). Rounding up unusual suspects: Facing the authority hidden in the history classroom. *Teachers College Record, 108*(10), 2080–2114.

Barton, K. C., & Levstik, L. S. (2004). *Teaching history for the common good* (1st ed.). Routledge.

Beers, K., & Probst, R. E. (2013). *Notice & note: Strategies for close reading*. Heinemann.

Bereiter, C., & Scardamalia, M. (1987). *The psychology of written composition*. Lawrence Erlbaum Associates.

Berkenkotter, C., Huckin, T., & Ackerman, J. (1991). Social context and socially constructed texts: The initiation of a graduate student into a writing research community. In C. Bazerman & J. Paradis (Eds.), *Textual dynamics of the professions* (pp. 191–215). University of Wisconsin Press.

Braasch, J. L., & Bråten, I. (2017). The discrepancy-induced source comprehension (D-ISC) model: Basic assumptions and preliminary evidence. *Educational Psychologist, 52*(3), 167–181.

Bråten, I., Britt, M. A., Strømsø, H. I., & Rouet, J. F. (2011). The role of epistemic beliefs in the comprehension of multiple expository texts: Toward an integrated model. *Educational Psychologist, 46*(1), 48–70.

Bråten, I., Stadtler, M., & Salmerón, L. (2017). *The role of sourcing in discourse comprehension*. In M. Schober, D. N. Rapp, & M. A. Britt (Eds.), *Handbook of discourse processes* (pp. 141–168). Routledge.

Breakstone, J., Smith, M., & Wineburg, S. (2013). Beyond the bubble in history/social studies assessments. *Phi Delta Kappan, 94*(5), 53–57.

Bunch, G. C. (2013). Pedagogical language knowledge: Preparing teachers for English learners in the new standards era. *Review of Research in Education, 37*(1), 298–341.

Bunch, G. C., Kibler, A. K., & Pimentel, S. (2014). Shared responsibility: Realizing opportunities for English Learners in the Common Core English Language Arts and Disciplinary Literacy Standards. In L. Minaya-Rowe (Ed.), *Effective educational programs, practices, and policies for English Learners* (pp. 1–28). Information Age Publishing.

California Common Core State Standards. (2013). *English language arts & literacy in history/social studies, science, and technical subjects*. https://www.cde.ca.gov/be/st/ss/documents/finalelaccssstandards.pdf.

California Department of Education. (2000). *History-social studies content standards for California public schools: Kindergarten through grade 12*. https://www.cde.ca.gov/be/st/ss/documents/histsocscistnd.pdf.

California History-Social Science Project. https://chssp.ucdavis.edu.

Canagarajah, S. (2002). Multilingual writers and the academic community: Towards a critical relationship. *Journal of English for Academic Purposes, 1*, 29–44.

Celce-Murcia, M., & Larsen-Freeman, D. (1999). *The grammar book: An ESL/EFL teacher's course* (2nd ed.). Heinle & Heinle.

Chinn, C. A., Barzilai, S., & Duncan, R. G. (2021). Education for a "post-truth" world: New directions for research and practice. *Educational Researcher, 50*(1), 51–60.

Cho, S., & Reich, G. A. (2008). New immigrants, new challenges: High school social studies teachers and English language learner instruction. *The Social Studies, 99*(6), 235–242.

Christensen-Branum, L., Strong, A., & Jones, C. D. (2019). Mitigating myside bias in argumentation. *Journal of Adolescent & Adult Literacy, 62*(4), 435–445.

Coffin, C. (1997). Constructing and giving value to the past. An investigation into secondary school history. In F. Christine & J. R. Martin (Eds.), *Genre and institutions: Social processes in the workplace and school* (pp. 196–230). Bloomsbury.

Coffin, C. (2004). Learning to write history: The role of causality. *Written Communication, 21*(3), 261–289.

Coffin, C. (2006). *Historical discourse: The language of time, cause and evaluation.* Continuum.

Cowgill II, D. A., & Waring, S. M. (2017). Historical thinking: Analyzing student and teacher ability to analyze sources. *Journal of Social Studies Education Research, 8*(1), 115–145.

Crammond, J. G. (1998). The uses and complexity of argument structures in expert and student persuasive writing. *Written Communication, 15*(2), 230–268.

Crossley, S.A. (2020). Linguistic features in writing quality and development: An overview. *Journal of Writing Research, 11*(3), 415–443.

De La Paz, S., Monte-Sano, C., Felton, M., Croninger, R., Jackson, C., & Piantedosi, K. W. (2017). A historical writing apprenticeship for adolescents: Integrating disciplinary learning with cognitive strategies. *Reading Research Quarterly, 52*(1), 31–52.

Derewianka, B., & Jones, P. (2023). *Teaching language in context* (3rd ed.). Oxford University Press.

di Gennaro, K. (2013). How different are they? A comparison of Generation 1.5 and international L2 learners' writing ability. *Assessing Writing*, 18, 154–172.

Digital Inquiry Group. https://inquirygroup.org.

Digital Public Library of America. *Dear Los Angeles friend . . . please don't buy grapes.* https://dp.la/item/d8f88dff38301a20abf182cb024e8274.

Erduran, S. (2007). Methodological foundations in the study of argumentation in science classrooms. In S. Erduran & M. P. Jiménez-Aleixandre (Eds.), *Argumentation in science education: Perspectives from classroom-based research* (pp. 47–69). Springer Netherlands.

Fang, Z., & Schleppegrell, M. J. (2010). Disciplinary literacies across content areas: Supporting secondary reading through functional language analysis. *Journal of Adolescent & Adult Literacy, 53*, 587–597.

Ferretti, R. P., & Graham, S. (2019). Argumentative writing: Theory, assessment, and instruction. *Reading and Writing: An Interdisciplinary Journal, 32*(6), 1345–1357.

Flores, N., & Rosa, J. (2015). Undoing appropriateness: Raciolinguistic ideologies and language diversity in education. *Harvard Educational Review, 85*, 149–171.

Galguera, T. (2011). Participant structures as professional learning tasks and the development of pedagogical language knowledge among preservice teachers. *Teacher Education Quarterly, 38*, 85–106.

Garcia, O., & Solorza, C. R. (2020). Academic language and the minoritization of U.S. bilingual Latinx students. *Language and Education, 35*, 505–521.

Gilbertson, N. (2012). Literacy acquisition using historical methods and content: Teaching cause and effect in history texts. *Social Studies Review*, 14–23.

Goldenberg, C. (2013). Unlocking the research on English learners: What we know—and don't yet know—about effective instruction. *American Educator, 37*, 4–11.

Goldman, S. R., Britt, M. A., Brown, W., Cribb, G., George, M., Greenleaf, C., Lee, C. D., Shanahan, C., & Project READI. (2016). Disciplinary literacies and learning to read for understanding: A conceptual framework for disciplinary literacy. *Educational Psychologist, 51*(2), 219–246.

Göksun, T. (2020). The bases of the mind: The relationship of language and thought. *Medium.* https://medium.com/kocuniversity/the-bases-of-the-mind-the-relationship-of-language-and-thought-a0bf30375528.

Graham, S., Bruch, J., Fitzgerald, J., Friedrich, L., Furgeson, J., Greene, K., Kim, J., Lyskawa, J., Olson, C. B., & Smither Wulsin, C. (2016). *Teaching secondary students to write effectively*. National Center for Education Evaluation and Regional Assistance (NCEE), Institute of Education Sciences, U.S. Department of Education.

Graham, S., Harris, K. R., & Santangelo, T. (2015). Research-based writing practices and the common core. *The Elementary School Journal, 115*, 498–522.

Graham, S., & Perin, D. (2007). *Writing next: Effective strategies to improve writing of adolescents in middle and high schools—A report to Carnegie Corporation of New York.* Alliance for Excellent Education.

Guldi, J., & Armitage, D. (2014). *The history manifesto*. Cambridge University Press.

Halliday, M. A. K. (1978). *Language as social semiotic.* Edward Arnold.

Halliday, M. A. K. (1994). *Introduction to functional grammar* (2nd ed.). Edward Arnold.

Halliday, M. A. K., & Matthiessen, C. M. I. M. (2014). *Halliday's introduction to functional grammar* (4th ed.). Routledge.

Harman, R., & Burke, K. (2020). *Culturally sustaining systemic functional linguistics: Embodied inquiry with multilingual youth*. Routledge.

Howell, M., & Prevenier, W. (2001). *From reliable sources: An introduction to historical methods.* Cornell University Press.

Humboldt, W. (1999). *On language: On the diversity of human language construction and its influence on the mental development of the human species.* Cambridge University Press.

Jessner, U. (2008). A DST model of multilingualism and the role of metalinguistic awareness. *The Modern Language Journal, 92*(2), 270–283.

Kanno, Y. (2022). *Preparing multilingual learners for college and career success* [Webinar]. Center for Applied Linguistics. https://www.cal.org/resource-center/research-to-policy-series/multilingual-college-career.

Kanno, Y., & Cromley, J. G. (2015). English language learners' pathways to four-year colleges. *Teachers College Record, 117*, 1–44.

Kellogg, R. T. (2008). Training writing skills: A cognitive developmental perspective. *Journal of Writing Research, 1*(1), 1–26.

Kim, Y.-S. G., & Graham, S. (2022). Expanding the direct and indirect effects model of writing (DIEW): Reading–writing relations, and dynamic relations as a function of measurement/dimensions of written composition. *Journal of Educational Psychology, 114*(2), 215–238.

Kuhn, D. (1991). *The skills of argument*. Cambridge University Press.

Kuhn, D. (2005). *Education for thinking*. Harvard University Press.

Kuhn, D. (2019). Critical thinking as discourse. *Human Development, 62*(3), 146–164.

Lunsford, A. A., Ruszkiewicz, J. J., & Walters, K. (2016). *Everything's an argument*. Bedford St. Martin's.

Maamuujav, U. (2022). *Unpacking adolescent writers' texts: A systematic investigation of the language features in the academic writing of linguistically diverse students.* ProQuest Dissertations & Theses Global.

MacArthur, C. A., Jennings, A., & Philippakos, Z. A. (2018). Which linguistic features predict quality of argumentative writing for college basic writers, and how do those features change with instruction? *Reading and Writing, 32*(6), 1553–1574.

McCullagh, C. B. (2004). What do historians argue about? *History and Theory, 43*, 18–38.

McGrew, S., Breakstone, J., Ortega, T., Smith, M., & Wineburg, S. (2018). Can students evaluate online sources? Learning from assessments of civic online reasoning. *Theory & Research in Social Education, 46*(2), 165–193.

Monte-Sano, C. (2008). Qualities of historical writing instruction: A comparative case study of two teachers' practices. *American Educational Research Journal, 45*(4), 1045–1079.

Monte-Sano, C. (2010). Disciplinary literacy in history: An exploration of the historical nature of adolescents' writing. *The Journal of the Learning Sciences, 19*(4), 539–568.

Monte-Sano, C. (2012). What makes a good history essay? Assessing historical aspects of argumentative writing. *Social Education, 76*(6), 294–298.

Monte-Sano, C., & Allen, A. (2019). Historical argument writing: The role of interpretive work, argument type, and classroom instruction. *Reading and Writing, 32*, 1383–1410.

Monte-Sano, C., & De La Paz, S. (2012). Using writing tasks to elicit adolescents' historical reasoning. *Journal of Literacy Research, 44*(3), 273–299.

Moon, Y., Steiss, J., Wang, J., & Collins, P. (2024, April 11–14). *Effectiveness of a writing intervention in history classrooms: Do they vary by teacher- and student-factors?* [Roundtable session]. American Educational Research Association Annual Meeting, Philadelphia.

Moshman, D. (2013). Epistemic cognition and development. In P. Barrouillet & C. Gauffroy (Eds.), *The development of thinking and reasoning* (pp. 13–33). Psychology Press.

National Center for Education Statistics. (2019). *Technical summary of preliminary analysis of NAEP 2017 writing assessments.* Institute of Education Sciences, U.S. Department of Education. https://nces.ed.gov/nationsreportcard/subject/writing/pdf/2017_writing_technical_summary.pdf.

National Council for the Social Studies. (2010). *National curriculum standards for social studies: A framework for teaching, learning and assessment.* Washington, DC: National Council for the Social Studies.

National Council for the Social Studies. (2013). *Social studies for the next generation: Purposes, practices, and implications of the college, career, and civic life (C3) framework for social studies state standards.* Washington, DC: National Council for the Social Studies.

National Governors Association Center for Best Practices & Council of Chief State School Officers. (2010). *Common core state standards for English language arts and literacy in history/social studies, science, and technical subjects.* Washington, DC: Authors.

National Writing Project (2018). *Civically engaged writing analysis continuum for public writing: Analyzing public writing that focuses on civic issues of significance to the writer, community or the public.* https://cewac.nwp.org/wp-content/uploads/2018/03/CEWAC_2.0.pdf.

Nokes, J. D. (2013). *Building students historical literacies: Learning to read and reason with historical texts and evidence.* Routledge.

Nokes, J. D. (2017). Exploring patterns of historical thinking through eighth-grade students' argumentative writing. *Journal of Writing Research, 8*(3), 437–467.

Nokes, J. D., & De La Paz, S. (2023). Historical argumentation: Watching historians and teaching youth. *Written Communication, 40*(2), 333–372.

Olson, C. B., Maamuujav, U., Steiss, J., & Chung, H. (2023). Examining the impact of a cognitive strategies approach on the argument writing of mainstreamed English learners in secondary school. *Written Communication, 40*(2), 373–416.

Olson, C. B., Scarcella, R., & Matuchniak, T. (2015). *Helping English learners to write: Meeting common core standard, grades 6–12.* Teachers College Press.

Paris, D., & Alim, S. H. (2014). What are we seeking to sustain through culturally sustaining pedagogy? A loving critique forward. *Harvard Educational Review, 84*, 85–100.

Perfetti, C. A., Britt, M. A., & Georgi, M. C. (1995). *Text-based learning and reasoning: Studies in history.* Routledge.

Perie, M., Grigg, W., & Donahue, P. (2005). *The nation's report card: Reading 2005.* National Center for Education Statistics.

Probst, R. E. (1988). Dialogue with a text. *The English Journal, 77*, 32–38.

Ray, A. B., Graham, S., Houston, J. D., & Harris, K. R. (2016). Teachers' use of writing to support students' learning in middle school: A national survey in the United States. *Reading and Writing, 29*, 1039–1068.

Read.Inquire.Write. https://readinquirewrite.umich.edu.

Reid, J. (2006). "Eye" learners and "ear" learners: Identifying the language needs of international students and U.S. resident writers. In P. K. Matsuda, M. Cox, J. Jordan, & C. Ortmeier-Hooper (Eds.), *Second-language writing in the composition classroom: A critical sourcebook* (pp. 76–88). Bedford/St. Martin's.

Renier, G. J. (2016). *History: Its purpose and method.* Routledge.

Richter, T., & Maier, J. (2017). Comprehension of multiple documents with conflicting information: A two-step model of validation. *Educational Psychologist, 52*(3), 148–166.

Rogoff, B. (1990). *Apprenticeship in thinking: Cognitive development in social context.* Oxford University Press.

Rouet, J.-F., & Britt, M. A. (2011). Relevance processes in multiple document comprehension. In M. T. McCrudden, J. P. Magliano, & G. Schraw (Eds.), *Text relevance and learning from text* (pp. 19–52). IAP Information Age Publishing.

Rouet, J.-F., Britt, M. A., & Durik, A. M. (2017). RESOLV: Readers' representation of reading contexts and tasks. *Educational Psychologist, 52*(3), 200–215.

Schall-Leckrone, L. (2022). Equipping all teachers to teach disciplinary language: Toward a developmental continuum in teacher education. *TESOL Quarterly, 56*(2), 840–851.

Schall-Leckrone, L., & Barron, D. (2018). Apprenticing students and teachers into historical content, language, and thinking through genre pedagogy. In L. de Oliveira & K. Obenchain (Eds.), *Teaching history and social studies to English language learners.* Palgrave Macmillan.

Schleppegrell, M. J. (2001). Linguistic features of the language of schooling. *Linguistics and Education*, 12, 431–459.

Schleppegrell, M. J. (2004). *The language of schooling: A functional linguistics perspective.* Lawrence Erlbaum Associates, Inc.

Schleppegrell, M. J., & Achugar, M. (2003). Learning language and learning history: A functional linguistics approach. *TESOL Journal, 12*(2), 21–27.

Schleppegrell, M. J., Achugar, M., & Oteiza, T. (2004). The grammar of history: Enhancing content-cased instruction through a functional focus on language. *TESOL Quarterly, 38*, 67–93.

Schleppegrell, M. J., & de Oliveira, L. C. (2006). An integrated language and content approach for history teachers. *Journal of English for Academic Purposes, 5*(4), 254–268.

Schleppegrell, M. J., Greer, S., & Taylor, S. (2008). Literacy in history: Language and meaning. *Australian Journal of Language and Literacy, 31*(2), 174–187.

Schleppegrell, M. J., Sun, S., & Monte-Sano, C. (2023). The value of models to support students' voice in middle school social studies argument writing. *Journal of Second Language Writing, 61*, 101043.

Seixas, P., & Morton, T. (2013). *The big six historical thinking concepts.* Nelson.

Sembiante, S. F., & Tian, Z. (2021). Culturally sustaining approaches to academic languaging through systemic functional linguistics. *Language and Education, 35*, 101–105.

Shanahan, T., & Shanahan, C. (2012). What is disciplinary literacy and why does it matter? *Topics in Language Disorders, 32*(1), 7–18.

Shapiro, S. (2022). *Cultivating critical language awareness in the writing classroom.* Routledge.

Shulman, L. (1987). Knowledge and teaching: Foundations of the new reform. *Harvard Educational Review, 57*, 1–22.

Steiss, J., Krishnan, J., Kim, Y. S., & Olson, C. B. (2022). Dimensions of text-based analytical writing of secondary students. *Assessing Writing, 51*, 100600.

Steiss, J., Wang, J., Kim, Y. S., & Booth Olson, C. (2024). Challenges and dimensions of secondary students' source-based argument writing in history. *Written Communication, 41*(2), 693–725.

Stoel, G. L., van Drie, J. P., & Van Boxtel, C. A. (2017). The effects of explicit teaching of strategies, second-order concepts, and epistemological underpinnings on students' ability to reason causally in history. *Journal of Educational Psychology, 109*(3), 321–337.

Strauss, S., & Feiz, P. (2014). *Discourse analysis: Putting our worlds into words.* Routledge.

Swain, M. (2006). Languaging, agency and collaboration in advanced second language proficiency. In H. Byrnes (Ed.), *Advanced language learning: The contribution of Halliday and Vygotsky* (pp. 95–108). Continuum.

Tate, T., & Collins, P. (2022, April 21–26). *Multiple lenses for understanding source-based analytical writing development* [Symposium]. American Educational Research Association Annual Meeting 2022, San Diego, CA, United States.

The Martin Luther King, Jr., Research and Education Institute. (2024, March 1). *Montgomery bus boycott.* https://kinginstitute.stanford.edu/montgomery-bus-boycott.

Toulmin, S. E. (1958). *The uses of argument.* Cambridge University Press.

U.S. Department of Education, National Center for Education Statistics. (2012). *The Nation's Report Card: Writing 2011 (NCES 2012–470).* Institute of Education Sciences, U.S. Department of Education, Washington, DC. https://nces.ed.gov/nationsreportcard/pdf/main2011/2012470.pdf.

Van Boxtel, C., & van Drie, J. (2018). Historical reasoning: Conceptualizations and educational applications. In S. A. Metzger & L. McArthur Harris (Eds.), *The Wiley international handbook of history teaching and learning* (pp. 149–176). John Wiley & Sons.

van Drie, J., & Van Boxtel, C. (2008). Historical reasoning: Toward a framework for analyzing students' reasoning about the past. *Educational Psychology Review, 20*(2), 87–110.

VanSledright, B., & Maggioni, L. (2016). Epistemic cognition in history. In J. A. Greene, W. A. Sandoval, & I. Bråten (Eds.), *Handbook of epistemic cognition* (pp. 140–58). Routledge.

WIDA. (2020). *WIDA English language development standards framework, 2020 edition: Kindergarten-grade 12.* Board of Regents of the University of Wisconsin System. https://wida.wisc.edu/teach/standards/eld.

Wiley, J., Griffin, T. D., Steffens, B., & Britt, M. A. (2020). Epistemic beliefs about the value of integrating information across multiple documents in history. *Learning and Instruction, 65*, 101266.

Wineburg, S. (1991). Historical problem solving: A study of the cognitive processes used in the evaluation of documentary and pictorial evidence. *Journal of Educational Psychology, 83*, 73–87.

Wineburg, S. (2001). *Historical thinking and other unnatural acts: Charting the future of teaching the past.* Temple University Press.

WRITE Center. http://www.writecenter.org.